HERITAGE
AND
CHALLENGE

HERITAGE AND CHALLENGE

THE HISTORY AND THEORY OF HISTORY

by

Paul K. Conkin
Vanderbilt University

and

Roland N. Stromberg
University of Wisconsin–Milwaukee

FORUM PRESS, INC.
ARLINGTON HEIGHTS, ILLINOIS 60004

Copyright © 1989
Forum Press, Inc.
All rights reserved

Library of Congress Cataloging in Publication Data

Conkin, Paul Keith.
  Heritage and challenge.

  Rev. ed. of: The heritage and challenge of history.
1971.
  Bibliography: p.
  Includes index.
  1. Historiography. 2. History—Philosophy.
I. Stromberg, Roland N., 1916–   . II. Conkin, Paul
Keith. Heritage and challenge of history. III. Title.
D13.C635 1988   901   88-30968
ISBN 0-88273-286-2

Cover design: Roger Eggers

Manufactured in the United States of America
92 91 90 89 88 CC 1 2 3 4 5

CONTENTS

Preface   VII

Part I. The Heritage of History
1. The Roots of Western History: The Ancient World   3
2. Medieval Historical Writing   20
3. History in the Early Modern Period   32
4. The Eighteenth Century and "Enlightened" History   47
5. The Nineteenth Century: The Golden Age of History   61
6. History in Our Own Time: The Twentieth Century   86
7. Recent Trends   III

Part II. The Challenge of History
8. What Is History?   129
9. History and the Generalizing Sciences   149
10. Causation   170
11. Objectivity   192
12. Use   217
Epilogue   239

Selected Bibliography   246
Index   255

V

PREFACE

WHEN the first version of this book was published, in 1971, it was gratifyingly well received as an introduction to the study and writing of history. In time it inevitably came to need revision to bring it abreast of advances in scholarship and changes in perspective. The original book has now been considerably revised and rewritten as *Heritage and Challenge: The History and Theory of History*. The attempt to combine a survey of the history of historical writing with a critical analysis of the theoretical issues and problems that have emerged from this history still seems to us both sound and interesting. The differences in our views and approaches only add to this interest. We both find the subject endlessly fascinating; it is the attempt to understand humanity's attempt to understand itself. Fledgling historians should of course realize how much more there is to this large enterprise than this short book indicates; it is meant to start them on their quest.

In the preface to *The Heritage and Challenge of History*, in the aftermath of the turbulent sixties, we noted that historians then felt more disquietude than at any other time in the recent past. Perhaps they still do. The historical profession remains severely fragmented in definition, methods, and purposes. It is not clear that young people value historical knowledge any more today than they did in 1971. Perhaps people still sense an almost complete discontinuity between past and present. Yet the very stresses and strains of contemporary life suggest a need for historical-mindedness, for a recognition of continuities. This need is no less pressing whether most of our past merits our celebration or deserves only our condemnation.

Any profession can succumb to myopia, particularly in times of prosperity. Until recently, historians often relaxed in the comfort and security of an old, well-established profession. They rarely questioned the legitimacy or the long-range usefulness of their inquiry. Much more than social scientists, they remained aloof from definitional and meth-

odological controversies. No more. Gentility and decorum still grace
our conferences and soften our controversies, but the decorum is forced.
No true community of historical scholars exists.

One result of such differences is the increasing self-consciousness of
historians. Many are now willing to engage in the most subtle philosophical analysis. An unprecedented contemporary interest in history
by professional philosophers has not only stimulated historians' concerns but provided them with the intellectual resources needed for
disciplined self-analysis.

The most basic questions for the historian have always been: What
are the defining characteristics of history? What is unique about it as
a field of empirical inquiry? The answers to these questions implicate
all the other controverted issues: Is history a science? How does it relate
to other disciplines? Is historical inquiry a unique pathway to truth?
Does historical explanation differ from other types of explanation? What
is the place of causation in history? Can a history be true? Can it be
objective? What role does value play in historical writing? What are the
proper tools for dealing with historical evidence? And, perhaps the most
tantalizing question of all, what is history for—what social roles does it
play?

These questions, and others of the same type, are not new. Perhaps
some of the answers are new. Since the the time of the ancient Greeks,
both historians and philosophers have asked and proffered answers to
such questions. Thus in Part I of this book Roland N. Stromberg presents a brief account of the history of history in the West, focusing on
the most notable epochs, on the greatest historians, and even more
particularly on developing conceptions of history. In this sense, he has
written a brief history of historical self-consciousness, and in the process
uncovered the knotty problems of subject, method, and purpose which
Western historians have faced through the centuries.

In Part II, Paul K. Conkin turns from history to analysis. In topical
chapters, he tries to bare the theoretical issues of greatest concern to
contemporary historians. He is particularly concerned to clarify some
of the unending problems of definition, and to reveal at least the range
and subtlety of philosophical issues that attend historical inquiry. For
each major problem, he presents his own tentative resolution. These
views can be compared with others referred to in the text or identified
in our bibliography.

We hope the bibliography will guide the dedicated student in more
intensive study and be helpful to teachers of historiography. We believe
all history departments should offer such courses. Most graduate students in history now take some introductory course in historiography.
But not enough end up with more than a smattering of information

about the rich history of their discipline, or with the skills needed to understand the enormously complex issues in contemporary critical philosophy of history. We hope this book will contribute to such needed knowledge and skill, not only for graduate students but for undergraduate history majors. They, too, need to confront the history and the theoretical challenge of their chosen discipline.

We believe the two parts of this book complement each other, as they represent two very different but equally necessary approaches to an understanding of history. We have divided our responsibilities in accordance with our individual interests, teaching experiences, and greatest competence. Except for mutual editorial assistance, Roland Stromberg alone wrote the historical section, Paul Conkin all the analytical chapters. We collaborated on the transitional chapter 7 of Part I, and on the final, brief epilogue.

In such a joint effort we recognize the difficulty of thanking adequately the many people whose expertise and goodwill have lightened our task, from librarians to typists. But we do want especially to note the contributions of the students in Stromberg's historiography seminar at the University of Wisconsin-Milwaukee, and in Conkin's courses in the philosophy of history, first at the University of Wisconsin–Madison, and now at Vanderbilt University. We also want to thank the readers of the manuscript, who made many useful suggestions for improvements.

PAUL K. CONKIN
ROLAND N. STROMBERG

Profitable philosophical discussion of any science depends on a thorough familiarity with its history and its
present state.

—Norwood Hanson, *Patterns of Discovery*

PART I
THE HERITAGE OF HISTORY

CHAPTER 1

THE ROOTS OF WESTERN HISTORY: THE ANCIENT WORLD

The Uniqueness of Western Historical-Mindedness

THE place of history in Western civilization has been a uniquely great one—a legacy of the dual tradition of Hebraism and Hellenism, of the Judeo-Christian sense of time and the Greek critical spirit. Few if any civilizations have possessed this sort of historical-mindedness.

It may be thought that no society can "escape history," and this is in some sense true. The past lies around us everywhere we look, in the form of physical mementos such as buildings, monuments, and objects of art and utility; and in the legends and tales preserved about memorable deeds, such as even savages relate. The past is a gigantic fact almost comparable to physical nature in its presence. Teaching about the past is a constant element found in all societies, some have asserted. Certain forms of historical consciousness doubtless exist even in primitive societies. Nevertheless, primitive people and some of our most highly developed civilizations, above all the Oriental ones, have not endowed time with the kind of value that Western people have always ascribed to it. In his interesting book *Cosmos and History: The Myth of the Eternal Return*, the distinguished historian of religions Mircea Eliade pointed out that traditional or "archaic" societies, the kind that most people have lived in during most of humanity's time on earth, typically "refuse history." Though they often believed in a golden age in the past (the oldest and most ubiquitous of all human myths), primitive or archaic people lived in a timeless dimension, ritualized around primordial acts in a way that seems determined to deprive time of any real meaning. And if we turn to a very sophisticated and old civilization, that of India, we see clearly that its modes of thought ascribe no significance or "ontological content" at all to time. It is without meaning. The Indian tradition posits huge time cycles of millions of years which always come back to the same place. Creation, destruction, and new creation go on

3

endlessly, rather like the explosion of the primeval atom followed by its eventual contraction back into that atom, in a cycle of some eighty billion years, which present-day astronomical science tells us is the pattern of the physical cosmos. There is no progress and no goal, only the endless turning of the wheel of time around and around. Under such conditions history can have no importance. Indian philosophy and religion—whether Brahman, Buddhist, or Jainist—have often taught people to aim at escaping the wheel of existence by transcending entirely the time-bound human condition, the goal being to attain nirvana, a realm of pure being unbounded by time and space.[1]

Great-cycle theories were familiar to the ancient Greeks, as readers of Plato know. Eliade seems to be correct in his belief that an annihilation of history rather than an acceptance of it has been typical of humankind, and that Western civilization has been atypical in its intense historical-mindedness. Western time has been rectilinear rather than cyclical and thus has been meaningful rather than meaningless. This idea came from the unique religion of the Jews, borrowed by Christianity (and later by Islam), which presupposed a god's intervention in human events and perceived a final goal of history. Western history has, moreover, usually been seen as at least partly determined by humans themselves rather than as externally determined by an inscrutable external will or fate. This idea came from the unique philosophy of the ancient Greeks, who invented rational and scientific thought. Just as the combination of Greek and Hebraic elements formed Western civilization in general, the combination of the two elements produced the Western sense of history: in origin, the meaningfulness of time was Judeo-Christian; human self-determination, Hellenic.

In the early kingdoms of the Near East where the first human civilizations arose—Egyptian, Sumerian, Babylonian—no history was written, really. People recorded and kept genealogies while kings boasted of their deeds. But we find no sense of history as it later came to be understood because they discerned no plan or pattern in the flow of events; things happened as they did because of the "incalculable whims of the Gods."[2] The creation of large unified empires run by efficient states helped in some ways to prepare the way for written history. In the first place, they provided significant units of history. No units extensive enough to have a significant history exist if people are dispersed in numerous small tribes or villages; a certain size and importance is necessary. We need only recall the extent to which history has flourished in modern times around the nation-state unit. Historians have told of the birth, rise, and growth of England, France, Germany, the United States, and so on. Where power became centralized, the story of this power took on importance. The deeds of Nebuchadnezzar and

Ramses II in ancient times were worth recording and boasting about, since these potentates were rulers of mighty kingdoms. Such recording of major action was a beginning of history. But the ancient storytellers seldom carried the matter any further; they never sought to explain those deeds, to discern their meaning, or to see them as a process.

The Assyrians, the Chaldeans, the Hittites, and the Egyptians of the New Kingdom (from c. 1500 B.C.) began the extensive preservation of documents in official archives. Theirs were highly developed states, fully in possession of the art of writing. No governmental bureaucracy is able to resist the impulse to preserve its records; it is a practical necessity as well as a badge of dignity. Yet it remained true that little or nothing that could be called history was written: no one undertook to narrate or describe the happenings of the past in coherent form. For all our recent upgrading of the achievements of these ancient peoples as our knowledge about them has grown (a veritable revolution since 1900, brought about by archaeological excavation), we still cannot make them historians. We must agree that critical inquiry into human affairs began with the Greeks and that the Jews were indeed a "peculiar people" in attaching so much importance to the events of human history.

The ancient Hebrews, once regarded by Christians and Muslims as well as by themselves as a people chosen by divine Providence for a unique and wondrous revelation, seem a bit less "peculiar" in the light of modern historical research. In the nineteenth century the first wave of higher criticism stressed the many similarities between Judaic beliefs and those of the more powerful peoples who surrounded the tiny Jewish state—Babylonians, Egyptians, Assyrians, and others. But if this view is true in some details, it is not true of the Hebrews' larger outlook. Their religion broke away from the prevalent pattern and became one of the greatest in world history. For our purposes, the significance of this spiritual revolution lies in its intense consciousness of history—its charging of temporal events with the greatest possible amount of "ontological content." And this vision of history was planted deeply in the consciousness of Western humanity by its expression in the Jewish Bible, constantly read, recited, and meditated on for so many centuries.

Harry Elmer Barnes has called the Jewish Bible a "story-telling masterpiece" and the first "truly historical narrative of considerable scope and high relative accuracy." It is much nearer to popular folk history than to scientific or critical history. It is mixed with myth; it is not critical; it is passionate and imaginative; and it contains its share of errors and oversimplifications. But it is more than a chronicle, usually more than the bare record of occurrences without context or interpretation which Babylonian and Egyptian kings left behind. It locates a purpose in history; it has a theme. History was part and parcel of the

religion of Israel; the Jews believed that each event of history testified
to the will of their god. They were the children of Yahweh, the one
god. But why did he raise them up and then cast them down? The
prophets attributed these calamities to Israel's sinfulness and called for
repentance and atonement. What lay ahead? A "history religion" such
as that of the Jews must see in the historical process some purposeful
direction and final goal. History would come to a grand climax. A Mes-
siah would come to redeem the Jewish people and restore their kingdom
and power. Or perhaps this final triumph would bring this world to an
end and usher in another and better one. Perhaps Israel would have
to suffer, a martyr to humanity, but it would at least serve a providential
purpose.

The Jewish messianic and eschatological consciousness was of course
handed on to the first Christians, who were also Jews. The Incarnation
and the future Apocalypse or Last Judgment were specific historic phenomena that made time, to the Christian, a linear dimension, charged
with meaning and divided into significant epochs. All history before the
birth of Jesus led up to this climax; afterward, one looked forward to
the Last Day, which might come at any time. (Certain hints and clues
in the Bible provided generations of Christians with the absorbing game
of figuring out just when it might come—a game played in almost every
decade, including quite recent ones.) It should be noted also that, for
the Christian, this was a universal plan, tying all humankind together
in the same providence, since Jesus offered his message of salvation to
all so that all could learn of it and accept it.

"The Christian religion is a daily invitation to study history," a modern
scholar, F. M. Powicke, has written. Rooted in concrete happenings, it
has caused even its foes to share that historical interest. What actually
did happen in Jerusalem some two thousand years ago? And had the
events been foretold? Is the Bible true and of divine origin, as Christians
have claimed, or could it be convicted of falsity? An incredible amount
of research has been devoted to such questions; it once was the chief
concern of scholarship. In later years Protestants and Roman Catholics
also disputed the history of the early church. More recently, beyond
the specific concern for the biblical narratives, this framework of reference has passed into the consciousness of many people who have
renounced literal Christianity. Many adherents of modern secular versions of millennial and eschatological history "live by what they choose
to forget," Jacques Maritain remarked. Atheistic socialists and agnostic
liberals silently adopted the framework. They wrote schemes of history
marked by progress toward a final goal without realizing that the structure of their history came originally from Judeo-Christian sources. Even
after abandoning Christianity, they could not escape its vision of history,

for that vision continues to shape the structure of modern secular ideologies.

Yet something else was needed to produce a satisfactory historical view. Despite their concern with aspects of historic time, devout Christians did not usually make the best historians. Not only were they often credulous, as some of the early Christian chronicles well demonstrate, but their range of interest was narrow and they lacked principles of explanation and selection. They recorded their troubles; they waited for the Day of Judgment; they invoked the wrath of God against pagan empires. While insisting (against the Greeks) that no event was the result of chance or blind fate but was part of a providential order, early Christians did not make this principle historically insufficient. One who thinks that all events are equally providential will attach significance to them and perhaps record them; but on what basis will one select and order them? No historian goes far in his work without realizing that he must select some events, from the inexhaustible supply of them, because they are for some reason more important than others; then he must order them according to some scheme of relationship. Precisely because they attached so much importance to each and every event—the fall of a sparrow comes before God's eyes as clearly as the fall of a kingdom— Judeo-Christian historians found it hard to select and organize.

After toying in the nineteenth century with the idea that secular history is virtually the same as divine purpose, Christian theologians have tended to return to an older view. We cannot discern God's will in secular history. We may need to know this history, but it is not the path to salvation. The Christian has faith that at the end of the road, somehow, the last trumpet that heralds life everlasting will sound; but we cannot see at all clearly the road that leads to that place. Truly Christian historiography has tended to find in each day fresh miracles, evidence of God's will, and yet no plan or pattern that merely human intelligence can decipher. For we see through a glass darkly, and only in another world will we see clearly. The Christian rejoices in the mystery and is content to believe that all will come out well despite the evidences of disorder in the world. If we must concede that the Bible lies at the heart of all Western consciousness of human time, we must also admit that biblical history is nothing like the modern kind of history, which wrests, or tries to wrest, from the past its secrets of cause and effect, sequence and orderly process. Some Christians regard such an effort as blasphemous.

Eusebius of Caesarea, the first significant Christian historian, did not organize his material well; his first work was a bare chronicle, and his deservedly praised *Ecclesiastical History* lacked a plan of development. Perhaps because he was a Greek, he was critical (though there was no reason why the works of Christian historians should not be critical and accurate; that the early ones often were not probably reflects only that they were written by poor and uneducated people). Eusebius was certainly industrious. But he cannot be compared with the great Greek historians Herodotus and Thucydides. Subsequent Christian historians would dwell upon the expansion of Christianity and the work of missionaries. It could be argued that Christians lacked sufficient sympathy with merely secular questions to have much interest in careful examination of them. In observing a war between rival kingdoms, a Christian might simply dismiss it as a judgment on the pagans; could he have analyzed it as exhaustively as Thucydides did the Peloponnesian War? A pronounced moralizing cast and a powerful prejudice operated on the Christian. So they do, arguably, on most historians. But some ingredients were lacking to make the best history—a more critical spirit, a more open mind, and a belief in more human freedom, all of which were contributed by the Greeks.

Jacques Maritain has observed that coherent historical writing requires freedom within a pattern of providence. If there is only chance and caprice, then no meaningful structure is possible; complete determinism allows no drama or interest. Christianity does leave humans the dignity of being free participants within the framework of a general providence (at least most versions of Christianity do); in Homer, by contrast, as an eighteenth-century English critic observed, "there is hardly a stone or javelin thrown, or an arrow shot, that is not either directed or turned aside by some god." So the Greeks did not always differ from the Christians in this respect. Nevertheless, Greek classical thought about humanity and fate, as developed in the great Athenian tragedies at the zenith of Hellenic civilization in the sixth and fifth centuries B.C., shows a remarkable balance between the two. Though accused by Christians of believing in blind fate and at times strongly addicted to cyclical views (there is little notion of progress in classical thought),[3] the Greeks nevertheless, as R. G. Collingwood has observed, "had a lively and indeed a naive sense of the power of people to control their own destiny."[4] It is exactly this tension between remorseless fate and proud human will that gives Greek drama its power. Strong individuals face the inscrutable necessity of things (not divine Providence in the Christian sense, but a fate bound up in the laws of existence) and are usually beaten, but they are often the victims of their own blindness or arrogance. They could have beaten fate had they known just a little more or had they overcome the tragic flaw in their characters. It is typical of Greek tragedy that an otherwise strong and noble person is finally defeated by a fatal flaw of this sort. Life is hard and searches out every human weakness. Heroes go to their doom. Yet a noble person is great even in defeat. Nor is his doom inevitable; it is conceivably within his power to overcome fate and evade his tragic destiny; though no such escape is seen on the Greek stage, the effect of the drama on the spectators is not to depress but to exhilarate them.

Sophocles and Aeschylus are not irrelevant to Herodotus and Thucydides, for the dramatists and the historians shared the same closely integrated Athenian culture and were even personal friends. Many a commentator has discerned in Thucydides' great *History of the Peloponnesian War*, one of the masterpieces of all historical literature, something akin to the structure of Greek tragedy. But the miracle of Athens in the Periclean age included more than its art and drama. Science and philosophy were the greatest Greek contributions to humankind. They were born as one in the Ionian isles of Asia Minor in the seventh century B.C., as a critical, inquiring, and above all ordered way of thinking, an effort to explain phenomena in terms of abstract ideas rather than of myth. Critical history was born about the same time. "The origin of Greek historiography, like Greek philosophy, lies in Ionic thought," writes Arnaldo Momigliano.[5] Herodotus was not the first Greek historian. Behind him was Hecataeus, behind him Xenophanes, and behind him probably some pioneer whose name has been lost—it is an irony that history does not know its own founder.

In the eyes of the Greeks the original historian was Homer, the supreme epic poet. Homer did indeed use an alleged historical event, the Trojan War, as subject matter. Historians still argue about whether such an event actually took place. Homer's treatment of it in any case is too fanciful to be "history." Between Homer and Herodotus—that is, between roughly the ninth and sixth centuries B.C.—prose replaced poetry as the appropriate language in which to record past events. The scientist's sober facts began to replace the mythmaking imagination, in part at least because of the widespread use of writing and record-keeping. The true parent of history was the alphabet, which the Greeks borrowed from the Phoenecians; the spread of literacy was its precondition.

Historical research of any quality depends on written records. In recent times students of African societies have faced the problem of trying to reconstruct history on the basis of oral traditions alone, and they have found the task difficult if not impossible. We need a variety of written documents and records as well as narratives of events before we can begin to put together an account of the past which has any claim to validity. The other main source of evidence is archaeological—the remains of physical artifacts used by humans. Taken alone, however, this evidence is normally too slender to yield more than sketchy knowledge about the human past. Oral records, however marvelously developed by the bards of premodern cultures (who committed to memory incredible amounts of material), can preserve only a partial account of the past, and they are usually pressed into coherence by a liberal use of fantasy.

The Greeks' development of a unique written language based on the phonetic alphabet—a language remarkable for its lucidity—accompanied the development of a uniquely critical spirit. The word "history" comes from the Greek word meaning "inquiry," and unquestionably we must credit the Greeks, who invented so many things intellectual, with the founding of history as an autonomous subject of inquiry rather than as a branch of religion or as a by-product of mythology. It was a part of that skeptical and critical Ionic revolt against traditional mythology which gave birth to philosophy, to science, virtually to thought itself. By the time this intellectual growth had reached fifth-century Athens, it had ripened and was ready to give birth to Socrates and Plato, to Aeschylus, Sophocles, and Euripides, to Hippocrates, to the Parthenon and the sculpture of Praxiteles, and to all the other glories of classical Greece. Herodotus and Thucydides represented the muse Clio in this amazing gallery of genius.

Despite what we have said about the importance of written records, it must be admitted that our first acknowledged historians in the Western tradition relied very little on archival sources, as few existed. They remedied this lack by writing largely about recent events and by searching out quantities of oral testimony, which they treated critically. Herodotus tells us when he has to leave his eyewitness sources and rely on tradition. Thucydides and Polybius were men of affairs with leisure and a wide acquaintance. They all traveled extensively in search of evidence. Polybius, indeed, insisted on reenacting the experiences he recorded; like a modern historian who duplicated the voyages of Columbus, he retraced Hannibal's footsteps over the Alps. And these early Greek historians developed a remarkable ideal of austerely objective research, with the goal of creating works of value for all time, not just an ephemeral account. Thucydides labored for thirty years on the 600 pages of his famous *History of the Peloponnesian War*. He boasted that he applied "the most severe and detailed tests possible" to his data and that he had left out "romance" to concentrate on "exact knowledge." It was a remarkable achievement.

The Great Greek and Roman Historians

Among the Greek and Roman historians, Herodotus, Thucydides, Polybius, Tacitus, and Livy are still widely read. Their works are still available in many editions, and presumably they always will continue to be read as long as there are literate people. They are "classics." Other historians, such as Xenophon, Sallust, Procopius, Suetonius, and the Romanized Jew Josephus, are not far behind them in popularity. Students of Greek and Roman history are acquainted with many others, most of whose works have been lost or survive only in fragments. Indeed, we have only portions of the output of the greater Greek and Roman historians—only 35 of Livy's 142 books, for example.

Herodotus, an inquisitive and much-traveled Greek from Asia Minor, has gained the title of "father of history." His major work on the Persian Wars of the Greeks was ridiculed by the irreverent Aristophanes, and he was long regarded as the father of lies as well as of history; yet he was held in deep respect throughout ancient times. Today the essential accuracy of Herodotus in most matters has been accepted. His work is less systematic and structured than that of Thucydides, who is generally regarded as the greater of the two. But Herodotus, who wrote in the middle of the fifth century B.C., has always appealed more to some readers because of what Johann von Herder termed his "wider humanity." Herodotus wrote in happier times than those of a generation later, when Thucydides took up a pen dipped in tragedy to analyze the bitter civil wars of the Greek cities. He wrote to "preserve from oblivion the memory of men's deeds, and to prevent the great and wonderful actions of the Greeks and the Barbarians from losing their proper share of glory; and to record the grounds of their quarrel." Herodotus tried to be critical and to give naturalistic explanations of events. He referred less often to divine intervention than Homer had done in his poetic account of the Trojan War several centuries earlier. He did not always avoid such providential explanations, however, and today we smile at some of his judgments. He was essentially a storyteller, and a most skillful one. He had a far-ranging curiosity about peoples and places, and his Greekness emerged in his concern to separate truth from falsehood by careful inquiry; he knew the value of firsthand testimony and sought, though in no very systematic way, to devise means to test the authenticity of accounts and the credibility of witnesses.

Unlike the Hebrews, the Greeks usually saw no long-range plan or purpose in the course of history. They studied particular events that revealed tragedy and human interest. The war that broke out in 431 B.C. between Athens and Sparta and their allies had both. Thucydides' great masterpiece was a study in contemporary history, as for the most part Herodotus' was too. It went far toward establishing the whole canon that ancient historical writers after them were to follow. The immortal preface declares proudly: "I have written my work not as an essay which will win the applause of the hour, but as a possession for all time." The style was brilliant, if rather tightly woven. Thucydides made up the speeches with which his work is liberally sprinkled, models of oratorical skill. This practice puzzled and sometimes repelled later scholars, but the speeches add to the effect; and they were, Thucydides claimed, essentially if not literally correct. They helped him in his examination of people's motives and dilemmas. J. B. Bury has called Thucydides' account "the longest and most decisive step that has ever been taken by a single man towards making history what it is today." This book by a former Athenian general (exiled after a military failure) could, perhaps, be criticized for its neglect of all but political matters, but its concentration on politics gives it unity and strength, too. Perhaps nowhere else have narrative power, rigorous analysis, and dramatic tension been so effectively combined. Behind this effort, which Thucydides never finished despite his thirty years' labor, lay the goal of learning in order to understand. His book is an anatomy of war and revolution, of the internal and external breakdown of order, written in the belief that future people might avoid such tragedies if only they could learn from history. It leaves divine intervention and miraculous happenings wholly out of the picture. Thucydides hoped "it may be judged useful by those who desire an exact knowledge of the past as an aid to the interpretation of the future, which in human affairs must resemble if it does not duplicate the past."

The hope that from the study of the past one might extract laws that could be applied profitably to the future was destined to prove illusory. The future not only fails to duplicate the past; often it does not even resemble it. There are always too many differences between the past and the present to permit past experiences to be wholly applicable to present circumstances. The unhistorical outlook of the Greeks—their failure to see much development or progress—is revealed here. We can expect to apply past lessons to future problems only if we assume that nothing changes very much, that people and circumstances stay substantially the same. Despite this fundamental criticism, which can be applied to almost all of classical historiography, Thucydides' work has indeed remained a possession for all time, and it dominated the entire ancient tradition of historical writing. For many years every historian wrote in the shadow of the two great Athenians, just as all philosophers were long disciples of Plato and Aristotle.

The names of a number of Greek historians after Thucydides are known, but the writings of only a few, including Xenophon and Diodorus, have survived. In the later, Hellenistic period a profusion of historians with a corresponding dilution of quality evidently signaled a certain decadence in the field, as in other areas of Greek thought and art. It was no longer the day of the *polis*, or self-governing city, but of

Alexander's empire and its successor kingdoms. The day is not long enough to enumerate them all, Dionysus of Halicarnassus wrote of these authors. Polybius inveighed against them on the grounds that they sacrificed truth to stylistic effects. For historians at all times one problem is how to be scholarly yet readable, analytical but not arid. Rhetoric gained ascendancy now in the realm of historical writing, evidently at the cost of austere Thucydidean canons of scholarship. The lack of professional organization doubtless encouraged those historical writers who sought easy popularity. It was an increasingly urban and culturally democratic age. Since little of this historiography survived, we cannot be sure that masterpieces were not lost. A vast body of writing about Alexander the Great seems to have mysteriously disappeared. We may speculate that, as a branch of rhetoric (the art or science of persuasion), lacking autonomy as a distinct discipline, history fell victim to partisan uses in an age when cultural consensus was weakening. Here is another fine line the historian always must walk, the line between objectivity and commitment.

At any rate, the originally unintellectual Romans now began to absorb Greek culture, and Clio's torch passed to a series of great Roman historians. The first to pass it, Polybius, was the last great classical Greek historian, one who can bear comparison with Herodotus and Thucydides. Captured in 168 B.C. and taken to Rome, Polybius became the friend and tutor of prominent Romans. He was one of the first to bring Greek literature and learning to the city on the Tiber, which, though engaged in conquering the world, was still almost barbarous in its thought. His imagination was struck by the meteoric rise of Rome, as well it might be: "Can anyone be so indifferent or idle as not to care to know by what means and under what policy almost the whole of the inhabited world was conquered and brought under the rule of a single city, and that within a period of not quite fifty-three years?" Such extraordinary occurrences are what stimulate historical inquiry, and of all rises and falls the greatest was that of the Roman Empire. Polybius watched its rise and wanted to know why it rose.

Such causal factors are extraordinarily difficult to establish with precision, and it cannot be said that Polybius succeeded in finding them. But his search was both stimulating and productive. Highly critical, admirably impartial, a man of affairs himself with much experience of the world and a splendid writer, Polybius is one of the greatest of all historians. The apprentice historian can perhaps learn more from him than from any other model. He had an extraordinarily keen eye for the apt illustration, the telling incident. But Polybius never quite solved the riddle of causes. His most notable answer to the question of why the Romans flourished pointed to the balance of the Roman constitution, in which he found a happy blend of the classic types of government—democracy, aristocracy, and monarchy—which allowed scope for common people, nobility, and a single ruler. He believed this balance enabled the empire to avoid the cycle of decay which the Greeks thought inevitably afflicted each of these orders in turn.

Polybius looked at republican Rome in its days of youth and success and admired the character of this sturdy people. The other outstanding Roman historians chronicle the process of decay. Titus Livy (59 B.C.–A.D. 17) wrote, it is true, at the beginning of the imperial era, in the Augustan age, and told in patriotic vein a story of success. But he was aware of deterioration in Roman character and institutions and wrote in part to revive the Romans' morale by showing them the stuff of which their forefathers were made. Livy may seem less of a historian than the others we have mentioned partly because he was unable to draw on documentary sources. He purveyed legends about the early history of Rome. But not only was he a gifted stylist, he also sought explanations and had the Romans' reverence for the past. This trait was far more evident among the Romans than among the Greeks. Neither Herodotus nor Thucydides was particularly concerned about tradition. It is clear that Livy was widely read and played a large part in that temporary Augustan recovery of morale to which Virgil's *Aeneid* also contributed. Here we see one of the practical functions history can serve: pride in one's race, nation, or other group. Noteworthy also is the fact that Rome's unification of the ancient world enabled Livy to adopt a global perspective, to see all the various local histories as part of one great stream.

For many readers, the greatest Roman historian, and perhaps their all-time favorite, was the scintillating Tacitus, who wrote from about A.D. 85 to 115, a time when the empire was reaching its peak of power and glory but was already beginning the process of internal decay and suffering from its persistent problem, the imperial succession. It is difficult to praise Tacitus' style too highly, style is above all what we can learn from him. He is compulsively readable; the brilliance of his writing leaves one breathless. It varies from epigrammatic brevity to full description, from sober narrative to poetic lyricism. His subject matter was largely court politics. The period between A.D. 30 and 112, about which he wrote (essentially the history of his own time), though we may think of it as Rome's silver if not golden age, was, he says, "rich in disasters, frightful in its wars, torn by civil strife, and even in peace full of horrors."

The devastating record of human weakness and depravity that Tacitus presents is rivaled only by the verse of his near-contemporaries Horace and Juvenal. With them we enter a different moral universe, which is very nearly that of the artist-intellectual alienated from his society. Tacitus is a moralizing historian, famous for his statement that "[h]istory's highest function is to ensure that noble actions are not left unrecorded and that evil words and deeds are held up to the reprobation of posterity." His criteria of selection are those deeds that were either "conspicuous for excellence or notorious for infamy." He found more of the latter than of the former. Tacitus is known also for his work on the Germans; in his praise of those uncorrupted barbarians one can read a reproach against his own civilization. It was once thought that the literary quality of the *Histories* and the *Annals* exceeded their factual reliability; James Westfall Thompson even said we should read Tacitus "as a great writer . . . but not as an historian." But the monumental researches of one of the greatest of modern classicists, Sir Ronald Syme, have gone far toward vindicating his integrity. Within his range, Tacitus is now generally accorded high honors. His frank moralism and bitter partiality (hardly consistent with his proclaimed desire to write *sine ira et studio*, without anger or bias) may seem strange to a modern historian; but, diligent in research and generally accurate in facts, Tacitus stands without rivals in the presentation of complex events and personalities.

Weaknesses of Ancient Historiography

It will be observed that Tacitus' range was narrow. He and the other ancient historians wrote almost exclusively political history, and almost exclusively of their own time. The reasons lay mainly in the nature of the materials on which they could draw for their sources. Livy had to rely on legends about early Rome because very few documents had been preserved. Thucydides excluded on principle any topic except one about which he could interview living witnesses. There were then no great collections of manuscripts in archives, nor were there numerous professional scholars to sort out such documents and publish their finding in learned journals. Thus, by modern standards, the scope of ancient historians was severely limited both in the time span they could cover and in subject matter. On the other hand, one cannot legitimately criticize a writer for not writing a book other than the one he or she did, nor can one deny the high significance of the subjects these first historians chose: the Greek wars, the rise of Rome, the moral decline of the Roman ruling class.

Ancient historiography has been criticized on more serious grounds. "Livy and Tacitus stand side by side as the two great monuments to the barrenness of Roman historical thought," Collingwood wrote in his *Idea of History*. He also turned thumbs down on Thucydides. These are extreme judgments, but Collingwood made some valid points. Despite Thucydides, the Greeks did not value historical work highly. Although some Greeks held other views, the dominant school of classical philosophy was rooted in what Collingwood called "substantialism," or essentialism; that is, philosophers searched for substances and essences, which they regarded in the Platonic manner as changeless and eternal, not transitory and evolutionary.

Plato, whose philosophy exerted a powerful influence on Western civilization for many centuries, held that the only real objects of knowledge are unchanging ideas or models that have a timeless reality; the changeable sensory world, a more or less imperfect copy of this eternal realm, is illusory and untrustworthy, and empirical investigation of its events is therefore not the main road to truth. Plato's particular view of history, as expressed in *The Republic*, was of a degenerative or cyclical process. From an ideal golden age mankind has decayed, as everything in nature must. But Plato suggests a cycle rather like that of his great student and successor Aristotle: from timocracy to oligarchy to democratic revolution leading back to elite rule and so endlessly around, though seemingly in a descending spiral. Thus Greek thought was not truly historical; it did not see the present as a product of the past, nor did it see anything as a product of the experience of such a past. The Greeks viewed human nature substantialistically: people have a given nature, which is their essence, and which does not change; the idea that such natures are shaped through time was uncongenial to the ancients. The school of Thucydides, rooted in a belief in the changelessness of things, believed that past and present situations could be exactly compared, as we have noted.

Herbert Butterfield, distinguished author of *The Origins of History* (1981), agreed that Greek habits of thinking tended toward "drawing the mind away from the changing and transient and fixing it upon the eternal and immutable." The Thucydidean outlook, echoing down through the centuries, was repeated by John Dryden in the seventeenth century:

> History helps us to judge of what will happen, by showing us the like revolutions of former times. For mankind being the same in all ages, agitated by the same passions, and moved to action by the same interests, nothing can come to pass but some precedent of the like nature has already been produced, so that having the causes before our eyes, we cannot easily be deceived in the effects, if we have judgment enough but to draw the parallel. [*Life of Plutarch*]

Their inveterate habit of looking for the general in specifics made the Greeks good scientists but poor historians, for history is not a generalizing science. Aristotle, who made the decisive pronouncements on Greek thought, ranked history below both philosophy and poetry, since it approaches neither perfect truth nor perfect beauty. It is the realm of probability and conjecture, of particular rather than general truth.

The failure of history to be accorded a place in the medieval universities, to be deemed the equal of philosophy and mathematics, was a legacy of this bent of mind. History was regarded as a practical subject, like engineering; it was thought to be of much value to politicians but of no philosophical interest. Or it was regarded as a subordinate branch of ethics, its function being to supply the examples of those principles discovered by reason. The Romans, more perhaps than the Greeks, certainly respected it highly on this level. In Cicero's famous definition, history is "the light of truth, the witness of time, the mistress of life." The first metaphor reflected the very worthy and very pronounced ancient belief that the historian must be unbiased, impartial, and critical. "History's first law is that an author must not dare to tell anything but the truth; its second is that he must make bold to tell the whole truth," Cicero declared. Lucian, a Greek in Roman service, whose manual *How to Write History* is about the only such formal treatise of methodology surviving from the ancient world, gave the same advice. His work says just about all any such manual has ever said on the need to examine sources critically, to use original sources, and to watch out for biased witnesses. Like Leopold von Ranke seventeen hundred years later, Lucian advises the historian to relate an event exactly as it happened, without intruding his own prejudices: "The historian's one task is to tell the thing as it happened. . . . He has to make his brain a mirror, unclouded, bright, and true of surface. . . . Historians are not writing fancy school essays."

As "the witness of time," history had pietistic value in keeping alive great deeds and great ideas, which otherwise would be lost to view. The Jews, like the Romans, a people with a deep sense of the national community, expressed this idea in the passage of Ecclesiasticus which begins "Let us now praise famous men": "Their seed shall remain forever, and their glory shall not be blotted out." We can hear Tacitus adding that neither should the memory of infamous men be forgotten, as a warning and a lesson to posterity. As "the mistress of life," history was "an instruction for the present and a warning for the future," a later humanist put it. We can learn lessons of conduct and polity from it. In these maxims Cicero summed up most of the classical thinking about history. It was hardly an ignoble testament. We seek truth; we preserve the best of the past to build civilization; we profit from the lessons of the past.

Yet the fact remains that all of the ancient historians were very un-historical by modern standards, for they did not understand the reality of change. They did not see any overall direction in history and believed events happened in a kind of eternal present. They did not sense process, evolution, organic change taking place. Perhaps this is why, despite the great genius of a few, the run-of-the-mill historical writing of the ancient world seems to have been pretty poor stuff. It tended to be rhetorical and bombastic. In fact, as a school subject it was placed under rhetoric; its function was to teach moral philosophy by example. In lesser hands, the Thucydidean set speech became an excuse for writing history by making up imaginary orations. Didacticism, which we see in Plutarch, reduced historical writing to polite essays on how "lives of great men all remind us we can make our lives sublime." The dangers of Tacitus' approach are obvious: history becomes indignant moralizing or political polemics. A tension remains between vowing, on the one hand, to write history without anger or prejudice (Tacitus) and, on the other, declaring its highest purpose to be the inculcation of sound morals and the den-unciation of vice.

For all its blind spots, ancient historical writing is a magnificent her-itage. At its best both critical and philosophical, it demonstrates a search for causes, an awareness that one must go beneath the facts to find their "purposes and reasons" (as Sempronius Asellio tells us), an ea-gerness for the truths that diligent study of past experiences can yield to lighten people's load in the future; in it we find rare gifts of style and a keen sense of drama. Like other facets of the Greco-Roman intellectual tradition, it dominated the conception of history in Western civilization for many centuries. Renaissance humanists would revive and disseminate these same concepts hundreds of years later. With delight, Machiavelli and Guicciardini would rediscover and read Polybius and Livy. In most respects, this classical view of history lasted down to the eighteenth century, not to be transformed until the most recent era of history. The great ancient historians exerted a deep influence in other ways: stylistic, of course, as among the leading masters of classical prose, and also political. The idea of a balanced constitution, of apportioning power among the three estates, is one example. John Adams included Polybius among the sources of the United States Constitution. The French Revolutionaries quoted Tacitus and Cicero, and Karl Marx was a persistent reader of Thucydides, as was Thomas Hobbes before him. In our own century some historians criticized the ancient ones for being too exclusively political in their subject matter and called for a more "relevant" or committed history. Ancient historiography from Thucy-dides to Tacitus (and including Julius Caesar, himself no mean historian) was relevant precisely because it was political.

Notes

[1]The Chinese, a rather more worldly people than the Indians, kept elaborate official records (political, administrative). Still, their cyclical, nonprogressive view of history made them relatively unhistorical by Western standards.

[2]Jacquetta Hawkes and Sir Leonard Woolley, *UNESCO History of Mankind*, vol. 1, *Pre-History and the Beginnings of Civilization* (New York: Harper & Row, 1963), p. 815.

[3]Ludwig Edelstein, in *The Idea of Progress in Classical Antiquity* (Baltimore: Johns Hopkins University Press, 1967), seeks to show that this traditional view is wrong. See also Robert Nisbet, *History of the Idea of Progress* (New York: Basic Books, 1980). Admittedly there were some exceptions to the general rule that the ancient Greeks held to the cyclical view; few if any ideas were totally unknown to those eager and wide-ranging inquirers. Still, beyond question the progressivists were a distinct minority, and—more important—their outlook did not survive.

[4]R. G. Collingwood, *The Idea of History* (London: Oxford University Press, 1946), p. 24; see also p. 41.

[5]Arnaldo D. Momigliano, "The Place of Herodotus in the History of Historiography," in his *Studies in Historiography* (New York: Harper & Row, 1966).

CHAPTER 2
MEDIEVAL HISTORICAL WRITING

AT one time the Middle Ages were seen as a vast cultural desert that the peoples of the West traversed in agony, dragging with them the little of the civilization that remained after the fall of Rome. As they struggled on they jettisoned ever more of it until at length they had but two or three battered books to guide them through the Middle Ages. At the end of the trail lay the fountains of the Renaissance, just in time to save the weary traveler from intellectual death. What little there was of literary creation during this eight- or nine-hundred-year period was monkish, poor, nasty, brutish, and short, the last four adjectives meaning much the same as the first. Therefore, one might dismiss the entire period in any account of serious historical work, save for, admittedly, a certain amount of quite primitive chronicling of battles, crusades, and feudal feuds.

Against this obviously distorted picture we might place a different one—that of a most lively and interesting age, disorderly but creative, in which Christianity developed fully, the Germanic barbarians brought their culture into contact with that of Latin Christianity, and a good deal of ancient classical culture was preserved and gradually added to, especially during the revival of intellectual life from the twelfth to the fourteenth centuries. Or we might protest that so long a period has little unity and choose to divide it up into several parts. How to handle those ambiguously titled Middle Ages still presents problems and is an object lesson in historical periodization.

On any showing, much history was written during this era (or these eras), though it perhaps cannot be said that a genuinely historical outlook prevailed. Western historiography owes a decisive debt to the best of the medieval historians for keeping alive a great tradition, even if they added little to the existing Christian and classical conceptions of history.

It might be argued that some of this "monkish" history was an improvement on that produced by the Romans. The Venerable Bede, who lived in Northumbria from about 675 to 735, wrote his much-admired *Ecclesiastical History of the English People* at Jarrow, a monastery that at that time was an unparalleled center of cultural convergence. Its intellectual life drew on the rich though abortive Irish civilization of early medieval times, on the zeal of the Roman church in the missionary age, and on the remnants of classical culture. Greek was known at Jarrow, which had a large library. Bede was acquainted with a wide range of writers, including the historians Eusebius and Josephus; the late Roman-Christian savants Marcellinus, Cassiodorus, and Gregory of Tours (author of a fine sixth-century history of the Franks, indispensable to our knowledge of this obscure period); and Isidore of Seville, a great scholar in Visigothic Spain. Eusebius was his chief historical model, but Bede meditated, like all literate Christians, on the brilliant writings of the Church Fathers—Ambrose, Augustine, Jerome, and Gregory I (the Great)—who set forth the grand role of the Church and Christianity, the City of God that survived the ruin of Rome, the Earthly City that a remorseless Providence had laid low in the most exciting of all historical events. It was this tremendous change that had drawn from Augustine his *City of God*—weak, no doubt, as history, but throbbing with the excitement of a great theme: how the spiritual kingdom, entangled here below with terrestrial empires, would march inevitably toward its eternal destiny. Bede imitated the great African's division of historic time into six ages corresponding to the days of the week and of God's creation—the seventh, equaling the Sabbath, being the Day of Judgment and eternal rest.

Bede sent to Rome for copies of documents in the papal archives and drew widely on other monastic libraries as well as on oral testimony. He was a fine historian. He had, E. W. Watson has said, "the statesmanship to know what was of permanent importance, and the skill to record it clearly and fully."[1] There is a suspicion that he had a touch of English patriotic pride, too. A predilection for the miraculous, some factual slips, and a robust Christian prejudice against pagans and heretics may remind us that we are in the Middle Ages; but no one can doubt that Bede had a vigorous, sharp mind and a fine style. His historical writing obviously represented a fruitful amalgamation of Christian and classical heritages. As a Christian, Bede was moved by a vision of Judgment Day and by a desire to learn how much time remained until the great moment: he began as a chronicler. He also approached history by way of that common medieval exercise, the lives of the saints. Hagiography led to historiography.

If to the devout Christian history is a record of God's incessant supervision of men's affairs, every event, however seemingly trivial, may be charged with the highest significance. But, as we observed earlier, the Christian's general interest in history, as the theater of divine Providence, seems often to have difficulty translating itself into effective historical writing. E. H. Harbison observed that "it is easier to say that God acts constantly in history than to say when and where."[2] Christians' disgust (in that age, at least) with the corruption and confusion of political power made them inclined, like Augustine, to turn away from the profane world after sketching an outline of its decay.

In Bede's case, the Church and the records of holy men provided him with his subject. It is obvious, though, that he had learned something from the pagan historians. Care, thoroughness, the critical method, exactness of analysis, and clarity of organization came from that source. Bede also stressed the moral effect of historical learning, in good classical manner: the past provides us with examples of virtue, and the concrete examples drive the lesson home. ("Sive enim historia de bonis bona referat, ad imitandum bonum auditor sollicitus instigatur": the reader of a good history about good deeds will be stimulated to imitate them.) To Bolingbroke, as late as the eighteenth century, history was "philosophy teaching by example"; to Bede it was Christian virtue taught by example. The concept of history in both cases was a classical one. Bede also made use of the famous Thucydidean device of the set speech.

Bede was admittedly a rarity even in 730: "there was nothing to be compared with him on the Continent at this time," an English scholar boasts. Gregory of Tours, the only early medieval historian to rank with Bede, was really a remnant of Roman culture living on for a time in southern France. In Bede's last years the Muslim tide swept across the Pyrenees. It was turned back but it dominated Spain and southern Italy and controlled the Mediterranean, thus, according to a celebrated historical interpretation, dooming Christian Europe to economic stagnation. The Northumbrian flowering showed what could have happened had it not been for these grave economic and political developments. There were to be other occasional flowerings as Europe struggled through the next few centuries. The great Irish and English monasteries were devastated by the Norse raids, but Alcuin, adviser to Boniface and Charlemagne, carried Northumbrian learning to the Continent. Many lesser Bedes chronicled the affairs of their localities or monasteries. The work begun by Bede was continued in the *Anglo-Saxon Chronicle*, which recorded the main events of English history through the twelfth century, and in the chronicles of Geoffrey of Monmouth (d. 1152) and the more philosophical works of John of Salisbury (d. 1180).

In Charlemagne's circle, too, was Einhard, born about 770 and educated at the influential abbey of Fulda, which Boniface had founded in Franconia and where his tomb is still lovingly preserved. A talented craftsman in all the arts, Einhard, perhaps about 817 to 821, after Charles's death, wrote a fine life of the emperor to whom he was so devoted, though a heavy reliance on the ancients is evident. (Einhard repeats the very words that Suetonius wrote about Roman emperors of the first and second centuries.) Carolingian annalists, in the *Royal Annals of Lorsch*, kept a faithful record of each year's chief events in the manner of the *Anglo-Saxon Chronicle*. Other biographies of kings and popes appeared, and a flood of hagiography. The falsest of the bromides about the "Dark Ages" is that they lacked literary culture. There is almost too much of it. Subject matter tended to be local, reflecting the fragmentation of the age. But when Charlemagne temporarily restored political unity, a renaissance in all the arts burst forth, an indication that cultural resources were present in abundance and needed only some degree of public order to allow them scope for growth. The emperor himself, an eager and omnivorous reader, tried to learn about Latin literature, astronomy, and indeed everything else in this naive infancy of the European mind. We know that he especially liked both Augustine's *City of God* and stories of *antiquorum res gestae*. This Germanic barbarian delight in tales of noble deeds done in the past should be added to the list of factors that conditioned the historiographical tradition. It gave rise to the great medieval epics and sagas.

It was the annals and chronicles of the monks, however, that constituted the chief contribution of the Middle Ages to historiography. Annals were not histories but more like newspapers or almanacs, unstructured daily or yearly recordings of events that seemed worth recording. They were extremely abundant. In an admirable survey of historical writing in England, Antonia Gransden found some 160 works produced between 550 and 1307, and noted that many others were written but failed to survive. Most but not all of the content describes local events. The chroniclers, every monk his own historian, recorded remarkable events, struggles to found, preserve, and extend the monastery, conflicts with kings, such news as reached their ears from the outer world, and many other things. They did so to edify, to entertain, to inspire, all familiar uses of historical narratives. The traditional "exemplarist" use of history is much in evidence: villainy is to be punished and virtue rewarded. They wrote sometimes to make known how "our predecessors sustained tribulations and oppressions, want and labor, for the hope of eternal glory." The most notable philosophical theme, apart from retribution and reward for deeds done, is perhaps *contemptus mundi*: the monks reflected on how the mighty are brought low and how human pride receives its comeuppance. "See how the honors and pleasures and glory of the world come to nothing." (We still find this a common theme in present-day histories.) The reporting of portents, wonders, miracles is common; such reports document the credulity of the age, no doubt, but also an eagerness for novelty quite like that of present-day devourers of sensational stories in the press or on television. Most monastic chroniclers were accurate and conscientious in their use of sources. They were the newspapers of the day, often richly illustrated (Matthew Paris, the chronicler of St. Albans, is credited with inventing the comic strip).

Though these clerical chronicles seldom rose above the level of an unintegrated string of chronological events, occasionally they produced a masterly historian. William of Malmesbury is the notable English example, a careful and critical researcher who seems quite modern in his methods and even in his mentality: skeptical of proclaimed idealistic motives, convinced that most people acted from self-interest, he sought to discover cui bono and enjoyed deflating myths. (He disbelieved the legends about King Arthur which other medieval historians swallowed.)

In time medieval Europe produced cities and universities as well as monasteries and cathedrals. The universities allowed little place for history as such; as in ancient times, it lacked autonomy. The interests of learned men of the High Middle Ages were logic, law, and philosophy. They clutched at these unchanging subjects because they had known too much disorder and fragmentation, and wanted something purer than the muddy political affairs of the world. (Perhaps Clio's reputation had been even further impaired by the association of historical research with the forging of false documents, practiced by certain sophisticated adepts of historical methodology.) "The scholastic method as it developed in the Middle Ages was an utterly unhistorical, if not anti-historical method," wrote E. H. Harbison. "History had little if any real interest for the profoundest thinkers of this age."[3] There were no chairs of history in the universities. Thomas Aquinas wrote nearly one hundred books, in which he had something to say not only about philosophy but about almost every other subject, including ethics, science, psychology, politics, government, and law; about the only subject on which he wrote little or nothing is history. He "had little sense of history, at least as we understand the word," remarks his editor, Thomas Gilby, in an understatement. "He treats his great forerunners as though they were speaking to him then and there."[4] Truth, to Saint Thomas, was not historically conditioned and not relative. He sought it in a timeless dimension. His powerful mind had no feeling for the dialectic of thought in history.

Of course, the apocalyptic mood continued. Such popular sects as the Joachites (followers of Joachim of Fiore) and the Taborites (who rejected everything that had no direct warrant in the Bible except war, which they waged with enthusiasm) pursued the millennium with unflagging (if sometimes flagellant) zeal, as poor men poured their hopes for a better life somewhat pathetically into these expectations of a great "New Deal" to come, suddenly, at any moment. The rich would be cast down and the humble raised up, all would be equal, and paradise would prevail on earth. The often arid logical analysis carried on by the Schoolmen in the universities found its opposite in this highly emotional popular chiliasm. But such unlettered enthusiasts were seldom capable of writing any history; their significance for history lies in their perpetuation of the lively Judeo-Christian sense of a time-goal in history. Most of these cults arose in the later Middle Ages. As Norman Cohn notes, such Joachite versions of the millennium ran counter to the teachings of the Church, since Augustine had made it clear that the Church itself was the realization of the Kingdom of God on earth and that there was no place for a further messianic fulfillment. And some of them went far beyond any possible version of Christianity to anticipate, in Cohn's words, "those latter-day philosophies of history which are most emphatically anti-Christian."[5] Joachim divided history into several ages, each characterized by distinctive features, in an ascending order, much as Condorcet and Comte and Marx were to do. The Middle Ages here bore within itself a whole school of "modern" revolutionary messianism which has deeply influenced present conceptions of history.

Though the temples of learning were in the control of metaphysicians and logicians, Clio was not so easily dismissed. History managed to survive. Biography continued to provide a point of entry; Joinville's life of Saint Louis had to be history as well as biography. The other most frequently reprinted and read historical writings of the high medieval period include the descriptions of the Crusades by Villehardouin and others; Bishop Otto of Freising's *Two Cities*, a twelfth-century work that strongly suggests Augustine's influence; and Froissart's *Chronicles of England, France, and Spain*, most notable for its account of the Hundred Years' War.

Otto, who wrote his *Civitas Dei* after the great investiture controversy had ended in the humiliation of the sacred power by the temporal, bitterly saw the Earthly City and the City of God as separating out into absolute evil and absolute good. Augustine, in his famous work written nearly eight centuries earlier, had seen these two impulses, the love of self and the love of God, intermingled in this world, not to be untangled until the Day of Judgment. As a model for the interpretation of historic events the two-cities concept was a fruitful one. We may translate it into more modern terms as a dialectic of ideas and matter, or of spirituality and power. The dialectic that Hegel and Marx saw as the key to history came, after all, out of the ancient world, from Plato to Augustine via neo-Platonism.[6] The medieval "philosophy of history" is not all that different, *mutatis mutandis*, from modern ones.

Froissart, a fourteenth-century Frenchman, was steeped in the romances and poetry that flourished during the Age of Chivalry—those tales of knights who were not merely bold and brave but courteous and gentle and frequently amorous as well. Froissart was a composer of chivalric tales and love songs. The later Middle Ages civilized the feudal warrior into a high-minded idealist and a well-groomed lover, at least in song, and we have reached the decadence of a ruling class in some respects. But in Froissart's time the great war of England and France broke out, and Froissart, as a Frenchman in the service of England, was in a good position to observe it and to appreciate its drama. (Later he returned to France and served French patrons.) He was a good war reporter and accumulated a great deal of battlefield information. A cosmopolitan writer and diplomat, he traveled back and forth between France and England, in a way typical of those prenationalistic days. He also traveled to Spain to learn what was going on in the war between Aragon, Castile, and Portugal.

In chronicling the events of the Hundred Years' War, Froissart seems remarkably objective. His objectivity comes to appear less remarkable, however, when we understand that he had friends on both sides. In addition, there was a relative lack of national feeling in this war, which has been called the first of the wars of modern nationalism but might more appropriately be seen as the last of the feudal wars. Froissart was not concerned, as a modern reporter doubtless would be, to justify or favor the cause of one side or the other. He was, in quite a singular way, concerned with the nobility of the actions, with the degree to which they met chivalric standards, rather than with the cause itself. It matters not who wins or loses, but how one plays the game, Froissart thinks. He admires warriors who lose gracefully as well as those who win nobly, without regard for the side they are fighting on. In this respect, Froissart reflects his age and class and intellectual training. He is the historian of chivalry.

Every history reflects in part the intellectual outlook of its time. The aristocratic and chivalric elements in Froissart's book, which may not appeal to all modern tastes, reflected an interest that was dominant in his time, and one that commanded his enthusiasm. (He was a devotee of that somewhat sentimental type of late chivalry which created the Order of the Garter and the Knights of the Golden Fleece.) It seems odd to us, no doubt, if not downright sinful, that he looked at the

Peasant Revolt of 1381 largely in this light, disapproving of it because it was led by rather lowbrow and uncourteous types. He was not interested in revolution or in social change in its own right. His work is an interesting study in the preconceptions of historians. This period saw the birth of modern nationalism and a new social and economic order—the things that engage the interest of present historians. Froissart was interested—not quite entirely, but predominantly—in noble deeds done on the field of battle. "It is of little value to criticize him for not being what he never intended to be," a recent writer about him sighs—nor, we should add, what he could not have been.

Historians are themselves products of history. Froissart could sketch a scene and describe a battle splendidly. In seeking to get at the truth as critically as he could, he demonstrated the perennial quality of the historian. Because he did not have enough evidence, he often failed. He supplies a good deal of colorful incident in his excellent prose. Ironically, later historians found him a mine of information about things he put in only as background for knightly battles. They were not interested in the battles but were fascinated by the incidental details that shed light on life and work in his time. This would certainly have surprised Froissart.

A source of knowledge to later historians, as were Bede and Einhard and Gregory of Tours and a large number of medieval chroniclers—a great, invaluable source—Froissart was not quite a historian himself. He was more a romantic war correspondent, offering superb vignettes of battles and of other dramatic events of his time. He did not put them together in any connected way to supply a single sustained account of a process or a period. In all likelihood, he could not have understood the value of such an enterprise; if he had been able to understand, he would not have been interested in it. Enough for him to have found a chivalrous action, a knightly encounter, a glorious deed! He expressed one of the basic themes of the Middle Ages, as did Bede (the Church), Joachim (the Apocalypse), the Scholastic doctors, and others. Each age must deal with the past in its own way.

Byzantine and Arabic Historical Writing

Learning and the arts in the Middle Ages were far superior in areas adjacent to backward Europe with its poverty, its feudalism, and its lack of populous cities. We are perhaps fonder of this poor old Europe because it is our direct ancestor in the line of civilization and because it was after all rather endearing despite its faults. But historiography, like other branches of knowledge, did much better elsewhere. A prominent

student of Byzantine studies declared that "no other nation, with perhaps the exception of the Chinese, has such a rich historical literature
as the Greeks."[7] At a time when most people of western Europe were
living in mud huts, the Roman Empire withdrew to the banks of the
Bosporus, became fully Greek (its intellectual side had always been primarily Greek), and for several centuries carried on the ancient classical
traditions at the great city of Constantinople. The Byzantine historians
were more numerous and more sophisticated than those of western
Christendom. They had access to great libraries and were supported by
a powerful state at a time when Europeans were terrified by barbarian
bands and scarcely knew what lay beyond their village or monastery.
Yet this Byzantine ghost of the Roman Empire was remarkably con-
servative and tradition-bound and scarcely aspired to break new ground
in cultural affairs. It produced both chronicles and histories. The histories dealt with contemporary or near-contemporary subjects, were
written in classical Greek, and were highly stylized. In brief, they were
well within the Thucydidean tradition. Speros Vryonis, in his *Readings
in Medieval Historiography*, chooses three of them to reprint: those of
Procopius, sixth-century historian of Justinian's memorable reign; Michael Psellus, a versatile eleventh-century professor, author, and politician, rather superficial but brilliant (we can think of many examples
closer to home); and Anna Comnena, a daughter of the emperor Al-
exius, who wrote in the twelfth century amid signs of the empire's final
decline. Comnena is a good storyteller. She avows her dedication to her
parents from earliest infancy, even from the womb, and although she
tells us that she labored to make her account objective, her failure to
achieve this goal is quite evident. She writes to preserve from oblivion
the memory of actions that otherwise would be drowned in Lethe's
gulf—a fine traditional motive for historical writing and, as we know,
one shared by all literate peoples. "The tale of history forms a very
strong bulwark against the stream of time, and to some extent checks
its irresistible flow," she declared. Hers is an appealing personal history,
but it is no more than that.

There is nothing wrong with a good story. We may inquire why our
historian does not go beyond the events themselves to tell us the "causes,"
perhaps the "underlying causes," implying for this function both a more
useful and a more philosophical status. But the full story itself is one
way of presenting the "causes." If we ask why team *A* defeated team *B*
in last week's football game, we may find that some general factors were
involved, such as the better conditioning, the superior ability, the greater
enthusiasm, or the abler coach of team *A*; but then the game itself, all
that happened in it, is part of the explanation, too. The luck of the
game, the dropping of a pass at a crucial moment, an injury to a key

player—everything that happened during the game is part of the reason why one team won. (Causation and explanation are discussed further in Chapter 10.)

But the problem of selection always stares the historian in the face. She cannot possibly put everything in. She must extract the significant elements from the infinite abundance of human experience. So even a descriptive account must focus carefully on the crucial events, pass over the less important ones, and show why those that are included are important. In its exuberance of detail and its fondness for events on purely personal grounds, Comnena's history falls short of this ideal.

As it happens, we have from an only slightly later period an outstanding example of quite a different kind of history, one that aspired to interpretation at the highest level. The Arabic historian Ibn Khaldun (1332–1406) was a ripe product of that brilliant Islamic civilization which in his era was in rapid decline both in Spain and in the Middle East, its twin axes, before the advance of Christians and Turks, respectively. It had, however, far surpassed the civilization of western and even eastern Christendom for several centuries. It produced many other historians, though Khaldun's fame has much overshadowed that of the others. In its great cities with their magnificent libraries it had preserved and added to the ancient classical heritage. The Arabs were the teachers of Europe in the twelfth century; both Scholastic philosophy and the literature of chivalry owed a large debt to them, as is well known.

Ibn Khaldun was born in northern Africa of a family that had once lived in Spain but had been pushed out by the Christian reconquest. He spent most of his life, which he described in an autobiography, in active political work in the Arab principalities of North Africa and southern Spain, even venturing as far as Syria, where he met the great conqueror Timur the Lame. He found time to compose a preliminary volume and six main volumes of his *Universal History*. Arnold J. Toynbee declared that the *Muqaddimah*, or introductory volume to Ibn Khaldun's *Universal History*, is "the greatest work of its kind that has ever been created by any mind in any time or place." Ibn Khaldun was certainly interested in a very sweeping attempt to comprehend nothing less than the causes of the rise and fall of civilizations, as Toynbee was. He had experienced the decline of an Arab empire that had expanded fabulously in the seventh and eighth centuries to embrace most of the Mediterranean shores, only to decline and fall like Rome's. He was aware that there had been other empires that rose and fell in Asia. Ibn Khaldun's deeply inquiring mind was impatient of most earlier historiography. Muslim historians there had been; but he remarks that not only were they uncritical, failing to reject nonsensical stories, but above all "they did not look for, or pay any attention to, the causes of events and conditions." History, he tells us, is popular; both kings and common folk aspire to know it. But what kind of history? Gossip about political leaders, "elegantly presented and spiced with proverbs." There is another dimension, "the inner meaning of history," which is truly philosophical and involves going behind the events to discern their significance.

Every historian worth his pay has come to the same realization. But Ibn Khaldun was perhaps the first to seek the ultimate meaning of history by comparing various civilizations in search of nothing less than the laws that govern the origins, growth, and decay of institutions and cultures. The idea was taken up by Vico and Montesquieu during the European Enlightenment, by a number of nineteenth-century theorists, and more recently in a more extensive way by Arnold Toynbee. It is a task fraught with difficulties and is perhaps inherently impossible despite its allure. It is a measure of Ibn Khaldun's stature that he was aware of all the dimensions of the problem—physical, geographic, psychological, social, and economic. His work was almost grotesquely incomplete; yet it was for centuries a giant pioneering effort without a parallel. The work became known to Europe only in the early nineteenth century, but indirectly it may have seeped in earlier to influence Montesquieu.[8] If Ibn Khaldun arrived at any one explanation for the growth and decay of societies, it was a psychocultural one in which success spoils a people; originally hardy people are rendered effete, corrupt, and selfish by wealth and power, and they fall to a fresh barbarian conquest. (This idea seems to be something like the dynastic-cycles theory of the Chinese historians.) But his work is far more subtle than this crude statement suggests. It touches strongly on intellectual history and on economic history as well; the speculations are those of a far-ranging inquisitive mind. Perhaps only in the twilight of a distinguished civilization are such works possible. Ibn Khaldun's work was almost lost in the darkness that settled over the Arab world not long after his death.

Notes

[1]In A. Hamilton Thompson, ed., *Bede: His Life, Times, and Writing* (1932; New York: Russell & Russell, 1966), p. 59.

[2]E. H. Harbison, *Christianity and History* (Princeton: Princeton University Press, 1964), p. 118.

[3] Ibid., pp. 271–272.

[4]Saint Thomas Aquinas, *Philosophical Texts*, selected and translated by Thomas Gilby (New York: Oxford University Press, 1960), pp. xxi–xxii.

[5]Norman Cohn, *The Pursuit of the Millenium: Revolutionary Messianism in Medieval and Reformation Europe.* . . (New York: Harper Torchbooks, 1961), pp. 100–102.

[6]See chap. 1 of Leszek Kolakowski, *Main Currents of Marxism*: vol. 1, *The Founders* (New York: Oxford University Press, 1978).

[7]Carl Krumbacher, quoted in Speros Vryonis, ed., *Readings in Medieval Historiography* (Boston: Houghton Mifflin, 1968), p. 130.

[8]Such is the conjecture of an article by Warren E. Gates, "The Spread of Ibn Khaldun's Ideas on Climate and Culture," in the *Journal of the History of Ideas* (July–September 1967).

CHAPTER 3
HISTORY IN THE EARLY MODERN PERIOD

The Renaissance

THE time-honored division of Western history which puts "Renaissance and Reformation" together in one basket might perhaps be questioned. Recent social historians have questioned the entire "Ren./Ref." category; looking at popular rather than elite culture or socioeconomic rather than intellectual-cultural elements, they find no significant break in the period from about 1450 to 1650, the traditional if rather vague boundaries of the era. From still another perspective, the rise of the modern territorial state beginning in the later Middle Ages and climaxing in the seventeenth century is the most significant process. Nowhere is the arbitrary nature of periodization more evident than in this "premodern" epoch.

Novelty was not the goal of the men and women who led the two movements of Renaissance and Reformation. The humanists of the Renaissance wanted to go back to ancient Greece and Rome; the reformers wanted to go back to the earliest Christianity. The two movements were not much connected with each other, except in a chronological overlap: it is difficult to imagine minds more different than Machiavelli's and Luther's. For the purpose of a history of history, they stand in the same ambiguous light. Both have been credited with bringing to birth "modern historical scholarship," yet neither intended anything of the sort. If they performed this feat, they did so unintentionally and in quite different ways.

Modern historiography has frequently been traced back to the humanist scholars of the so-called Renaissance but not because of any new conception of history, since in this respect they did not wish to differ from their adored masters, the ancients. First, they revived interest in these historians, in Livy and Polybius and Cicero. Second, they had a "historical" way of looking at things, if by that term we mean a personal and descriptive way as contrasted with the logical abstractions of Scholasticism. This sort of "realism" is a familiar feature of the Italian humanists. "To move from the Golden Legend to the Discourses of Machiavelli is to move from a gloomy Gothic-revival landscape to a brightly lighted Renaissance interior," E. H. Harbison wrote. Machiavelli was not a very good historian; in fact, he was an extremely poor one. (Let anyone who doubts this judgment be condemned to read through all of that endless and formless chronicle of political intrigues, his *History of Florence*.)[1] But he had a feeling for the texture of specific, concrete things and events, as he showed in his famous political writings. He was really interested in a science of politics, and he supposed that he could use the data of former political situations to this end. Such situations are all similar, he held, since human nature does not change and the way of a man with power is constant and perennial. The evening hours that he spent in the courts of old were to Machiavelli an exact substitute for the days he used to pass in the court of Florence. Like Thucydides, Polybius, Josephus, Ibn Khaldun, and many other historians, Machiavelli had once played a part in the world of affairs and wrote about politics partly out of frustration. He was a *homo politicus* who eagerly explored every political experience. But, like the ancients, he possessed little or no sense of historical development. To him, as Felix Gilbert has pointed out, "historical writing was an instrument to disclose the laws of politics."

The Renaissance humanists were inhibited by their classical tastes. They adored and slavishly imitated the ancient historians. Who could presume to supersede Titus Livy?[2] The humanists really had little interest in history as such. As far apart as Erasmus and Thomas Aquinas were on other matters, they were alike in one thing: neither had a historical dimension. If Aristotle spoke to Saint Thomas in the present tense, so spoke Socrates to Erasmus and Paul to Colet. The humanists accepted Aristotle's verdict that poetry outranked history and tended to look upon history as only a branch of literature. They did not value it highly. They confined history to (mostly contemporary) political subjects, considered it to be "philosophy teaching by example," wrote it with rhetorical flourish, and saw it in no context of progression. But a new periodization came into being as a result of the humanist position. Humanists, looking back to an idealized antiquity, inescapably saw the in-between period as a "dark age" and themselves as the age of revival or renaissance. Thus a golden age–dark age–renaissance scheme of periodization, which was new, emerged naturally. The ancients in the main saw, as we know, no general goal in history, but rather an ebb and flow in which the basic situation stayed much the same. The Christians might entertain radically apocalyptic notions of a final destiny, but Renaissance humanists were too moderate, too worldly to have such an outlook. They were seldom really anti-Christian, but their Erasmian Christian humanism played down drastic elements in favor of an ethical code for everyday living. They did inadvertently father a new time scheme, containing elements of the primordial golden age in the past and adding to it a fall from grace (familiar through the Christian doctrine of the Fall) extending over the long period from about A.D. 400 until the revival of culture in the Italian cities in the fourteenth and fifteenth centuries. False as it is seen to be in many respects in the light of our knowledge today, the idea of a long Dark Age, an utterly sterile thousand years between Rome and Florence, strongly shaped modern conceptions of the past. In general, the humanists shared an intense awareness of time. They were keenly conscious of living in a certain age, at a certain moment.

The Renaissance humanists advanced historical scholarship by their antiquarian interests and in their collections of materials. They collected documents out of a veneration for antiquity, especially for those great and noble writers of classical times whose phrases came ringing down the centuries. Their interests were largely philological, not historical; but their textual labors heaped up matter for future historians and made their tasks easier.

The critical method was scarcely new; humanists followed in the footsteps of the ancients here, of course, and medieval monks showed as much ingenuity in forging documents for the Church as Valla did in exposing them. Lorenzo Valla's analysis of the forged Donation of Constantine, a prime foundation of the papacy's powers, became a classic of critical methodology. Based as it was on the detection of anachronisms and thus on a feeling for the period, this critique had a distinct historical dimension. Could a man have written this way in the fourth century? Was this phrase in use then, or was this knowledge then available? Such were the tests Valla applied.[3] Leonardo Bruni's demolition of the myth of Florence's founding by Caesar was a similar exercise. They used archives.

No doubt, the "erudites" of the sixteenth and seventeenth centuries brought textual criticism to the level of a science for the first time. When Owen Chadwick declares that "the Renaissance, the Reformation, and the Counter-Reformation gave that impetus to historical studies which begat modern historical writing," he has in mind this skill in the detection of forged or garbled documents, the editing and assembling of them in usable collections, in general a "new awareness of evidence." This awareness does not in itself produce history but it provides the foundation of evidence without which an adequate history cannot exist. Such skills were then cultivated not because of a scholarly concern for finding the truth about the past but for urgent practical reasons. Kings, for example, fought legal battles with feudal lords which often turned on the exposure of fraudulent titles (Valla's famous tour de force is just a lofty instance of this kind of detective work.) During the Reformation, Protestants and Catholics vied to find documentary evidence concerning the power of the popes, the principles of the early Church. The Bible itself constituted the greatest of textual challenges, enlisting the energies of a legion of scholars from that time to this.

From all this activity concerned with authenticating and correcting documents—legal, literary, religious documents—there emerged a kind of science of textual criticism; handbooks were published, rules established. Fabulously erudite scholars made sometimes sensational discoveries, redating or emending long-accepted texts. On the solid foundation of such authoritative evidence subsequent historians might build. We get, too, the beginnings of the great libraries—Vatican, Medici, Bibliothèque Nationale.

Renaissance historiography, like that of the ancient world, failed to sustain itself perhaps because it lacked a professional base. Before fairly recent times, historians were always something else first and only incidentally historians. The great ones of antiquity tended to be retired generals or politicians, though Livy was a "man of letters." Medieval recounters of events were of course mainly churchmen, discharging their religious duty to work, to meditate, to study God's providence; others were crusaders and soldiers. The Renaissance produced a somewhat new type, described as the secretary–man of letters or the humanist scholar: such men as Machiavelli, who served a secular ruler as adviser and diplomatist. In an interesting way such men combined literary and practical political aptitudes, but they were not professional historians. Learned societies and specialized journals had not yet been born.

History, moreover, was not particularly well defined as a genre. It spilled over into fiction, biography, political commentary, and other genres as well: natural history, travel literature, philosophical essays, providential theology. Vasari's well-known *Lives of the Most Eminent Painters, Sculptors, and Architects* (1550–1568), which covered the most remarkable achievements of Renaissance Italy and was truly innovative in its subject matter, was, as its title indicates, a succession of biographies, not an integrated history. Rosemary Colie in her work on Renaissance genres notes the "many competing and overlapping notions of what 'history' was or ought to be."[4]

When all is said, the humanists produced little in the way of historical writing of any merit. Their genius and greatness lay elsewhere, though the by-products could affect history. Felix Gilbert has indeed argued that if Machiavelli was not a great historian, his Florentine colleague

Francesco Guicciardini was: Guicciardini's *History of Italy* was "the last great work of history in the classical pattern, but . . . also the first great work of modern historiography."[5] If it was, it is an exceptional case (though Bruno Aretino's *History of Florence* has also received praise). And though Guicciardini did undeniably have a stronger awareness of history than Machiavelli, the latter's influence and reputation far exceeded his.[6]

The Reformation

The by-products of the Reformation, too, affected the emergence of modern historical-mindedness, and even more powerfully than those of the Renaissance. The most significant of these by-products was the appeal to the past for support in this mighty battle of contending opinions. An important part of the Protestant case—indeed perhaps its crux— involved such an appeal to history. Turning their backs on the Church of Rome, the Protestants endeavored to show that Rome had wrongly usurped authority from the bishops and communicants of the primitive Church, and that doctrine was sounder and life purer before the papacy assumed control. Between 1559 and 1574 the famous Magdeburg Centuries came forth to bombard the papists with ammunition from an armory of ancient documents. The first chair of history in Europe apparently was established at Heidelberg University under Protestant auspices.[7] Later, the Calvinist university of Leyden in the Netherlands became the greatest center of historical studies. The Catholics, slow to respond, finally did so with a vengeance. Between 1588 and 1608 the *Ecclesiastical Annals*, edited by Baronius (Cesare Cardinal Baronio, an Italian member of the Oratorio of St. Philip Neri, an order established during the Reformation period which became famous for its scholarship), sought to silence the Magdeburg guns, and after this initial salvo whole batteries of Catholic guns were rolled up. Catholic historians explored the early church and particularly the patristic age in an effort to prove that papal authority and the Roman church were legitimate.[8] The result of this competition was possibly the most fabulous flowering of scholarly virtuosity of all times. Nothing less than religious zeal could have inspired such mighty labors. The early compilations were uncritical, crudely propagandistic, and utterly biased; yet out of this beginning grew notable scholarly work. The seventeenth-century *érudits* combined Renaissance techniques with Reformation motivation.

Clearly in some ways these efforts were most unhistorical: passionate partisanship dictated a course whose purpose was not to disclose the pattern of the past but to support a current ideological position. Still, such essentially propagandist motives can prove to be the most powerful of incentives to scan the past. What begins as narrow partisanship can turn into something less biased, and a closer look at some of these religious historians reveals that this was often the case. They were not propagandists in any cynical sense even to begin with, for they sincerely believed that truth was on their side. They were not manufacturing evidence to order. Thus they were the readier to follow where truth led. Quite often their materials and their quest took possession of them, gradually and unconsciously, at the expense of their *parti pris*. We can see the same sort of thing happening today. Young people, seized by that lofty and narrow idealism to which intelligent youth seems peculiarly susceptible, have often embarked upon their studies with the most intense commitment to some cause or crusade. But it is a function of historical study to tame such fanaticism; few can honestly find in the data support for an extreme position. E. H. Carr has written that every historian worth his salt begins with a bee in his bonnet, an invigorating impulse to prove or disprove something. In the end, the historian who reaches scholarly maturity will transcend the narrower sort of bias. In any case, it is clear that many Reformation historians failed to come out by the same door where in they went. The strictly orthodox often were somewhat disquieted.[9]

The variety of views adopted by Reformation scholars was bound to induce a skepticism from which historical objectivity could profit. The ultimate product of all this controversy was the skeptical Pierre Bayle, that lapsed French Calvinist who virtually began the Enlightenment later in the seventeenth century. In demolishing each other the rival religionists ended by casting doubt on all truth; such was not their intention, but they succeeded perhaps too well in their attacks on each other's version of the truth. It was a part of the larger story of the Reformation: in the end, people wearied of the strife and turned away in disgust to pursue other interests.

Meanwhile, some irenical trends appeared. Possibly one of the functions of historians is peacemaking. We can see that function at work quite frequently. It appears, for example, in Robert Aron's post–1945 work on Vichy France, in Spanish accounts of the bitter civil war of the 1930s, and in some accounts of the world wars. The historian, habitually inclined to explain and not condemn, able to see both sides, soothes the corrosive hatreds that have divided a community: he exerts a healing influence. The historian may or may not deliberately hold in mind such a social function. It may be that the issues raised in the fury of controversy simply cry out for clarification and so patently cannot result in a simple victory for one side or the other that a lucid mind is driven to explain what the question really is. Propaganda is frequently the parent of "objective" history.

So it was, clearly, after the initial phase of Reformation controversy. A good example is the striking sixteenth-century French school that included Jean Bodin, François Baudouin, and La Popelinière. Baudouin tried to bring religious peace to a divided France on the eve of the Huguenot wars. He gradually drifted back to Rome from Calvinism, but he always hoped for a reconciliation. The failure of his dream did not destroy Baudouin's irenic ideals, which contributed to the unusually high valuation his group put on history. Jean Bodin placed history at the top, "above all sciences." It appears to be significant that this French school arose during the long era of civil and religious strife from 1561 to 1593 which nearly destroyed France. Students of this group also point out that it emerged not from the rhetorical or literary tradition but from the law. History had been held in thrall for centuries by literature, and humanists in some ways threatened to perpetuate its servitude. It now made its escape by way of law. Lawyers are perhaps not the most imaginative people, but they have many virtues, among them a concern to establish facts by careful and judicious inquiry, a dislike for emotionalism, and a commitment to the peaceful solution of conflicts and quarrels. There is a strong case for their having fathered modern historiography.[10]

Jean Bodin, the universal genius whose *Methodus ad facilem historiarum cognitionem* (1566) was the leading tract of its time on historical methods, received a humanist education, studied theology, and then turned to the study of legal institutions. His arguments for religious toleration and his studies in the political theory of state sovereignty are classics, and he ranks also as one of the pioneers of modern economic theory. In talent and versatility he challenges Vico, if not Leibniz; he exerted an influence on Vico, Montesquieu, and other pioneers of the social sciences who gained greater fame than he. But his *Methodus* is marked by a baroque disorder; J. G. A. Pocock calls it a "strange semi-ruinous mass."

The Venetian friar Paoli Sarpi, author in the early seventeenth century of a multivolume *History of the Council of Trent*, is sometimes honored as the greatest historian to come out of the Reformation. His was polemical history, for Sarpi was a product and indeed a hireling of a Venice that was, though not anti-Catholic, quite antipapal; his purpose was to discredit the Council of Trent, which had strengthened the papacy, and so to discredit the power of the popes. But for learning and acuteness his work belongs with that of the fabulously learned Protestant champion, Isaac Casaubon, who undertook virtually a page-by-page refutation of Baronius. Milton, Johnson, and Macaulay—Protestants all—regarded Sarpi's as the best historical opus of its age. Lord Acton, a Catholic, was far less pleased. A careful modern student of the great council, Herbert Jedin, calls Sarpi's *History* one-sided, as obviously it was. Yet it was a brilliant job of research and writing and seems to mark a coming of age after the cruder propaganda of just a few decades before. Out of this furious and sustained battle of books, precipitated by ideological hatred, came some wisdom and maturity at last. Sarpi's work has endured.

The Reformation carried on in a most intense way that popular revolutionary tradition of Christian millenarianism which we mentioned in connection with the medieval Joachimites and Taborites. On every hand we meet poor men excited by the ideas found in the biblical books of Daniel and the Apocalypse of John. There had never really been a lapse in this tradition. The Taborites, for example—the radical wing of the Bohemian Hussites, who arose early in the fifteenth century and thus anticipated Martin Luther and the high Reformation by a century— were extremely chiliastic, believing in an earthly kingdom of God to follow the Day of Wrath; all sin and pain would then be purged from the world, the poor would enter into their own, and everybody would live in perfect bliss. Toward this end they were quite prepared to do violence to the rich. Such movements inevitably failed, not merely because they drew onto themselves the fearful wrath of outraged authority but because they had absolutely no concrete ideas for organizing the new order, since they expected an automatic utopia. The German and English Reformation bore similar fruit. The radical millenarianists of the sixteenth century, like their predecessors, were mostly unlettered poor people whose imagination distilled visions of an earthly paradise out of their misery and the intoxicating prose of biblical apocalyptic passages. "The Saints shall have a kingdom here on earth," the millenarianists declared. This colorful chapter of social and intellectual history has importance for us because it kept alive, now with a secular interpretation, the time sense of Western civilization—the idea of progress. We have here a crude but recognizable version of what Hegel and Marx were to proffer in the nineteenth century. Drenched in biblical imagery, Reformation millenarianism nonetheless painted what was in effect a secular utopia at the end of the historic road and inspired revolutionary action to attain it.

The Seventeenth Century

It is clear that the Reformation had set in motion all kinds of powerful new forces that would break through the old structures to produce new ones not dreamed of by Martin Luther when he first questioned a dubious ecclesiastical practice. Of the many revolutions that belong to this period—the discovery and exploration of the New World, the invention of the printing press, the whole scientific revolution from Copernicus to Newton, and the rise of the consolidated territorial states under monarchical leadership—none was without its influence on historical writing. Intellectually speaking, probably it was science and nationalism that had the greatest impact on it. But the new sciences worked partly against history. In the aftermath of the sensational discoveries of Kepler and Galileo about the laws of physical motion and the configuration of the universe, a majority of thinking people began to inhabit this frontier of knowledge. A mighty inquiry had been initiated which would not be deflected from its course before Sir Isaac Newton unveiled the laws of motion and of gravitational attraction in the 1680s. The historical school of Bodin and Baudouin, which had looked so promising about 1590, was overtaken by this other, more exciting train of thought and faded into obscurity. We may think that there should have been room enough in the world for both. But when people still took for granted a kind of speculative monism in which one key conception guided the whole culture, as had been the case in the Middle Ages, they hardly had the capacity for more than one intellectual revolution at a time.

The scientific rationalism advanced by René Descartes and his followers took over the intellectual dominion of the seventeenth century and did not surrender it until well into the eighteenth century. This school of thought was quite incompatible with the kind of skeptical and empirical study that history is, and in fact the Cartesians openly disparaged history on grounds Plato would have found familiar: it does not attain certain truth; it is an inexact and confused study; it cannot be reduced to mathematics. Moreover, the Cartesians, intoxicated by the success of science, boldly claimed control over areas of thought that are now considered to bear little relation to science. Hobbes sought an exact science of politics, Spinoza one of ethics, the French neoclassicists one of art. The chief contribution of the great Frenchman himself was to be a scientific method of universal applicability, which he hoped would unify the realm of knowledge. Though Leibniz, at the end of the century, had more sympathy for history, he still thought such a method possible.

In some incidental ways, history surely profited from the great scientific revolution. What we rather vaguely call the scientific method embraces rigorously exact and critical standards of thought, both in the framing of hypotheses and in the testing of their validity by experimentation. Such an attitude is applicable to historical studies, and some of it rubbed off on scholars whose prime interest was not in the physical sciences. Contacts between the two cultures of science and the humanities were somewhat closer, perhaps, than they came to be later. The Hellenistic scientist Eratosthenes, for example, had been a founder of critical chronology; the seventeenth-century master of philological erudition, J.-J. Scaliger, was led to similar interests through the scientists' rediscovery of Eratosthenes. In such ways the scientific movement spilled over in the direction of historical studies. Isaac Newton pursued biblical textual studies and enjoyed a friendship with the great philologist Richard Bentley. Other seventeenth-century thinkers whom we associate with the Cartesian spirit—Spinoza is the outstanding example—exhibited a passion for deciphering the correct texts of the Bible and for establishing their authorship and dates. That this sort of inquiry was of potentially great significance for history is obvious. It involved the dating of documents and led ultimately to the higher criticism of the Bible. Such caveats must be entered against any sweeping dismissal of the scientific movement as wholly irrelevant to history. Nevertheless, its basic orientation was in an entirely different direction.

There is more truth in a single principle of metaphysics than in all the books of history, declared the seventeenth-century philosopher Nicolas de Malebranche. The historicity of the "social contract" did not concern Thomas Hobbes and John Locke, who argued that such a contract was a logical necessity and need not have actually happened at all. The shining lights of the Century of Genius were virtually all scientists or rationalist metaphysicians. Nevertheless, even science could not quite monopolize the teeming seventeenth century. It has been described under other rubrics by historians—as an age of power, for example. The great states of modern Europe began to take shape, creating bureaucracies and fighting wars. The Puritan Revolution in England combined religious issues with a struggle to determine the shape and substance of the new national state.

Elizabethan England had produced what has been called a historical revolution. The spirit that produced it may be seen in Shakespeare's proud cycle of history plays. Shakespeare displayed an intense interest in every moment of royal drama—

A kingdom for a stage, princes to act
And monarchs to behold the swelling scene!

—and an intense love for England, "this land of such dear souls, this dear dear land." William Camden's celebrated *Annals of the Reign of Queen Elizabeth*, written in a florid and grandiloquent Latin and not very critical, was of a quite traditional type in its formal aspects, but it

radiates a similar love of England and reflects what A. L. Rowse has
called "the Elizabethan discovery of England." Needless to say, there
was much to boast about in this glorious age, when Drake singed the
beard of the king of Spain, Ralegh planted colonies in the New World,
Shakespeare molded the English language, and Queen Bess dazzlingly
presided over it all.

We recognize here history's well-known function as the natural propaganda of the social order. It has frequently been associated with patriotism, nationalism, and group integration of all sorts. The tendency
to glorify our own is very human, and we need not disparage this sort
of history unduly even if it is far removed from the critical or philosophical domain. When people feel deeply about an institution, a cause,
or a community, they naturally wish to preserve the records of its life
and dwell on them lovingly. Shakespeare's love of England, in the dawn
of national consciousness, was spontaneous, and he was in no cynical
sense writing propaganda. In the United States, the rise of black studies
has allowed Americans of African ancestry to glorify their race by ex-
alting its traditions; this is an essential part of a discovery of identity
and thus of dignity. A nation, as Ernest Renan once observed, is shaped
from the common memory of deeds done in the past. Who can imagine
the modern nations without their Shakespeares and Macaulays, their
Bancrofts, their Treitschkes, and their Guizots? This sort of history steals
into schoolbooks and may fill young heads with tales that are both untrue
and pernicious. Youngsters learn that George Washington never told
a lie, that Charlemagne was a Frenchman, and that King Alfred was the
soul of unselfish generosity. So we may resent this sort of history and
correct it by going to the opposite extreme of debunking. Nevertheless,
it is likely that this folk use of stories about the past will continue as
long as new and vital institutions arise. We see the process every day
at the level of family or neighborhood life, as people fondly preserve
stories and mementos of the past, frequently embellished. In the age
of Elizabeth it emerged at the national level, in written works, and
helped to shape a national consciousness.

In the molding of historiography, however, of greater importance
was the new battle of historical propaganda touched off by the English
revolutions of the seventeenth century. As Parliament and king, Puritan
and Cavalier contended for the state, both sides in the great dispute
appealed to history. History became a handmaiden of propaganda, and
yet historical work of enduring value emerged. Each side commissioned
a historian to make the past disgorge proof that either the Crown or
Parliament had precedent on its side, and to write a partisan account
of the revolution itself.[11]

When Thomas Macaulay said that some of the greatest issues of English politics had turned on the researches of antiquarians, he had in mind primarily the Puritan Revolution. The peculiarly precedent-minded nature of the British political and legal system made this appeal to the past more urgent in the case of England. A good example of these seventeenth-century legal-historical inquiries dictated by political controversy was John Selden's *History of Tithes*. Selden, a gifted and learned man much admired by his contemporaries, undertook this bit of antiquarianism because of an important issue raised in the revolutionary period. Had the payment of tithes to the clergy existed before the development of the common law, as a divine-right prerogative of kings, or were tithes a creation of the common law, and so might legitimately be regulated by that law? Selden wanted to find evidence that not only would decide a rather crucial issue but would help to resolve the larger issue in this great conflict between Crown and Parliament. It was important to discover precedents, which he could then use as ammunition; the precedents were not necessarily decisive but they were significant evidence of a sort that carried much weight in England. Here again, lawyers played an important part in the development of history.

It could of course be said again that such interesting exercises in political controversy were not fully historical. It was not merely that they had a propagandistic motivation, for we are never likely wholly to escape such impulses, and it is in many ways good that history should be relevant to some current situation. But this was not an interest in the past which people pursued in order to see how it shaped the present. The inquiry was directed to the much narrower goal of finding out what practices had existed in the past so that Englishmen might know how to guide and justify present practices, the assumption being that usage and custom bestowed a kind of right. This was the doctrine that Edmund Burke, a century later, called prescription. The Englishman's inclination to root his political constitution in historical continuity was much older than Burke and was clearly marked in the memorable debates and conflicts of the seventeenth century. For the English evidently more than for any other people, inquiry into the past became not merely an academic exercise but a matter of immediate and urgent importance, a matter of their very life. The English almost became a people who had to find out what their ancestors did yesterday in order to know what they should do today. Nothing could do more to encourage antiquarian research, and we immediately see why history and the law have so often gone hand in hand in England; why one of England's greatest modern historians, F. W. Maitland, dedicated himself to a history of the common law. Nevertheless, the lawyer's search for precedents is at best a very narrow concern. He does not wonder why the social order changes or why people once lived and thought differently; indeed, he may be committed to the view that they lived and thought much the same then as they do now, since the rules that governed them should govern us. Yet this sort of research did contribute both to the birth of critically trained historians and, indirectly, to a feeling for history and a love of the past. The French jurists even tended to replace the universal, abstract authority of Roman law (the Justinian code and corpus) with a national law rooted in French social conditions, and to study the law comparatively.

The Earl of Clarendon's *History of the Rebellion and Civil Wars in England* was the one masterpiece, composed in the high Thucydidean style, that the seventeenth-century English revolutions produced. Like many another great historical work, Clarendon's was aided by the perspective of a person able to achieve some objectivity because he was out of sorts with both sides. A one-time member of Parliament, Clarendon had also been a chief counsellor of both Charles I and Charles II; his daughter was to marry the last of the Stuart kings, James II. So he had participated in the great decisions of that great revolutionary era. In the 1640s he had advised more moderate policies than the unfortunate Charles I pursued. He was forced to flee after the Royalists' defeat in the civil war of 1642–1648, but with the Restoration of 1660 he became a minister of the executed king's son. In 1667, however, he fell out of favor with Charles II disfavor and again went into exile. Originally Charles I had asked him to write a partisan history of the conflict between king and Parliament in reply to the Puritan accounts, but at length he decided to make it a true history—one, in the Thucydidean tradition, both solemn and impartial, and philosophical in the sense of searching for causes. He would also include character sketches and set pieces, the speeches and "scenes" of classical historical writing. What seems more important to us is that Clarendon was a disillusioned Stuart partisan, with inside experience of one of the greatest of all historic events plus the literary skill to write a well-evidenced history.

Clarendon's history, written over the years from 1667 to 1674, was a work of considerable merit. It retained a royalist bias and a personal one, in that Clarendon inevitably tried to show that had Charles followed his advice he would not have lost his throne, and assumed that this outcome would have benefited Britain. It is interesting that no Puritan or Whig history of the civil wars written in that era comes close to rivaling Clarendon's. The Whig partisans turned antihistorical. It has been suggested that their attitude can be traced to their inability to make a strong case for Parliament against the king on grounds of precedent. Their appeal was to Reason ("Reason, equity, and the Law of God," said the Levellers during the Puritan Revolution). John Locke's famous defense of the Glorious Revolution of 1688 (which overturned the last legitimate English monarch and established parliamentary supremacy) postulated a primeval "state of nature" but treated it only partly, and casually, as a real historic phenomenon; to Locke the foundation of government was a matter of moral principle and logic, not of fact. He was concerned to refute Sir Robert Filmer's Tory argument that government evolved from the family, but again Locke considered this question to rest more on logic than on history. What mattered was less what *did* happen than what *should* have happened. Locke's philosophical epistemology, his famous "way of ideas," was empirical, but he related it to natural science and ethics, not to history or sociology. Here was the Cartesian spirit, rather contemptuous of historical knowledge because it was contingent, fluctuating, imprecise. The eighteenth-century Enlightenment was to be very strongly influenced by this scientism, with its demand for stable "laws" governing everything.

At least one student of this period of historiography, F. S. Fussner, has described it as a "historical revolution" that swept us to the edge of the modern age of historical consciousness, with its relativistic and time-conditioned outlook, its tendency to see everything as development and evolution.[12] But he may have exaggerated, for the Cartesian influence was in the ascendant, and the great eighteenth-century Enlightenment exhibited, all in all, a decidedly ambivalent attitude toward history.

Notes

[1] In *Machiavelli and Guicciardini: Politics and History in Sixteenth-Century Florence* (Princeton: Princeton University Press, 1965) Felix Gilbert has pointed out that Machiavelli had no particular interest in writing a history of Florence but received a commission to do so from the city fathers. In writing the histories of their cities, the humanists followed the classical model as they gratified their local pride. Such histories were popular; indeed, they treated virtually the only permissible subject other than war.

[2] The humanists awarded Livy the palm. They thought the Romans in general somewhat superior to the Greeks, who reminded them of the Scholastic philosophers; and the style of Tacitus, who lived too long past the golden age, was not pure enough. They admired Sallust beyond his merit because he lived at the right time, but to them Livy was the greatest.

[3] Joseph M. Levine has pointed out the contrast between Valla's philological methods and the still Scholastic, medieval ones of Reginald Pecock, who criticized the Donation of Constantine independently of Valla at about the same date. Lacking Valla's methods of detecting anachronisms, Pecock could only range one authority against another, choosing the ones he preferred without any compelling reason for the preference. It was not that he was uncritical, but

that he lacked the tools. As a grammarian and student of literature Valla could show convincingly that the Donation must have been written much later than the fifth century. See Joseph M. Levine, "Reginald Pecock and Lorenzo Valla and *The Donation of Constantine*," *Studies in the Renaissance*, 20 (1973), 118–143.

[4]Rosalie L. Colie, *The Resources of Kind: Genre Theory in the Renaissance* (Berkeley: University of California Press, 1973), p. 95.

[5]Gilbert, *Machiavelli and Guicciardini*, p. 301.

[6]Eric Cochrane, in his valuable *Historians and Historiography in the Italian Renaissance* (Chicago: University of Chicago Press, 1981), found historical books not especially popular, constituting at most 10 percent of published titles.

[7]In 1557; but the title was Professor of History *and Poetry* still.

[8]In England, where in the seventeenth century learning of this sort rivaled that of the Continental schools, savants labored to defend on historical as well as theological grounds the peculiar position of the Church of England, which based its legitimacy on episcopal but not papal authority.

[9]See, e.g., Bruno Neveu, *Un historien à l'école de Port-Royal: Sebastien le Nain de Tillemont, 1637–1698* (La Haye: Martinus Nijhoff, 1966). One of the orthodox wrote to Tillemont that if he continued his history of the early church, it would be necessary to reform the breviary and forget most of the saints (p. 280). In the eighteenth century Edward Gibbon drew on the researches of Tillemont, his "patient and sure-footed mule," to produce his anti-Christian *Decline and Fall of the Roman Empire*.

[10]See particularly Donald R. Kelley's *Foundations of Modern Historical Scholarship* (New York: Columbia University Press, 1970).

[11]John Rushworth's *Historical Collections* (1659) was a parliamentary and Cromwellian account of the events of the revolution; the Royalists commissioned John Nelson to reply. Daniel Neal's *History of the Puritans* (1732–1738) was a subsequent defense of the Puritans against the Restoration reaction. In *The Ancient Constitution and the Feudal Law* (New York: Norton, 1957), J. G. A. Pocock closely examined the historical debates between the Royalists and the partisans of Parliament and the common law.

[12]See also Joseph H. Preston, "Was There an Historical Revolution?" *Journal of the History of Ideas*, April–June, 1977.

CHAPTER 4
THE EIGHTEENTH CENTURY AND "ENLIGHTENED" HISTORY

WE have reached the eve of the modern epoch. It is obvious that some exciting things happened to history during the so-called Enlightenment, that reputed seedbed of the modern mind. This great era had an apparent historical dimension. Pierre Bayle, who almost began it, wrote a *Historical and Critical Dictionary*. The eighteenth century began with a quarrel between ancients and moderns which raised the whole question of progress, and they never stopped arguing about it. Montesquieu's great *Spirit of the Laws* combined history with sociology to begin the quest for a true science of human society. Voltaire, this century's giant, wrote much history, and has been ranked as one of the founders of modern historical methods. David Hume, too, was a historian; his investigations mark a significant break with the tradition by which philosophers would have nothing to do with anything so imprecise as history. And the Neapolitan philosopher and savant Giambattista Vico appears as a pioneer of really modern historical thought. The "enlightened" ones, under the influence of Newton and Locke, tended to react against the abstract rationalism of the Cartesians in the direction of an empirical, experimental approach to reality much more suited to historical work. Edward Gibbon is only the most illustrious of many eighteenth-century historians; a list of all their names would fill a large catalog.

The wars of religion well behind them, the *philosophes* were thoroughly secular-minded, thoroughly critical, thoroughly "modern." Still interested in physical and natural science, they were much more interested in humanity, and they brought into existence all the social sciences. At the same time, their delightful style and talent for organization make them far more readable than the ponderous polymaths of the previous century, those *érudits* who made a heap of all they found. In the time of Voltaire, Hume, and Gibbon, history became genuinely popular as well as scholarly and "philosophical." It also achieved a surer definition of its genre, its identity. In a century that also witnessed the emergence, virtually the invention, of the "novel," a fictionalized but often realistic depiction of human events, history emancipated itself to a degree from its tutelage to literature and rhetoric and moved under the wing of those "social sciences" that Enlightenment thinkers so loved.

Yet it must be said that the Enlightenment has frequently been found wanting in true historical-mindedness. Collingwood declared that during the Enlightenment "no attempt was made to lift history above the level of propaganda." Notoriously unfair to the Middle Ages and to the era of the Reformation, Voltaire and his friends really had no conception of continuity. They even, in a sense, wished to abolish the past; more than once they said as much. And they wished, adds José Ortega y Gasset in reference to the ideals of the French Revolution, to abolish the future as well. For the ideal society was a static one; it had much in common with the "natural order," that concept which so permeated the thinking of the eighteenth century. Despite a few atypical specimens such as Vico, mechanism and not process remained a guiding concept until nearly the end of the century. When Lafayette suggested in 1788 that one might well begin the study of French history with the year 1787, he was only slightly exaggerating a tendency shown by most of the eighteenth-century historians. The past was useful only for exhibiting dreadful examples of how badly people had always behaved and for demonstrating why they they had failed to find the road to utopia. It was a record of "crimes, follies, and misfortunes," of superstition, ignorance, and error, illuminated by only an occasional burst of reason and common sense. Can historians be biased against the past? Eager to pursue their vision of a new moral world, major Enlightenment thinkers could almost be accused of such bias.

Typical champions of enlightenment remained primarily neoclassical in their tastes. They held to unchanging standards of excellence and idealized the ancients, dismissing the Gothic style as barbarous.[1] Oliver Wendell Holmes, Jr., once wrote that Montesquieu "was not able to see history as an evolution, he looked at all events as if they were contemporaneous."[2] In this respect, the *Spirit of the Laws* differed from Machiavelli's *Discourses* only in its richer empirical content. "Exemplarism," the familiar use of the past as a storehouse of lessons or examples—"philosophy teaching by example"—remained in vogue. Lord Bolingbroke's widely read *Letter on the Study of History* (1735) was a notable instance of this attitude. To Bolingbroke, Pocock has written, the only conceivable purpose of studying the past was to "inculcate the moral and practical lessons of statecraft." He saw it as an aid to the statesman but regarded historical inquiry for any other reason as absurd antiquarianism, unsuitable for a gentleman of cultivated mind.

Despite a certain fascination with the question of whether there had been progress (and the Enlightenment philosophers did not agree that it had occurred in all fields, certainly not in the arts, religion, or morality), until near the end of the century the dominant outlook on the past remained almost as cyclical as that of the ancients. Renaissance historians had celebrated a classical golden age, lamented a dark age that followed, and then rejoiced in the recovery of this golden past. Voltaire saw then another relapse during the Reformation era, with its ghastly wars of religion, then a recovery in the time of Louis XIV, followed perhaps by another decline. Voltaire saw his own century as falling short of the great era of Racine and Moliere, and he certainly thought Locke and Newton had spoken the ultimate words in science and philosophy. Thus historians such as Voltaire saw more discontinuity than continuity in the past; the past was a record of rather inexplicable alternations of light and darkness. Many eighteenth-century thinkers permitted themselves the hope that, now that Newton and Locke had enlightened the world, a permanent turn for the better had set in. Yet their optimism should not be exaggerated. "We preach wisdom to the deaf, and we are still far indeed from the Age of Reason," Diderot confessed to David Hume. That the vast majority of people were superstitious and fanatically religious and perhaps always would be was an idea congenial to the *philosophes*. Any consistent idea of progress or of development as the theme of history had to await the very end of the century. Arthur O. Lovejoy, that keen student of ideas, even asserted that Enlightenment historians basically held a "negative philosophy of history": they believed that if change had occurred, it had been, on the whole, a change for the worse, a deterioration since the golden age of antiquity.[3]

It was a complex and contradictory age, and that is part of its fascination. Yet we must come back to the invigoration it provided for all fields of inquiry, and not least for history. Even if the Enlightenment was not genuinely historical-minded, its stimulus to inquiry meets us at every point, and history must acknowledge a giant debt to it.

Probably most challenging and exciting to historians is the typical Enlightenment conviction that beneath the accidents of events, we may uncover the larger trends and processes. The great *philosophes* asserted this proposition boldly. "There are general causes, moral or physical, at work in every monarchy," Montesquieu wrote in *Grandeur and Decay of the Romans*, "which elevate it and maintain it or work its downfall; all accidents are the result of causes; and if the chance of a battle—that is, a special cause—has ruined a state, there was a general cause at work which made that state ready to perish by a single battle. In a word, the main current carries with it all the special accidents." We often find such magnificent assurance that inquiry will disclose a fundamental and somewhat simple order of things. This was the "faith of reason" that scholars inherited from Newton, and they did not doubt it could be applied to human studies. People in the eighteenth century were much better at proclaiming this faith than at carrying it out—better at conjectural or speculative history than at actual detailed empirical investigation. (Such investigations might have interfered with the clarity of their vision!) They almost seemed ready to say, with Rousseau, that the facts are irrelevant; if they do not fit the framework, they ought to. But this confidence in reason was bracing. They embarked on the historic quest with an assurance that they could find significant generalizations.

Enlightened intellectuals cherished the practical and the useful. History had always been considered primarily a practical subject, and without challenging this classical view these scholars upgraded it. The mechanical arts and the practical sciences, once despised, experienced a renaissance at the hands of the Encyclopedists, who delighted in magnifying the down-to-earth useful things at the expense of vain metaphysics and idle imagination. "The only scope of History is *Utility*," wrote Peter Whalley, in *An Essay on the Manner of Writing History* (1746), adding that history is "the noblest, and most deserving of our serious attention, of all studies." This utilitarianism was close to the heart of the age. The eighteenth-century *philosophes*, so called, wished to distinguish themselves from previous "philosophers," who were vain seekers after answers to unanswerable questions, lost in a fog of abstractions and mystifications. Metaphysics, rejected by Locke and ridiculed by Voltaire, was to be abolished in favor of unvarnished facts systematically analyzed. Imagination and "enthusiasm" were deeply suspect; private fantasy, partly because it was associated with religious fanaticism and political revolt, had to be checked sharply. All this worked to the advantage of a discipline that claimed to rest on ascertained facts and to be objective.

Finally, of course, the eighteenth-century writers wove wit and literary skill into all they wrote. This was a part of their basic *esprit*: their enterprise was in part a rebellion against seventeenth-century metaphysics and seventeenth-century erudition, against the baroque with its complexities and sinuosities, against incomprehensible philosophies and indigestible learning. They demanded that things be clear and a delight to the reader. In pursuit of this goal they might outrageously oversimplify, but they were never dull. That is why they became the most influential writers of all time and why they are still read and always will be. The combination of seriousness with wit and style is, after all, the quintessence of Voltaireanism, a quality shared by Rousseau and Diderot and Hume. The style was elegant neoclassical, and by the time we reach Gibbon, near the end of the century, it has almost lost its savor, becoming too pat and in need of the drastic revitalization that romanticism was to provide. Yet it is always clear and comprehensible. In an age of prose, the enlightened ones created a style admirably suited to exposition, which all historians can read to their profit and should read again and again.

One student of eighteenth-century historiography isolated the following ingredients: (*a*) From Bayle came the critical, skeptical mentality; drawing on the methods of the earlier *érudits*, this strain becomes bolder, more iconoclastic during the Enlightenment. It subjects all the old tales, even those of Scripture ("the fables of a barbarous and ignorant people," says David Hume), to critical examination. (*b*) From Montesquieu, the search for deterministic general causes in human affairs. (*c*) From Voltaire, a sense of *esprit du temps*, or the special flavor of a particular period, seen as expressing or embodying a distinctive mentality and culture. (*d*) Appearing late in the century, in the writings of Turgot and Condorcet, an idea of orderly development in the human past; in brief, the idea of progress. While scarcely complete, this list includes some important elements. None of them, it may be noted, was in itself fully historical in the modern sense, but combined they added up to something like a full-fledged historical outlook.

Some Eighteenth-Century Historians

Eighteenth-century historians brought specific innovations to the art of history. Biased against Judeo-Christian religion, Voltaire called for a widening of the scope of history to include other peoples and religions: "It is time to stop insulting all other sects and nations as if they are mere appendages to the history of the Chosen People." The great deist did not himself carry out his exhortation to learn more about the Chinese, the Hindus, and the Muslims. In fact, Voltaire was so much a victim of the eighteenth century's inability to conceive of people as different— of, as Lovejoy put it, its "uniformitarian" view of human nature—that he made deists out of the Chinese and natural philosophers out of the American Indians. He refused to believe that ritual prostitution could have been practiced in Babylon, that there ever could have been a time when private property did not exist (as against his enemy Rousseau's entirely speculative ideas in *The Origins of Inequality*), or that the Crusades were motivated by anything but a desire for plunder. This "rationalist fallacy," as it has been called—the belief that people and cultures are everywhere much the same—was a large obstacle in the way of any appreciation of other ages and civilizations. Yet at the same time

Voltaire is credited with being the first to demand a widening of horizons to include world history.

Even more important was Voltaire's demand for an extension of history to include subjects other than politics. His most eloquent passages were on this theme. Instead of battles and intrigue, why do we not hear about "a canal which joins two oceans, a painting of Poussin, a fine play," or about population, how people made their living, what the laws are and how they got that way, why some provinces are rich and others poor, and a hundred other inquiries? "These are a thousand times more precious than all the annals of courts or accounts of campaigns in the field." Yet all past historians had neglected these really interesting questions. This is an astonishing and a memorable call for a revolution in historiography. Voltaire did not carry it out, but he tried. His foremost historical work, *The Age of Louis XIV*, included topical chapters on government, economics, literature, science, the Church, but he never integrated these subjects successfully into his political narrative; the chapters on writers, artists, and scientists tended to become mere catalogs. His *Essai sur les moeurs* was by general agreement a very unsatisfactory book. This is only to say that Voltaire did not have the needed materials and had not worked out the methodology of his new conception of history. We may still be working on such a methodology. But he broke through the confines of tradition to announce that history knows no boundaries and that its interests extend to every phase of human activity. This is a proposition that all contemporary historians accept. Voltaire can well claim to have originated the idea of economic history, social history, intellectual history, and cultural history.

How critical were the eighteenth-century historians? It is not necessary to say that Voltaire and his fellows boldly subjected all manner of orthodoxy and authority to critical examination. But a really adequate historical methodology seems to require more than a skeptical spirit. It requires many tools and a consistent body of principles. Beginning late in the eighteenth century at the University of Göttingen, German scholars began to develop such a systematic science of criticism. They made Voltaire and even Gibbon look like amateurs. The great *érudits* of the previous century, such as Mabillon and Duchesne, had forged some tools in the areas of paleography and diplomatics, the sciences of deciphering and testing handwriting and official documents. Voltaire's criticism of sources was rather hit-and-miss, sometimes inspired and sometimes wholly wrong. In his critical zeal, for example, he insisted erroneously that Cardinal Richelieu's *Testament* was a forgery.[4] His use of sources, too, was somewhat old-fashioned in its reliance on oral testimony, though he did make use of some archival material.

Biased, incomplete, victims of the rationalist fallacy, lacking a sense of historical development; yet eager inquirers into human affairs, able to see the larger patterns, anxious to broaden the scope of history, brilliant writers who valued history highly—such were the *philosophes*. We may acclaim them as the fathers of modern history, as we have so many others, or we may see them as still enslaved to a substantialist view of reality which had changed little since the time of Plato and Aristotle. One might choose to say that what has been called the "terror of history" had not sufficiently abated. To Voltaire, the past was still "a disordered collection of crimes, follies, and misfortunes amid which we can find some virtues, a few happy moments as one discovers set-tlements strewn here and there through wild deserts." Another French *philosophe*, the economist Mercier de la Rivière, called the record of the past "the shame of humanity, each page a tissue of crimes and madness." Perhaps this is indeed what it was. If so, why not ignore it? Why should we remember such a chamber of horrors? But we do need to recall the rare moments of happiness and virtue, so that we may try to imitate them. Such, in the main, was the Enlightenment philosophy of history.

Another of the eighteenth century's greatest minds—in the strict sense a much greater philosopher than Voltaire—wrote an important work of history. That was David Hume, the Scottish philosopher, who was part of a whole renaissance that burst forth in Scotland in the eighteenth century. This Scottish Enlightenment produced such other notable the-orists as Adam Smith and Adam Ferguson, pioneers of the social sci-ences, and another important historian, William Robertson. But Hume was the greatest of them and ranks as one of the eighteenth century's foremost philosophical intellects. His *History of England* has been crit-icized as too much the work of a philosopher, destined to be overtaken by later research. But it was Hume's most popular work in its day and retains many admirers.

Hume followed Clarendon in the lineage of histories of the Glorious Revolution, that central event in the making of modern Britain and one of the grandest of subjects for historical interpretation. Written to cor-rect the "misrepresentations of faction," his work aspired to that irenic role which we have noted as so frequently the historian's specialty; but it did not succeed in convincing Whiggish England of its impartiality. Against the Whig-Puritan interpretation of Stuart rule as a tyranny that it was the glory of England to have defied, Hume tended to defend Charles I, arguing that "it is better to be deprived of liberty than des-titute of government." To this Tory interpretation he added an acute analysis of the "anatomy of revolution," anticipating Edmund Burke's discussion of the French Revolution more than a century later. Revo-lution, by overthrowing legitimate authority and engendering a struggle among the various revolutionary factions, leads finally to "the arbitrary and despotic government of a single person." Cromwell had been the inevitable upshot of the Puritan revolution, as Napoleon and Stalin would culminate later revolutions.

Hume also argued that we ought not judge one age (or one people) by the standards of another: the fallacy of presentism, as we might call it. This sense of varying values and knowledge in different periods and places was historically minded. Yet Hume could also write that "mankind are so much the same, in all times and places, that history informs us of nothing new or strange in this particular. Its chief use is only to discover the constant and universal principles of human nature." This conception, which seems unhistorical, was persistent in the Enlightenment and it is rare to find it contested. Fontenelle, the French Cartesian and a pioneer *philosophe* of the later seventeenth century, did argue (in his *Digressions on the Ancients and Moderns*, 1688) that while politics and social institutions exhibit external sameness beneath the surface phenomena, *mind* has a true history, because it advances with the accumulation of knowledge, and may even change its basic tenor: an age of science or reason can replace an age of religion or superstition. Here was the germ of the idea of progress, which slowly grew during the eighteenth century.

The first volume of the most famous of all eighteenth-century works of history, and indeed one of the world's most famous books, first reached the public in 1776, the year of Adam Smith's *Wealth of Nations* and the beginning of the great era of democratic revolutions. Perhaps at this memorable moment history's golden age was launched. But Edward Gibbon's *Decline and Fall of the Roman Empire*, like the works of Hume and Voltaire, was still poised halfway between the old and the new. The work of an amateur and a *philosophe* (the eccentric Gibbon lived for some years on the Continent and greatly admired the French writers), it was based on a considerable acquaintance with the older erudition but also lacked the rigor of modern scholarship; one reads it today primarily as a classic and a work of literature. Gibbon was unusual in his celebrated dedication to this one project, which he made his life's work; it is a kind of prologue to modern professionalism in this regard, perhaps, though Thucydides, the founder, had also given his whole creative life to one subject. Its peculiar appeal, which makes it still probably the most widely known—and read?—of all histories, lies chiefly in its style and tone, on which Gibbon set the seal of an inimitable literary personality. In this personalism it may be, paradoxically, the child of the dawning age of romanticism as much as it is a classic of the Age of Reason. Jean-Jacques Rousseau had already written (in the 1760s he became a household name); the unique subjective self had

made its debut. It is worth noting that Gibbon wrote about six auto-
biographies, all different.

The *Decline and Fall*, six volumes of delightful rumination on the
collapse of the greatest of all empires, is a unique work. Certainly it did
much to make serious history popular. It almost established the persona
of the historian: in turn grave, stirring, ironic, drily witty, its sonorous
periodic sentences do justice to the complexities of human affairs. In
the end it preaches another sermon on *contemptus mundi*. But Gibbon
did not see a repetitious cycle; the fate of Rome would not await the
modern world, for too much had changed.

Off the beaten track then but later elevated to the supreme position
among eighteenth-century pioneers of historicism was Giambattista Vico.
He was less a historian than a theorist of history, but his influence on
historians was to be enormous; in many ways he anticipated Hegel and
Karl Marx.

Writing in remote Naples and not well known outside his own region
for some time, Vico contributed to history a philosophical refutation
of the old view that we cannot have exact knowledge of the past. The
Cartesians had insisted that whereas we can gain exact knowledge of
physical nature by measuring its properties and framing precise math-
ematically expressed laws, we can never do the same in the study of
history. Vico held that, on the contrary, we cannot fully understand
physical nature because God made it and we are alien to it; but we *can*
understand human history because people like ourselves made it all,
and the workings of their minds we can grasp. Moreover, the study of
the past permits us a fuller understanding of human nature, which is
the greatest goal of knowledge. In general we understand things only
when we know their origin, growth, and experience. This was a truly
genetic approach and appears as a profound break with all previous
thought. Vico today is usually presented as *the* founder of modern historical thought. In Patrick Gardiner's anthology *The Theory of History*,
Vico comes first. Benedetto Croce and R. G. Collingwood, those influential twentieth-century historians of historical thought, accorded him
the same honor. If it remained for Herder, Kant, and Hegel fully to
develop this strain of thought, the seed was planted by Vico.

It must be conceded that Vico's *New Science* (first published in 1725,
revised in 1730 and 1744) was written in so curious and difficult a
manner that it is hard to read, a shortcoming that impeded its ready
acceptance. It was exactly this sort of wearisome jargon that the *philosophes* most despised. No one today is likely to turn to the book for
pleasure; it joins a long list of writings that exerted profound influence
despite their graceless style (a list that might include such varied names

as Copernicus, Jeremy Bentham, Karl Marx, and John Dewey). Nevertheless, the Italian rises to eloquence in expounding his central insight:

> In the night of thick darkness enveloping the earliest antiquity, so remote
> from ourselves, there shines the eternal and never-failing light of a truth
> beyond all question: that the world of civil society has certainly been made
> by man, and that its principles are therefore to be found within the mod-
> ifications of our own human mind. Whoever reflects on this can but marvel
> that the philosophers should have bent all their energies to the study of
> the world of nature . . . and that they should have neglected the study of
> the world of nations or civil world, which, since men have made it, men
> could hope to know.

Does Vico's *verum factum* meet the objections of the critics who have
always said (and still say) that history is a failed science because it rests
on too slender a basis of evidence? By far the greater part of the past
has vanished without a trace; of the little that has survived in memory
or in artifacts the traces are faint and contradictory. Past events are not
present to hand but gone, so that we can know them only indirectly.
Attempts to reconstruct them from the meager evidence are guided by
the notions of people living in the present, in a different climate of
thought, often with a different language or *episteme*. What is written
down can never be "the past," for words on a page represent a different
order of reality, and this reality is essentially present thinking about the
past, not the past itself.

In reply to this criticism Vico argued in essence that the past is not
a dead and vanished thing lying "out there" to be rediscovered, but
something alive, embedded in our language, our customs, our feelings,
our institutions. All of our science, religion, art, all culture and institutions are creations of human history. Descartes's allegedly exact truth,
that of mathematics, is itself a creation of human history! So all understanding is genetic, historical; we find nothing outside this process
of human development, and so we really have no choice but to study
history. Vico's faith that if we study the past properly, we can understand
it, rests on a sense of "understanding" that differs from other sorts of
scientific knowledge: it is imaginative and intuitive, in the sense that we
say we "understand" a person or a human relationship. The Vichian
conception of history must of course be evaluated (Part II of this book
addresses such questions). That it proved powerfully influential is beyond doubt.

In his skirmishes with history Vico advanced a cyclical theory with
stages. Vico's age of gods, age of heroes, and age of men bear some
resemblance to August Comte's famous nineteenth-century stages, the
theological, the metaphysical, and the positivist or scientific (perhaps

they could be called, in Saint-Simon's categories, the theocratic, aristocratic-feudal, and democratic stages). The last stage ends in refinement, dissolution, and finally breakdown, whereupon we revert to barbarism and begin again—a sequence not far from that of Ibn Khaldun. Vico sees interesting analogies between the European Middle Ages and the Homeric period of ancient Greece. Some scholars have interpreted Vico's *corso, ricorso* (flux and reflux) to mean not a mere repetition but a spiral ascent, a progression through cycles of the sort that Toynbee posits in his *Study of History*. The validity of such ideas is not entirely clear, but the stimulation and excitement they afford are apparent.[5] For the most part this was merely speculative history of a kind that abounded in the later Enlightenment period. Such speculations preceded and stimulated the more pedestrian labors of testing them against the evidence.

Vico also provided some rules to guide historians or, more exactly, he identifed some prejudices he hoped they would avoid. These pitfalls might be compared with Francis Bacon's famous "idols" or false standards that mislead us in our attempts to reason (Idols of the Tribe, the Marketplace, the Theater, the Cave, in Bacon's picturesque metaphors). Some of Vico's precepts subvert the old habit of seeing all people as alike. We should *not* assume that other people are like ourselves; we should *not* suppose that other ages were in the same state of development, and hence intellectual condition, as our own. Vico worked his way (after long travail, he tells us) out of the "rationalist fallacy." Another of his perfectly valid points is that we should not suppose that the ancients knew more about themselves than we can know. They may have been deceived about their own time, and we can learn more about them than they knew, since we have the ability to correct errors, accumulate data, and see matters in a broader perspective. (We do know more about the Greeks and Romans today than they did; that is, a modern trained historian has much greater knowledge about those times than anyone then alive could have had.)

This amazing thinker was also keenly interested in language and in myth as keys to an understanding of the past. He knew that myth may contain valuable clues to reality. He was aware that primitive people thought metaphorically or poetically and he decried the tendency to view them as rational thinkers. In all this and more, Vico sounds very much up to date, and we recognize him as a true creator of our ways of thinking. His contributions to legal thought and philosophy were equally great; he has been seen as a precursor of Hegel and Marx and even Nietzsche; perhaps he founded anthropology. Far less famous in his own time than Montesquieu or Voltaire, he was more profound if less readable then either, and has come into his own only in this century. It is difficult to quarrel with the enthusiastic Vichians who raise the cry

"All hail to mighty Vico, John the Baptist of modern social science!" In the teeth of such adulation, it may be comforting to learn that Vico was so careless of mere factual detail that he got his own birth date wrong. Unhappily, such inadequacy in small things ("Confound details!" said Voltaire) often accompanies profound speculative brilliance of the sort that Vico demonstrated.

Vico saw Providence or the divine will as guiding or underlying the course of history. If there is a plan, where does it come from and why should it exist? The meaningfulness of history implies some sort of larger purpose, which must be part of a cosmic order. Is all that happens then necessary? Such a conclusion seems to deny human freedom. Are we puppets jerked about by unseen forces? This position seems to cause difficulties for Vico's doctrine that "man makes himself." The Neapolitan professor pondered such questions without reaching a conclusion. Vico tended to see God's will as immanent in the historic process, expressing itself in and through the development of human society—which, however, has its own laws. A person who appears to be a free agent *unwittingly* serves the higher purposes of the divine plan. This is the reasoning that ties Vico to the German philosophers, to Hegel and Marx. Something similar may be seen in the eighteenth-century German *philosophe* Gotthold Lessing, whose *Education of the Human Race* postulated a progressive revelation, God choosing to reveal himself gradually through the course of history rather than through one message delivered in ancient times, as traditional Christianity would have it.[6]

And indeed more than one late-eighteenth-century thinker wrote what the Scotchman Dugald Stewart called "theoretical or conjectural history." Stewart was only one of a whole Scottish school of such historians; in France, Turgot and Condorcet provide the most famous examples. Written in the aftermath of the French Revolution, Condorcet's *Sketch . . . of the Progress of The Human Mind* presented a progressive scheme of ten stages. In Condorcet's exceedingly simplistic view, the human mind, moving ever onward and upward, was now in the next-to-last phase of its development and soon would arrive at the nearest thing possible to perfection. But Condorcet's greatest significance lies in his ability to see civilization as a whole: it is not just one kind of progress but the movement of entire cultures that is in question, and it is in knowledge and general welfare that progress manifests itself. Condorcet's pamphlet became famous.

Of the various schemes devised to explain historical development, the most significant were those of Kant, Herder, and finally Hegel. With these figures we are close to the boundary that divides the Enlightenment from the romantic period, and the eighteenth century from the nineteenth. But with Kant and Herder we are still in the eighteenth century, and the giant figure of Kant belongs as much to the Enlightenment as to the next era; he was virtually a transition in himself. Though dedicated primarily to issues of epistemology and metaphysics, with special reference to scientific and religious knowledge and the boundary between them, Kant wrote one notable essay on history. This interest he passed on to Herder and to the German idealist philosophers. In his essay "The Idea of a Universal History from a Cosmopolitan Point of View" Kant argued that there must be some cosmic teleology or providential plan if history is to make sense. Individuals work toward the realization of ends of which they are unconscious. The full development of reason, of the human capacity for understanding, requires the whole species: it is not open to a single individual, and it must develop through time. All that has happened will be found to have existed for some purpose. Thus wars are the means of driving people toward a world government. Everything that happens has its purpose, though that purpose may not be evident to us. Thus Kant reveals to us "a consoling view of the future, in which the human species is represented in the far distance as having at last worked itself up to a condition in which all the germs implanted in it by nature may be fully developed, and its destination here on earth fulfilled."

Herder immediately took up this idea. It would take a good part of the next century to work out the details of this edifying prospect. The Enlightenment, which began in the rather bitterly pessimistic skepticism of Pierre Bayle and with Voltaire sadly disenchanted by such events as the Lisbon earthquake, ended in an optimism that sprang from ruminations on history. Scholars rediscovered the exciting idea of a providence in history which differed from the old Judeo-Christian providence in *evolving* in a sustained and logical way through the natural workings of the social and historical process. God (or, if you choose, Reason) revealed himself (or itself) in history, as humanity marched toward perfection. "The total mass of the human race," Turgot tells us, "through alternating periods of calm and excitement, good and evil, marches steadily, if with slow steps, toward a greater perfection."[7]

Notes

[1]The neoclassical artists were fond of using "historical" (classical) themes; plays about Cato, Caesar, and other ancients proliferated, and "history painting" was accorded the most prestige in the graphic arts. There was thus a strong feeling for at least one phase of the past, but not for others.

[2]Introduction to the 1900 edition of *Esprit des lois*, reprinted in *The Mind and Faith of Justice Holmes*, ed. Max Lerner (Boston: Little, Brown & Co., 1943), p. 381.

[3]See Arthur O. Lovejoy, "The Parallel of Deism and Classicism," in his *Essays in the History of Ideas* (1948; rpt. Westport, Conn.: Greenwood Press, 1978).

[4]See the introduction to Henry Bertram Hill's edition of *The Political Testament of Cardinal Richelieu* (Madison: University of Wisconsin Press, 1961).

[5]It may be worth noting that the greatest of twentieth-century novelists, James Joyce, fell under Vico's spell: *Finnegans Wake* is based on the eternal *corso, ricorso.*

[6]It seems that the Germans received more of a feeling for history through their universal genius, Leibniz, than did the French through Descartes. "What philosophy, more nearly than his, has prepared the way for Hegel?" asks Yvon Belaval in a study of Leibniz, *Leibniz critique de Descartes* (Paris: Gallinard, 1960). Friedrich Meinecke began his classic account of the growth of modern historical consciousness (*Die Entstehung des Historismus*) with Leibniz.

[7]Turgot, *Discourse on the Progress of the Human Spirit* (1750).

CHAPTER 5

THE NINETEENTH CENTURY: THE GOLDEN AGE OF HISTORY

Varieties of Historicism

BY the end of the eighteenth century, history had become more philosophical and philosophy had almost become historical. Condorcet declared that philosophy had outlived its usefulness and that all the important truths were to be found in the study of the past. If, as the German philosophers suggested, the record of past human experience was similar to the revelation of Reason or Divine Will, then the equivalence of philosophy and history was obvious. From another perspective, Edmund Burke, in his much-read attack on the French Revolution, found a safer foundation for political and social life in the past, in the continuity of a people as expressed in their rooted institutions, than in the abstract formulations of political theory. Burke's mistrust of "the fallible and feeble contrivances" of individual human reason led him to lean, like Hume, on the collective wisdom of the people as summed up in those practices and structures that had sprung from their long experience.

During the first half of the nineteenth century, thinkers on the political left and right alike tried to make the past not merely a source of examples and a road to wisdom but a revelation of the purposive force that controlled human destiny. If conservatives were Burkean, and if Hegel's vast scheme perhaps belonged in the center, socialists such as Louis Blanc also believed (before Karl Marx took up the notion) that "history follows a path traced for it by the hand of God" or of nature. Saint-Simon agreed, and from him Comte borrowed much of his positivist historicism. Saint-Simon wrote that "the supreme law of progress . . . carries along and dominates everything; men are its instruments." Today we are inclined to be most suspicious of such schemes, which represent (in Karl Popper's unique use of the term) "historicism" or "metahistory" or, as some have termed it, "historiosophy." Such schemes were very widely taken for granted in the romantic era and go far to account for the enormous prestige and popularity that serious history attained at that time. If, as has recently been said, "history acquired in the nineteenth century an importance which it had never achieved before and does not hold today," such a historicism was the principal reason.

The major German philosophers in this age of philosophy nurtured Kant's suggestion of providence into a powerful statement of the case for metahistory. That truth was a matter of development, of movement, was their central insight. The error of all earlier philosophers lay in viewing the world statically; in fact, nothing stands still. All is involved in the continual flux, the *Werden*, or "becoming," of life. The dialectic, a process by which one position engenders its opposite and then embraces it to form something new, which in turn engenders its opposite, made its appearance in German philosophy before Hegel. Johann Fichte, a popular writer capable of reaching a larger audience than Kant—as he did with his famous *Addresses to the German Nation* of 1807—came to believe that basic reality is Ideal or Spirit, all of which is contained in a cosmic Ego of which our minds are a part. Philosophers who followed Fichte meditated on the relationship between the subjective and objective aspects of reality and on the creative interaction in which they engage. Hegel's ponderous genius put all these heady conceptions together in his vast *Philosophy of History*. History is a universal cosmic process that works toward the full realization of Absolute Spirit. It reveals a dialectical pattern; behind the somewhat incoherent record of external events (Hegel was not so naive as to deny its incoherence) we can perceive in each epoch a grand Idea, which is its contribution to the stupendous whole and which constitutes nothing less than the logic by which God realizes in time the purposes of the world. History is logic and logic is history; the real is rational and the rational is real. Hegel's view of history was not entirely a priori and theoretical: he left a place for the empirical investigator, for we must study the past to find the pattern. But when we think through the facts, we discover a theme or Idea behind them. And when we contemplate the whole sequence of ages and ideas, we find a logical order.

The tendency to trace all such ideas to Hegel is to be resisted. In the early nineteenth century, the concept of historical destiny was widely abroad in Europe; it was one of those beliefs whose time had come. François Guizot, a French historian and statesman who gained such popularity as a lecturer in Paris in the 1820s that he was admitted not only to the historical guild but to the political leadership of France as Louis-Philippe's first minister, had probably never read Hegel, few of whose works had yet been translated into French. Yet Guizot taught that history has a goal, a direction, a plan. Each age is destined to make its contribution to the evolution of European civilization: "For fifteen centuries Europe and France have been moving along the same road toward freedom and progress." To Guizot, the goal toward which humanity had been advancing steadily for so long included representative, constitutional government and national unification in a free society. A liberal (or whig), he saw in this slow and stately march a cause for extreme satisfaction; the Revolution of 1848 did something to disturb such a view. No liberal of the time doubted that, having come last, his own era had to be best; each could proclaim, with Tennyson, that he was "the heir of all the ages, in the foremost files of time."

Guizot's "fifteen centuries" is significant. As both the French nation and representative government had evolved primarily out of the structures of the Germanic tribes of early medieval Europe, Guizot put more stress on the Middle Ages than on classical antiquity. He saw a steady development reaching from the first "long-haired" Frankish kings down to the present. The romantics' interest in the Middle Ages helped to rescue this period from neglect, of course. We find even the socialist Saint-Simon arguing that "if historians had analyzed and examined the Middle Ages more deeply, they . . . would have recorded the gradual preparation of all the great events which developed later and would not have presented the explosions of the 16th and following centuries as sudden and unforeseen." This resurrection of the Middle Ages played a crucial role in the general renaissance of history, for it made possible a perspective on the past which stressed continuity rather than cyclical movement.

In this age of nationalism, an enthusiasm unleashed by both the French Revolution and romanticism and made possible by modern communications, the nation provided one obvious *telos* of history. Ranke said historical studies grew out of opposition to the Napoleonic idea. It is hard to deny that national growth was a slow development and thus a good historical subject. If this theme of the gradual emergence of the nation, of the shaping of a people, were taken away from nineteenth-century historiography, its most popular classics would be destroyed. Macaulay was the Guizot of England, Treitschke of Germany, and many other historians chose the same theme. For nineteenth-century Russia, struggling to find its national identity, Nikolai Karamzin played this role of historian-prophet.[1] Liberty, parliamentary government, and, for the somewhat bolder, democracy provided other popular themes. Hegel thought that the whole grand march of God through the world had culminated in the modern European nation under a constitutional monarch, with ordered freedom under law. Socialists saw the reign of equality and social justice as the end product, that one far-off divine event toward which all creation moved.

"The sense of history has everywhere awakened," Friedrich Savigny declared. In tracing the history of this rise of "historicism" in *Die Entstehung der Historismus*, the German historian Friedrich Meinecke called it "one of the greatest spiritual revolutions that Western thought has experienced." It was nothing less than the discovery of change. Much besides philosophical currents contributed to this discovery. Indeed, if we confined our explanation of the rise of nineteenth-century historical-mindedness to such belief systems, we might properly be accused of a one-sided idealistic interpretation of history. Even the simple fact of rapid change made people more conscious of the role of change. It can be argued that the French Revolution and the Napoleonic period, coinciding with the crucial impact of a so-called industrial revolution, brought sweeping and drastic change to Europe for the first time in its history—change that affected basic social structures and ways of life, not just political leadership. And the changes did not stop; they swept on with an irresistible momentum. "The age of historical preoccupation was made possible by the age of revolution," remarks Douglas Johnson, Guizot's biographer. After 1789 and 1815, people had a sense of being adrift on a stormy sea without a compass; accustomed to basic stability or to change so gradual as to be barely perceptible, they felt themselves being swept with fearful rapidity toward an unknown future. The old order was gone, and it was not clear whether a specific new order would emerge (and if so, what it would be like) or whether change would be continuous (and if so, what endless change would mean for people, for society, and for culture). The castaways looked anxiously about for landmarks.[2] But they were in a position to compare an old order with a new order, for the French Revolution and industrial developments opened up whole new historical perspectives.

Nevertheless, it is possible that the awakening sense of the past was primary and that it created the sense of change. Recent reconsiderations of the French Revolution find that it was far from the first revolution, did not bring about basic social change, and had as its ideology a warmed-over Christian millenarianism.[3] The nineteenth century produced a whole host of historicist interpretations now seen as largely myths. The imagination of the nineteenth century was historical, but it is not easy to say exactly why it was so. As historians of history we stumble over the problems of history, of which the most intractable is the difficulty of tracing causes.

A crucial factor in the advancement of historical research was an increase in access to the sources of history. The extensive use of archival sources was an outstanding feature of the history boom of the early nineteenth century. Scholars explored these sources with a sense of high adventure and of imminent discovery. Now at last, one could, in Leopold von Ranke's famous phrase, find out exactly what happened. Governments had begun to collect their documents in public archives, and scholars were given access to them. Most of the great public libraries and museums had been opened in the eighteenth century. The trend toward nationalism and the centralized state caused materials formerly held in private houses or local registries to be deposited at the national libraries, such as the British Museum and the Bibliothèque Nationale, where they were accessible and usable.

The University of Göttingen in Germany, where an important school of critical researchers had been centered since the latter part of the eighteenth century, took the lead in exploiting these resources. These scholars trusted nothing but the documents, the primary sources, and they were determined to plunge into the archives and to appraise them systematically. Out of the German universities came the seminar method of conducting graduate-school research. Why Germany took the lead is itself a matter for historical inquiry; it is a fact (according to Herbert Butterfield, who wrote an excellent essay on the subject) that as early as 1770 Germany was producing a far greater proportion of writings on history than any other European country.[4] Göttingen seems to have been the center of a kind of reaction against the feathery and superficial sort of historical writing identified with Voltaire and the French. The *philosophes* had once reacted against stuffy pedantry by becoming witty and popular; now in a reverse reaction, the *philosophes* were depicted as mere dilettantes who covered their laziness with cleverness. Germany of course experienced an intellectual renaissance in the age of Kant, Herder, Goethe, Fichte, and Hegel; it also experienced a nationalistic reaction after its defeat by Napoleon. It was the leading center of romanticism, that new spirit which exalted, among other things, folklore, national tradition, and medieval subjects, and reacted against the abstract universalism of neoclassical taste by stressing the concrete and the particular. Thus romanticism was closely associated with nationalism, and both were linked to history.

Nevertheless, the scholars at Göttingen were not in any obvious way romantic; they wanted to be solid, scientific, and exact. Their German pride in having their feet on the ground, in contrast to the "windbag-history" of Voltaire, is evident. They were interested in the Middle Ages, and of course, as they went back to the roots of the modern state in medieval times, the theme of national development tended to dominate in their studies. The stimulus to the quest for the roots of the modern state was provided by the absence, until 1871, of a unified national state in the German world. This was a source of much anguish to cultured

Germans, who hated the multiplicity of their petty states and yearned
for national unity and strength.

It would be a mistake to see all historians, even German historians,
as disciples of Hegel. The German historians came from a different
background, from the very precise and technical-minded school of archival research and systematic criticism; they did not much admire highly
speculative schemes of history written by philosophers. They agreed
with Herder's protest against Kant that "history is the science of what
is, not of what possibly may be according to the hidden design of fate."
They were content to begin in humble ways and shied away from theory,
yet they broadly shared the fashionable historicism of the day, of which
Hegel was the main philosophical spokesman. Leopold von Ranke and
his friends among the great German historians of the earlier nineteenth
century accepted the notion of a cosmic plan into which all ages and
peoples somehow fitted. Hence they felt justified in studying each phase
of the past with a sense of its own integrity and importance. In Ranke's
phrase, each was "equidistant from eternity"; each had its part to play
in the great pattern and hence deserved to be understood as it was.
This stance amounted to relativism; Ranke and his colleagues refused
to impose any yardstick of valuation, any "presentism," on the past.
Every part of it had a right of its own to exist. Guizot had said that
each age makes its own exact contribution; it does just what it has to
do, no more and no less, to help along the grand design. Ranke's equi-
distance from eternity expressed the same idea, which was Hegel's also.
This "Whatever is, is right" doctrine tended to silence all moralistic
criticism of the past. Whatever people did, they did rightly; they could
not have done otherwise. It remained only to describe these actions
accurately. Ranke was so wedded to the grand pattern that at the age
of eighty-five he started work on his *World History*, for he assumed that
his life's labors had been preparing him for just this task. The German
scholars, then, saw a potential unity to the whole human past. As its
chief constituent parts they tended to choose nationalities and states,
implicitly accepting Hegel's view that these were the principal vehicles
of historical destiny.

It bears repeating that the philosophical view of history adopted by
the German historians and some others actually strengthened their empirical investigations. Often it is said that the Hegelian system, being
abstract and speculative, was opposed to true historical inquiry. But in
fact it paved the way for a careful and neutral description of the past
by instilling in historians a belief that every part of that past was worthy
of being described—not condemned or praised, not judged, not yoked
to some present cause, but described. Ranke, who said that each phase
of the past was "equidistant from eternity," also enjoined historians to

"describe what actually happened." The two formulations go together. True, a commitment to a priori theories about the past can warp a historian's judgment, so that one finds what one has set out to find. This has been so notoriously the case with some of the less intelligent followers of that great disciple of Hegel, Karl Marx, that we may think of Hegelian-Marxian thought as the necessary enemy of honest historical investigation. It need not be so. Its strong faith that there *is* a pattern in events may operate as a powerful inducement to study those events with scrupulous care in an effort to describe them as they were. Of course, as we realize today, no one can help bringing to the study of events a mental framework. But in the era of Ranke and Mommsen and Niebuhr, philosophy worked to make historians think they were looking at the past "as it really was," and this was no bad thing. They had been cured of the vice of seeing the past entirely through the eyes of the present.

Belief in historical destiny, whatever its dangers, also produced a keen sense of the dramatic. The most romantic historians, such as Thomas Carlyle and Jules Michelet, felt the presence of great forces surging through history and communicated a tremendous excitement. To Michelet the people as well as the nation were mighty, awe-inspiring, sometimes terrible, carrying out the historical mission to sweep away the old order in the French Revolution. Like all great events, that one, of course, set in motion whole seas of historical writing. To Michelet it was the focal point of human history. The masses and mobs that made it were impelled by forces greater than themselves, forces they hardly understood. History has a will of its own; by its "cunning," to use Hegel's word, it uses people as tools.

The great strength of German historians was supposed to be their methods. "The Germans have taken the lead in historical inquiries," Will Ladislaw tells Dorothea in George Eliot's *Middlemarch*, "and they laugh at results which are got by groping about in woods with a pocket-compass while they have made good roads." In what did this vaunted German superiority consist? Was there some secret, or was it just an infinite capacity for taking pains? The Germans themselves would have said the latter. They tended to deny that they had any magic formula, any way of applying standardized tests to evidence to determine its value. "That hearsay evidence possesses only as much validity as the authority from which it derives is just about the only precept which the critical method can boast of," said the crusty Theodor Mommsen. Handbooks on historical methods appeared, but the real gain was simply in getting at the sources and in organizing them so that they could be used. These sources included not only the official and private papers of governments and statesmen but nonliterary sources as well. Mommsen organized the

Roman inscriptions at the beginning of that great archaeological revolution which dredged up new materials on the ancient Near East. Napoleon's invasion of Egypt began the study of the monuments, inscriptions, and artifacts of that ancient civilization (two hundred scholars accompanied the French troops and brought back numerous objects). A retired German businessman, Heinrich Schliemann, realized his life's dream of digging up ancient Troy. Persian, Assyrian, Babylonian, Cretan, and Hittite discoveries; the deciphering of ancient languages; the finding of prehistoric human relics—all were part of the unfolding story of historical craftsmanship. To assemble all the evidence, written and unwritten, and to order it in a way that made it useful was the essence of a new "scientific" methodology. It was not much different from the method Charles Darwin used to establish his theory about the way life evolves. A general theory of evolution was far from new; Darwin simply brought to it fertile theories and a mass of evidence. (Historians of science tend to see similar developments occurring in all branches of the scientific discipline during this time. It was the systematic professional *organization* of knowledge, even more than new ideas, that was behind the great nineteenth-century surge in scientific discovery.)

This historical tide seems to have crested in Darwin's decade, the 1850s. At the same time that Darwin was preparing his memorable *Origin of Species* (1859), another Englishman, Thomas Macaulay, completed the *History of England* he had rightly boasted would become England's favorite reading. (Both had been working on their masterpieces for more than twenty years.)[5] The French counterpart of Macaulay was Jules Michelet. Karl Marx set forth the outline of economic history which would partly materialize in the first volume of *Das Kapital* (1867). In Germany, Theodor Mommsen published his *History of Rome* (1853–1856); in the United States, Francis Parkman's *Oregon Trail* appeared in 1851. These are landmarks in the growth of historical studies. So is Alexis de Tocqueville's *L'Ancien régime et la Révolution* (1856), a work that still stands as possibly the most brilliant ever written on the causes of the French Revolution. And these were only the highlights. The aftermath of 1859 brought a spate of theorizing, often classified under the loose rubric of "social Darwinism," about possible laws of human social development corresponding to the processes of natural evolution set forth in Darwin's book.

Macaulay, Michelet, and Parkman were powerful imaginative writers as well as careful researchers; they produced masterpieces of literature while giving the general public the classic histories of their respective countries. Mommsen, closer to the new type of professional scholar, was a charismatic and popular personality. Marx's sweep and scope, of course, were unrivaled. In this era historians became influential public figures as they attained a new professional competence; for the first time, chairs of history occupied by leading academics become common in European universities.

Some observers have seen in this flowering of prestigious national historiography a kind of ideological legitimizing of the nineteenth-century social order. Certainly the great Victorian historians were far from impartial. Carlyle, Froude, Macaulay, Michelet, George Bancroft in the United States, and others breathed fire into their writings. But their causes were various, and some of them (such as Carlyle and Marx) were violent critics of the prevalent social order. Frequently, of course, the *telos* of history was the Nation, seen as the sacred mission of a People. But the goal might also be Liberty, Democracy, or Socialism. Usually it was some kind of progress. (But, in the case of one influential schema of world history, that of the Comte de Gobineau, the end was degeneration. Gobineau's opus on the inequality of races was another publication of the 1850s.) These works did more than reconstruct the past in a newly authoritative way. They invested it with moral and philosophical meaning.

The word "science" is involved here, too. Invoked not only by Marx, Comte, and Herbert Spencer but by the German academic savants with their cult of original sources, so-called scientific history raised questions about the validity of this claim.

History as Science

Perhaps a concern for accuracy which required bureaucratic organization and led to dry monographs was suitable to a bourgeois and industrial age. We may need to be reminded how surprisingly little people had once valued factual accuracy. In discussing Sir Walter Ralegh's *History of the World*, which the aging Renaissance and Elizabethan adventurer had undertaken in his idle moments during his imprisonment in the Tower of London, Philip Edwards remarks that "the notion of History as a faithful presentation of the events of the past for the reader to find what interpretation and derive what profit he can from them was quite foreign to Renaissance ideas. No historian considered an accumulation of accurate facts as his objective."[6] History was rhetoric plundering the past for instigations to present virtue or to action. Herodotus' reputation as the father of lies had no untoward effect on his reputation as a great historian. Even Voltaire, much more careful about his facts—as he cheerfully commented, in an increasingly critical age one just could not get by with making them up—did not imagine that one ought to begin by a systematic effort to uncover all of them. The

German scholars, with their archives and their seminars and their systematic critical methods, represented the trend that Auguste Comte was just then identifying as the basic intellectual revolution of modern times: the transition to an age of positivism, to the cult of the fact. Or, otherwise put, the age of science.

"Science" was a blessed word in the nineteenth century, and devotees of all manner of causes were eager to secure some of its benison. Socialists, campaigning for their essentially religious vision of a better society, claimed that they were scientific (the Owenites called their meetinghouses Halls of Science before Karl Marx decided that his was the only scientific socialism.) Virtually everybody wanted to be scientific, and it is not surprising that historians did too. They suffered from their failure to mount the sacred pinnacle. Thomas Buckle said flatly that historians were inferior to scientists because no Kepler or Newton had arisen to give them the dignity of all-embracing law. When we examine the innumerable assertions by nineteenth- and twentieth-century historians that they were being or trying to be scientific, we find that in actuality they meant rather different things. Quite often they meant merely being critical or systematic. Frequently they meant no more than that they were getting at the original sources, which, as we know, were intoxicating discoveries in the earlier nineteenth century. But sometimes they claimed to be finding general laws like those of the physical sciences, or in some other way uncovering the real pattern of the past. Comte and Marx and Herbert Spencer all thought they had found a plan that could be traced throughout history, a succession of stages or a progression that, having been decoded, revealed not only where humankind had been but even where it was headed. Others more modestly permitted themselves to hope or believe that solid research conducted by trained professionals would gradually provide the materials for an eventual science of history, so that generalization would become possible when scholars had accumulated enough indubitable particulars; someday, when all the bricks were at hand, they would complete the whole house of history.

This is not the place to discuss what science is and whether history can ever be scientific. (This matter is discussed later in the book.) Here we may observe only that when we call a body of thought scientific, we normally mean more than that it is orderly, critical, and systematic; otherwise, both cooking and the compiling of telephone books would be sciences. Moreover, in this sense no doubt Thucydides, Tacitus, Bede, Machiavelli, Sarpi, and Voltaire were scientific (perhaps without knowing it, like Moliere's bourgeois gentleman, who was astonished to learn that he had been speaking prose all his life). We mean by "science" a body of knowledge that takes the form of permanent, unchanging, and universal general principles or laws, which can be verified by experimentation, and which enable us to predict future events. In the nineteenth century a few people did argue for a science of history in this sense. Most of them were amateurs and speculative theorists, but not all. They tended to derive their ideas from Auguste Comte's positivism or, like Karl Marx, to be post-Hegelians.

Thomas Buckle, an Englishman who wrote in the 1850s and 1860s, argued that although history had not yet produced its Kepler or Newton, it could be expected to do so in the age of science. Intellectual progress does take place, Comteans thought, and on a scale of ascending difficulty sociology (the science of society) comes last but crowns all. The problem of such a science is complex but not in principle insuperable. Positivists believed in firmly excluding all except the "hard facts" (we learn not to speculate about God, ultimate reality, first causes, final purposes, because questions about such things are unanswerable); after establishing these facts, we detect regularities and relationships. Obviously, they argued, "laws" of predictive value do exist in human affairs. The rate of murder or suicide or divorce or undeliverable letters stays statistically rather constant, so that one may make forecasts, even though one can never predict which particular person will kill himself or fail to receive a letter.

But most positivists preferred sociology to history (in Comte's terminology, social statics to social dynamics), and few historians could ever really believe that the past repeats itself. Positivism in some ways was quite unhistorical, since it posited an unchanging lawfulness even in human affairs. Buckle wrote history, but it is hard to see that he carried out the program he announced. The same might be said of Hippolyte Taine, the French historian and critic. Nevertheless, at the end of the century we find Henry Adams, the American historian, disturbed at the failure of history to get anywhere. He updated the old hope of discovering great historical laws comparable to those of physics. (He suggested a historical second law of thermodynamics, according to which Western civilization had been dispersing its energy since the thirteenth century.)[7] Positivists were generally stimulating, often proposed interesting but dubious theories, and helped broaden the scope of history by their interest in broad social and economic trends or in intellectual patterns rather than in politics.

It might be possible to classify Herbert Spencer as a positivist. He takes us into the realm of that other exciting nineteenth-century school of thought, the evolutionary or Darwinian school; but Spencer's larger system of social evolution was positivist in that it boldly asserted certain laws of social development applicable to all societies. Other evolutionists also postulated laws of development or principles of change (adaptation) as constant and predictable. Though they linked primitive and civilized peoples in a single ascending ladder of evolution, their postulates applied more to anthropology than to history. Their schemes failed to stand up to the facts, and by the end of the century they had few adherents. T. H. Huxley described one of Spencer's ideas as "a beautiful theory slain by an ugly fact." The "science" of anthropology remained, as a careful and systematic investigation of various primitive peoples, but it found no single ladder that all ascended or even any invariable principles of development. It tended to discover that each people differs from all others in some ways and thus cannot be placed in any scheme of evolutionary ascent.

Darwin's memorable establishment beyond reasonable doubt of the truth of biological evolution—the derivation, by comprehensible processes, of all living species from one or a few simple original species— gave a boost to certain kinds of historical studies. Although Darwin had not discussed the evolution of human societies, others were quick to apply his ideas to that realm. Not only Herbert Spencer but, in another way, Marx and Engels claimed that they were doing for human social evolution what the great Cambridge biologist had done for the evolution of animal life: showing its exact laws of change, through struggle and adaptation. Apart from such sweeping claims, Darwinism encouraged a genetic approach to all subjects, not least those connected with human ideas and institutions. In some areas this enterprise proved revolutionary. Consider, for example, what Nietzsche called "the genealogy of morals," embodied in a more pedestrian form in such works as E. A. Westermarck's huge *Origin and Development of Moral Ideas* (1906–1908). Histories of morality were a frequent late-Victorian undertaking, in which such historians as W. E. H. Lecky joined anthropologists and philosophers. Such efforts reflected a naturalistic outlook on matters heretofore thought hardly appropriate for this sort of handling and may fairly be put down to the Darwinian influence. Instead of asserting rational proofs of some moral creed or presenting a new one, thinkers tended to describe and compare existing moral creeds, often on the assumption that this exercise would reveal a scientific ethic, resting on the firm authority of fact. All of human thought, including religion and philosophy, became subject to a genetic, historical approach rather than to a logical, analytical one; thus the consequences of Darwinism greatly extended the range of historical studies. In particular, Darwinists and Marxists raised the possibility of dealing with ideas and ideals—the intellectual "superstructure"—in a thoroughly naturalistic way.

Darwinism as well as Marxism continued the thrust initiated by Montesquieu in the eighteenth century: a determinism postulating the unity of history and explaining it by broad naturalistic processes. The chaos of innumerable absurd events gave way, when one read the underlying pattern, to a coherent whole linked by chains of connections. John Addington Symonds wrote that the evolutionist differed from previous inquirers mainly in seeing process as more than individual actions "independent of the volition of the men who affected them." Could one so reduce humans to the status of physical objects? The prospect was tempting in its bold simplicity but of course full of problems.

Historical "laws," comparable to those found by physicists, could conceivably be either (a) common *patterns* of development found in separate peoples, considered as isolated units, as in Spencer's claim that *all* societies progress from the simple and undifferentiated to the complex and specialized; (b) common *processes* that explain all change, exemplified in the Darwinian and Spencerian adaptation to environmental challenges, which kill off the individuals who do not adapt ("survival of the fittest" or "natural selection"); or (c) a discernible law of change that runs through the human race considered as one mighty stream or as a single tree. If we consider all history as one process, there obviously can be no "laws" in the physicists' sense of law, for "if a unique plant lived forever and suffered changes throughout its career," as Morris R. Cohen pointed out in *The Meaning of History*, "we should not be able to formulate any law in regard to its life cycle as a whole." If we attempt to compare a variety of civilizations or societies and find common patterns of growth and decline, as Arnold Toynbee has more recently done (1934–1954), we invite the criticism that in fact human civilizations have *not* been isolated from each other like so many disparate specimens. If we claim that such a principle as "adaptation to the challenge of the physical environment" explains all, we find that different peoples have reacted differently to the same environmental challenges. Obviously, the search for a science of society or history is incredibly complex, if not altogether impossible.

Marxism offered the most ambitious, certainly the most influential nineteenth-century historical "science of society." Marx was profoundly influenced by Hegel, under whose influence he studied philosophy (shortly after Hegel's death in 1831) at the University of Berlin. Hegel did not claim to be scientific; he was frankly metaphysical and argued cogently that empiricism always depends on a preliminary framework of thought, which is metaphysical—beyond science. Hegel did not despise the ordinary empirical investigations of the scientific "understanding" but thought them insufficient; the higher reason must give them their meaning.

Marx and others of the "young Hegelians" changed the master's thought without much difficulty into a scientific materialism that kept the providential plan but considered it to be simply what emerges from an empirical, scientific investigation. It has frequently been alleged that Marx illegitimately retained Hegel's speculative system. He kept this nonscientific framework while claiming, purely as an article of faith, that scientific investigation of the facts *does* prove it right. Whatever the legitimacy of it, Marx did maintain that there is a dialectical evolutionary pattern in the human past and that human history reveals a logical and purposive process. Beginning with primitive communism, human societies pass through several kinds of class structure, from ancient slavery to medieval feudalism to modern capitalism, each marked by the domination of one class and by a typical mode of production, until they achieve the classlessness of modern communism, the culmination of the historical process. It is not altogether clear whether Marx thought that human society constituted one great stream or that there were many human communities, all of which revealed the same pattern. The scheme seems obviously based on the Greek-Roman-Western model, but Marxists later tried to apply it to non-Western civilizations, such as China. It appears to fit such societies much less well. (Marx himself posited an "Asiatic mode of production" that early diverged from the Western pattern to produce a society that was essentially stagnant, until it was impinged upon by the West in modern times.) The motive force is, basically, Hegel's dialectic, transferred from ideas to matter: the eternal motion of things as they oppose and contradict each other. Marx's stress on technological and economic forces reflected the preoccupations of this age of great industrial changes, of the problem of labor and capital— the "Mechanical Age," as Carlyle called it.

Marx's fundamental assumption was that technological change results from human toolmaking impulses. From this "means of production" arise "relations of production" (who owns the tools, how the goods they produce are distributed) specific to the various stages of society; and on this base of productive forces *cum* relations of production there further grows a "superstructure" consisting of all the rest—political and legal forms, "ideologies" of all sorts. Revolution occurs rather suddenly as pent-up forces explode the old order, when the means of production advance to a point where the old relations of production are obsolete, a "fetter on production."

Marx was unique in linking a theory of history to a strategy of social change, and his imposing (if shatteringly incomplete) structure of thought suffered as much as it gained from this attempt at praxis. As a theory of history, at least, it turns out to be stimulating but oversimplified; its determinism (the economic base determines all the rest of culture, thought, government) and its evolutionism (society progresses through certain well-defined stages propelled by economic forces and defined by class structures) are either false or, if qualified enough to fit the evidence, not very meaningful. Marx and Engels themselves realized as much, and ridiculed the simple-minded versions of their ideas current among disciples ("Thank God I am not a Marxist!" said Marx). The gap between Marx the revolutionary propagandist and Marx the scientific student of history was at times a yawning gulf. (Ordinary workers almost never understood Marx's highly abstruse writings, which were obviously addressed to a sophisticated intellectual audience and had to be drastically bowdlerized for popular consumption.)

The historian J. H. Hexter has remarked, perhaps unfairly, that one can make Marxism stand up only by resolutely ignoring three-fourths of the evidence and asking no very bright questions about the rest. But Marx did combine a most dramatic (essentially romantic) picture of the inexorable destiny of humankind with a claim to being scientific. Not only that, he seemed to make history relevant by relating it closely to plans for revolutionary action; it provided a guide for changing the world which inspired the revolutionary socialist movement. At its roots perhaps lay something as simple as Joachim's medieval vision of the millennium. Yet until very recently, his loyal followers accepted at face value his claim to have deciphered the riddle of history and to have become the Newton of the social sciences.

History Popular and Professional

The new ideas and isms spawned in the early nineteenth century created a "generous confusion" of thought that has existed ever since. Conservativism, liberalism, socialism, romanticism, utilitarianism, positivism, anarchism, Hegelianism, Darwinism, Marxism, and many other doctrines competed in the marketplace of ideas. No longer did any one orthodoxy prevail. Christianity itself became ever more fragmented: Protestants into an ever-proliferating number of sects (the great revival of the first half of the century created a host of new ones), Roman Catholics into ultramontanists and nationalists, liberals and conservatives, and later modernists and traditionalists. The breakdown of intellectual authority tended for a time at least to elevate history. Skepticism about all merely intellectual formations may encourage people to lean on the historical process, which embraces them all and is a sort of hard and indisputable underlying reality. In the eighteenth century, David Hume had reached such a position: we retreat from our vain disputations, all of which end in uncertainty, to take refuge in that solid certainty, the world of people and events which, rooted in custom and nature, goes on with a sort of animal instinct.

Many Victorians looked to the past as a source of values, not, in the classical way, to find examples of values one already knew, but to discover values that one could find nowhere else. "By what Man has done, we learn what Man can do, and gauge the power and prospects of our race"; so said Benjamin Disraeli, statesman, disciple of Burke, and author of romantic novels. Walter Houghton, in his *Victorian Frame of Mind*, notes the large number of Victorian histories that celebrated heroic deeds and offered inspiration. Thomas Carlyle and Ralph Waldo Emerson shared the belief that the chief value of writing about the past is to show how great a person can be. As critics of a society increasingly commercial and devoid of heroism, they felt the lack of personal greatness more acutely. Carlyle's "great man" theory of history has often been condemned as a baleful influence. It is best seen as a response to the conditions of his own day rather than as an effort to find the right way to interpret the past. Carlyle was a moral critic who found modern humanity wanting in ideals, and he saw hero worship as an antidote to skepticism.

Let us again stress the great *popularity* of historical writing in the nineteenth century, especially in the first two-thirds of the century. Macaulay and Carlyle were followed by others in Britain who carried on a tradition of history which was by no means meretricious or *merely* popular. Such works, written by men who had first-rate minds, excellent pens, and some pretensions to real scholarship, were sometimes as eagerly read as a novel by Dickens or Hugo. Its authors are better termed men of letters than professional historians. In the United States the classic New Englanders, Francis Parkman, William Prescott, John L. Motley, John Fiske, and George Bancroft, filled this role. France had its Michelets and Guizots and Lamartines, the latter two combining active political careers with their literary work, as did Macaulay, Motley, Bancroft, and Morley. Edmund Wilson wrote (in *To the Finland Station*) that Michelet was "more like a novelist such as Balzac. . . . He had the novelist's social interest and grasp of character, the poet's imagination and passion."

In this connection we cannot overlook the popularity of historical themes among the greater poets and novelists. Robert Browning, Alfred Tennyson, and Matthew Arnold all spent a good part of their inspiration on long narrative poems, which later went out of fashion. Tennyson favored the Middle Ages and Browning the Renaissance. After the immensely successful Walter Scott, Charles Kingsley and many others satisfied the public appetite for historical novels. Even when they did not choose specifically historical subjects, as in Kingsley's *Hereward the Wake* and *Westward Ho!*, the greater Victorian novelists tried to examine the actual texture of events and of people in society in a basically historical or sociological way. George Eliot's *Middlemarch* plumbed the lives of "the number who lived faithfully a hidden life, and rest in unvisited tombs." The counterpart of medieval hagiography existed in such works as Samuel Smiles's *Self-Help* and *Lives of the Engineers;* the former was more popular than any novel. It has been noted that even in their treatment of love and other emotions the Victorians transformed romantic idealizations into *events*, things that developed and grew dynamically.[8]

John Ruskin made his great literary reputation, which extended into other fields, in art history: *The Stones of Venice, The Seven Lamps of Architecture*. These examples are all from England, but counterparts can be found in other European countries and to some extent in the United States. Viollet-le-Duc, the French architect famous for his medieval restorations, said that "the past is not dead. It is us, our life, our reason for existing. . . . He who does not remember is a barbarian." This passionate historicism was present too in the French novelists; Engels said he learned more social history from the novels of Balzac than from all the documents in archives. If Balzac was the counterpart of Dickens and Victor Hugo of George Eliot, then Alexandre Dumas resembled Walter Scott; later, in the Darwinian era, Émile Zola and Thomas Hardy were the twin stars of "naturalism." Zola's vast chronicle traced the working out of lives through heredity and environment in an allegedly scientific way. In the United States, Frank Norris, Theodore Dreiser, and Stephen Crane imitated those European naturalists.

The professionals in the British universities—Bishop William Stubbs, Edward Augustus Freeman, Samuel Rawson Gardiner—carried on a sometimes bitter rivalry with the powerful amateurs. James Anthony Froude, mid-Victorian historian of the English Reformation and the Age of Elizabeth, became the center of a violent historians' vendetta, as much for his alleged outrages against the facts as for his unconcealed Protestant bias (Mary Queen of Scots was simply "a bad woman," and Elizabeth was guilty of the sin of being insufficiently devoted to the Protestant cause). Froude was a vigorous and versatile Victorian with a lively style, a real gift for narrative, and a considerable talent for misreading his sources, though he certainly did consult many. We are inclined to forgive him when we think of him as a man of the world, with many other interests, to whom history was important but was not alone important. How well it was integrated into the very fabric of nineteenth-century life! Lord Acton, the great liberal Catholic who became Regius Professor of Modern History at Cambridge toward the end of the century, is another example: he was active in the affairs of the Church, editor of magazines, leader of the liberal faction at the great Ecumenical Council of 1870, friend and correspondent of Prime

Minister Gladstone, and withal a truly outstanding man of history even if he never quite got around to finishing his major works. Gladstone dabbled in history. German historians played an even larger part in political affairs, as leaders of movements or as advisers of statesmen. Louis-Adolphe Thiers followed Guizot in the lineage of French scholar-statesmen, which included Tocqueville. Innumerable amateurs wrote classic works in their spare time. George Grote was a banker; James Ford Rhodes, prominent American historian, was a retired iron manufacturer.

The professionals, more narrowly academic but also more accurate and painstaking in their work (and usually less biased), increasingly made life difficult for the amateurs. Freeman took careful aim at poor Froude and almost ruined his reputation. The great nineteenth-century amateurs were often so passionately committed that they could not be fair. Froude's extreme Protestant bias was shared by John L. Motley, the American historian of the Dutch revolt, whose massive account votes for the Dutch rebels on every page, as Bancroft's voted for Jackson (Motley has been corrected by the Dutch historian Pieter Geyl). Froude and Motley contributed to the "Whig interpretation," seeing modern history as largely the rise of liberty and making liberals of the early Protestants, a manifest error.

In 1894, when the Regius Professorship of Modern History at Oxford was to be filled, some scholars reacted with horror at the mention of the name of Frederic Harrison. Positivist, political radical, brilliant essayist, man of letters, Harrison admired Carlyle and deplored the trend toward a narrow specialization, which allowed a major scholar to spend his life mastering "ten years in the fourteenth century." It has since become a familiar complaint. But Harrison was insufficiently expert to meet the requirements. Earlier Froude had received the post despite his professional failings; Harrison did not (it went to York Powell, whose name few people recognize today). Professionalism had taken over.

The professionalization of history spread to other nations from Germany in the 1870s and 1880s. In England it is often dated from the appointment of William Stubbs as Oxford's Regius Professor in 1866; it arrived in France by 1881. The first graduate schools offering specialized training on the German model appeared in the United States in the 1870s. Of thirty-four authors who contributed to Justin Winsor's *Narrative and Critical History of America* (1884–1889), only ten were professors and only two were professors of history. In the American Nation series (1904–1907), twenty-one of twenty-four works were by university professors. In a memorable passage in the introduction to his *Study of History*, Arnold Toynbee recalled his dismay as he watched the books change on the shelves in the home of a distinguished professor he often visited as a child in the 1890s, from general works to "the relentless advance of half a dozen specialized periodicals"; and he recalled that Theodor Mommsen, the great German scholar who wrote *The History of the Roman Republic* in his younger days, turned his talent to the editing of inscriptions and the writing of monograph articles for learned journals. To Toynbee this was industrialism advancing on the humanities—a depressing spectacle. He was not alone in his lack of enthusiasm for this trend. A notable holdout, George M. Trevelyan, nephew of the great Macaulay, wrote in the 1900s with some bitterness, "The public has ceased to watch with any interest the appearance of historical works, good or bad. The *Cambridge Modern History* is indeed bought by the yard to decorate bookshelves, but it is regarded like the *Encyclopaedia Britannica* as a work of reference." The market for public reading was being supplied, he thought, by "prurient journalism," since "serious history is a sacred thing pinnacled afar on frozen heights of science, not to be approached save after a long novitiate."[9] The complaint that historians write not for the general public, as Carlyle and Macaulay did, but for each other is a familiar one and is still heard. Even in the 1830s, Carlyle had inveighed against the "Dryasdusts."

But professionalism was taking over in all walks of life in the late nineteenth century. The professional classes gained in numbers and in status; they represented the increasing division of labor in an increasingly complex society. The general education that had so long served Europe, based on close reading of a comparatively small body of classics— the great Greek and Roman writings and the Bible—was under fire and gradually gave way, though it still constituted the core of an English gentleman's education down to 1914. Specialization meant expertise and gains in competence. It also meant a weakening of ties to the general culture. Once there had existed a reading and thinking public, a culture, which consisted of people who had received a liberal education—quite a small group in Victorian England, in comparison with the total population, but it had unity and cohesiveness. The members of that culture not only had learned the same things but had even gone to the same schools. (Oxford and Cambridge remained the only two universities of social distinction, though new ones, such as the Benthamite University of London, were rising. By and large, the English utilitarians, followers of Jeremy Bentham, showed much more interest in economics and sociology than in history.)[10] This general culture was threatened not only by the coming of professionalism and educational specialization but by the rise to prominence of a genuinely popular culture, a mass culture, which lacked roots in any traditions and was fed by the yellow press. This was a cultural crisis that affected all of intellectual life.

When Nietzsche wrote "The Use and Abuse of History" in the 1870s, he found it alarming that the past should be dealt with in such a dispassionate manner by the "chilled spirits" of academia. Their molelike activities reflected the fragmentations of a decadent era: "The mark of every literary decadence . . . is that life no longer dwells in the whole." Instead of living thought that grappled with serious questions and satisfied the thirst for culture, one had a sort of mechanical regurgitation of past thoughts. The great historian Jacob Burckhardt, Nietzsche's friend and a student of Ranke's, "never dreamed of training scholars and disciples in the narrow sense," and himself published little in comparison with the gargantuan labors of the succeeding generation. (The bibliography of Theodor Mommsen numbered 1,513 items; "in the course of his life," Michael Grant comments, "Mommsen did the work of about ten or twenty first-class scholars.") Thus a certain crisis of confidence afflicted the first generation of historians after the exuberant ones of mid-century.

But the gains from expertise should not be minimized. Though Toynbee was distressed to see Mommsen turn from a broad interpretation of Roman history to the editing of inscriptions; today those collections of inscriptions are a vital part of the equipment of every historian of the Roman era, and it is hardly too much to say that they revolutionized the field by adding a large and well-organized body of information to the meager literary sources surviving from ancient times. Most historians regard this solid addition to knowledge as a finer achievement than Mommsen's somewhat subjective and perhaps dubious interpretation of the Roman Republic (he greatly admired Julius Caesar as dictator and imperialist). One can go on forever spinning interpretations of the past out of one's prejudices and imagination, and there is little to choose between them on any rational grounds. But to add some real knowledge where none existed before, knowledge that will last forever afterward and be used by all future historians—is this not a worthier achievement?

Fin de Siècle

The nineteenth century was diffuse and many-sided. It produced a bewildering variety of ideologies. The socialist tradition in historiography, for example, includes notable works on the French Revolution by such great French socialist intellectuals as Louis Blanc and Jean Jaurès (a labor carried on in the twentieth century by Albert Mathiez) as well as historical studies by Germans of the Marxist school such as Karl Kautsky. The English Fabian Socialists fell back on history after having rejected the a priori economic theories of David Ricardo and Marx; when they found these rationalistic "proofs" of human exploitation faulty, they appealed to the simple facts of the case. Sidney and Beatrice Webb wrote histories of the trade unions, local government, and social welfare; Charles Booth produced a monumental history of life and labor in the city of London (1892–1897) from the position of an earnest social reformer. In Germany the "socialists of the chair," led by Gustav Schmoller, similarly converted theoretical economics into institutional or historical economics.

More numerous were historians in what Herbert Butterfield calls the Whig tradition (his *Whig Interpretation of History* is a popular essay on the ideological presuppositions of history), who saw modern history as the story of the winning of liberty from tyrants. From Macaulay to Charles Trevelyan to George Trevelyan to John Fiske, they perpetuated the outlook of the Puritans and Whigs of the seventeenth century. John Bright read Hallam aloud to his wife. John Vincent, historian of the Liberal party, observed that "the real compass of thought uniting the middle class, or the Liberal section of it, was . . . a view or recollection of English History." This powerful political tradition, that of nineteenth-century liberalism, thus rested at bottom on a certain set of ideas about the past, pointing toward the destined triumph of civil liberty and constitutional government through long courses of evolution.

Those who reacted against modern liberalism and socialism also entered the lists. The French Revolution sparked a battle between republicans and monarchists which lasted a century in France. In England the Whig interpretation never had the field to itself, though works in that tradition were the more brilliant. A now forgotten *History of Europe*, written in the 1830s by Archibald Alison, a Scottish lawyer and sheriff, sought at great length to prove, as Disraeli said, that God was on the side of the Tories. It may be said that everybody tried to show by writing history that God, as revealed in the historical process, was on the side of his or her party or cause.

Lord Acton and Johann Döllinger of Munich tried to establish Roman Catholic theology on the basis of historical development. Research in biblical history—the so-called higher criticism—raised fundamental questions about the literal truth of events related in the Bible and stirred up a tremendous row that shook all churches in the last decades of the century.

The fact that no movement or creed or intellectual position was without its historical writings suggests the enormous authority people accorded history in the nineteenth century. It also suggests that that authority was bound to weaken in time. Could history really support so many conflicting causes and positions? The skeptical view, already expressed by Napoleon—history is a set of lies agreed upon (*une fable convenue*)—gradually gained adherents throughout the century. In 1864, Froude expressed it this way: "It often seems to me as if History was like a child's box of letters, with which we can spell any word we please. We have only to pick out such letters as we want, arrange them as we like, and say nothing about those which do not suit our purpose."[11] Voltaire had said something similar a century earlier. Yet we know how potent the conviction had been that history was an orderly, logical, purposive, and scientific discipline, and hence that it would reveal to us not only exactly where we had been but even where we were going. "It is not I to whom you are listening, it is history itself that speaks," Fustel de Coulanges told his enraptured audience. Writing in 1887 in the *North American Review*, Gladstone declared that "complex and diversified as it is, history is not a mere congeries of disjointed occurrences, but is the evolution of a purpose steadfastly maintained, and advancing towards some consummation." Faith in historic order, purpose, and knowability dominated the nineteenth century. At least it dominated the first half of that century, which has often seemed to be very different from the latter half: the first half optimistic, enthusiastic, a bit naive, somewhat confused but brimming over with vast projects for wholesale reform, full of messianic hopes and dreams; the second half (the revolutions of 1848 forming the boundary line) increasingly disenchanted, weary, realistic, skeptical, and even decadent—a time of alienated artists and cynical politicians.

The element of bias in "scientific" history was rather sorrowfully revealed in 1870, when the big guns on both sides of the Franco-Prussian War—Fustel de Coulanges led the French, Mommsen the Germans—lined up to a man on the side of their own country. The French made history prove irrefutably that Alsace was French; the Germans, that it was German. Such episodes doubtless made it increasingly difficult to believe that history spoke through even the best-trained historian. Whose history? At this time currents of thought coursed through Western civilization which induced a greater skepticism in general. Marxists were saying that all thought is class-conditioned (except of course Marxist thought, which somehow was an exception). Bourgeois historians, they held, give us only disguised propaganda for capitalism, whatever their advertised pretensions to scientific objectivity. Darwinism led to the view that all knowledge serves the purpose of adaptation, helping people survive, a profoundly naturalistic vision that in the hands of a Nietzsche undercut the claims of any thought to be outside the struggle for life. Furious historical controversy was going on not only between nations and between classes but between the faithful of all religious persuasions as they debated the higher criticism. It cannot be said, of course, that historiography had ever been without controversy. Yet in an age when the sciences were performing so many other miracles, the claims of scientific and professional historiography to be able to end such controversy and find the truth had gained some credence. Now these claims seemed dubious. The scientific professionals were themselves bitterly at odds when it came to anything that mattered!

A glimpse of one *fin-de-siècle* historian would then not be amiss. Jacob Burckhardt, the Swiss historian of the Italian Renaissance and of ancient times (*The Age of Constantine*) published his *Civilization of the Renaissance in Italy* as early as 1860, but it did not receive recognition as a classic until the 1890s. It coincided with the vogue for Renaissance studies, such as the work of Walter Pater, which became virtually a manifesto of the esthetic movement of the 1880s and 1890s, in what was manifestly a desire to escape from the modern age. The rejection of an ugly and materialistic society was extremely apparent in this fastidious stylist, who withdrew to teach and write in the quiet old backwater of Basel—a city rich in humanistic traditions (Erasmus had worked there) and somehow apart from the modern world of industry and democracy and nationalism.

Burckhardt was disillusioned with these modern ideals, which represented to him a debasement of culture. In imagination he would return to the aristocratic Italian Renaissance, which was saturated in art and made an art of life itself. Burckhardt was a thorough professional in his research methods but he differed from most of the Rankean school in caring less for politics than for culture and in seeing far less progress in human affairs. In an age of ugly Bismarckian nationalism and, to Burckhardt, an equally ugly plebeian democracy, politics had turned sour, and he could not believe that this Europe of belching smokestacks, yellow-press-fed masses, and tasteless bourgeois society was an improvement on the past. He conceived of the historian's task in a new age of barbarism to be that of keeping alive the vivid image of other, more civilized times. Development plays relatively little part in Burckhardt's historical work. He strove to depict a civilization or culture at its one ideal moment of completion. A mature civilization, such as that of the Italian cities in the age of the Renaissance, had to be a whole, a unity, as was Athenian culture in its golden age of antiquity. To paint the portrait of such a high civilization is to create a work of art as well as of scholarship. It involves careful selection of materials, and one must first steep oneself in the best sources, as Burckhardt told his students, in order to get a feeling for the period and an awareness of what is typical. But the writing of such a book demands above all else a gift of style and an artistic imagination.

Burckhardt came close to carrying out Voltaire's program for a *Kulturgeschichte*, and he inspired others (Karl Lamprecht and J. H. Huizinga among them) to do the same after him. Another aspect of Burckhardt's modernity was his awareness of how subjective such portraits are. He knew that someone else would see things differently:

To each eye the outlines of a given civilization probably present a different picture. . . . On the vast ocean upon which we venture, the possible ways and directions are many; and the same studies that have served for this work might easily, in other hands, not only receive a wholly different treatment and interpretation, but might also lead to essentially different conclusions.

As his friend Friedrich Nietzsche wrote, there are as many truths as there are pairs of eyes. When we reach this level of sophistication about the process of historical creation—when we undertand that it is an art as much as a science, that it has subjective as well as objective aspects, and that its truths, like all empirical truths, are tentative and incomplete—we have reached the end of one age of history and the beginning of another.

Ernest Renan, the post-Comtean French positivist and higher critic who was a major literary figure of the later nineteenth century and who shared to the fullest his century's interest in history, tried to use the past as a bulwark against skepticism and declining faith. He looked to it to provide values. Like Matthew Arnold, he would go forth into the past to find and cull from it the best that people had thought and said and done. He would cure modern skepticism by a recourse to history. But this quest was bound to fail, for we cannot make events, whether of history or of any other sort, yield values. We may place a valuation on them; they themselves are simply there. The past itself does not really vote for either Brutus or Caesar, Protestants or Catholics, Whigs or Tories. This great realization was bound to come, and when it did come, the prevailing conception of history was bound to change. Twentieth-century historical writing has largely fallen under the influence of this moral relativism.

Notes

[1]Karamzin's twelve-volume *History of the Russian State* (1819–1826), widely read in nineteenth-century Russia, assured anxious Russians of the distinctive and valuable qualities of their national civilization. "There are sounds of the Russian heart, play of the Russian spirit in the creations of our literature which will unfold yet more richly in the future." The Russians, of course, suffered from an exceptional case of identity crisis, complicated by an inferiority complex vis-à-vis Europe. A useful discussion of this subject may be found in Hans J. Rogger, *National Consciousness in Eighteenth-Century Russia* (Cambridge: Harvard University Press, 1960), chap. 5.

[2]"When . . . the French Revolution took away the naive acceptance of things, and at the same time failed to inaugurate the reign of Reason, many of those whose horror of meaningless drift could not be stilled by reliance on Divine

Providence turned . . . to History as the guarantor of meaningful purpose and promise of inevitable denouement": J. L. Talmon, *Political Messianism: The Romantic Phase* (New York: Praeger, 1960), p. 229.

[3]See François Furet, *Interpreting the French Revolution* (Cambridge: Cambridge University Press, 1981); William Doyle, *Origins of the French Revolution* (Oxford: Oxford University Press, 1980).

[4]Herbert Butterfield, "The Rise of the German Historical School" in *Man on His Past: The Study of the History of Historical Scholarship* (New York: Cambridge University Press, 1955). One explanation of the Germans' flair for history was given by Lord Acton's friend Johann Ignaz Döllinger: "The Germans . . . are the most adaptable of all nations," the most cosmopolitan. See Döllinger, *Addresses on Historical and Literary Subjects*, trans. Margaret Warre (London: John Murray, 1894), pp. 31ff. His argument was essentially that the Germans, as a people of the Holy Roman Empire, had less definite national characteristics than the French and English but a wider range of sympathies for all cultures, and for this reason had a strong historical sense. It was a popular argument.

[5]In 1837 the young Karl Marx, reading Hegel, suddenly felt, with the force of a revelation, the idea that human nature is a creation of culture through history and changes in each generation. This was the moment when Darwin found his theory of evolution through natural selection, when Macaulay began his *History of England*, and when Thomas Carlyle published the *History of the French Revolution*—among many such landmarks. Perhaps 1837 should be honored as the birth year of modern historical consciousness.

[6]Philip Edwards, *Sir Walter Ralegh* (London: Longmans, Green, 1953), pp. 150–151. The notorious carelessness with which premodern historians failed to cite their authorities in footnotes and even cribbed whole passages without acknowledgment reflected not dishonesty but simply a lack of concern about the exact establishment of fact as such.

[7]"Since Gibbon the spectacle was a scandal. History had lost the sense of shame. It was a hundred years behind the experimental sciences. For all serious purposes it was less instructive than Walter Scott and Alexander Dumas": *The Education of Henry Adams*. An article by Keith Burich, "Henry Adams and History," in *Journal of the History of Ideas*, July–September 1987, carefully explains how Adams saw in the second law of thermodynamics a possible hypothesis for history.

[8]Patricia Bell, *The Heart's Events: The Victorian Poetry of Relationships* (London, 1976).

[9]G. M. Trevelyan, *Clio: A Muse, and Other Essays* (London and New York: Longmans, Green, 1913), p. 52.

[10]Bentham was too much an absolutist rationalist to be guided by history, though he used it as a storehouse of edifying examples of reform. John Stuart Mill, Bentham's foremost disciple, rejected Hegel but adopted Comte, and could praise "that series of great writers and thinkers from Herder to Michelet, by whom history, which was till then 'a tale told by an idiot, full of sound and fury, signifying nothing,' has been made a science of cause and effect." But like most positivists, Mill embraced sociology at the expense of history in the long run.

[11]James A. Froude, "The Science of History," in his *Short Studies on Great Subjects*, ed. David Ogg (1864; repr. Ithaca: Cornell University Press, 1967), p. 1.

CHAPTER 6

HISTORY IN OUR OWN TIME: THE TWENTIETH CENTURY

New Views of History

HISTORICAL writing has always been susceptible to the influence of general ideas in the surrounding culture. Historians reflect pervasive interests and concerns when they select and group their empirically discovered facts. They readily take on the coloration of their times. In a romantic epoch they wrote romantic history; in a nationalistic one, nationalistic history. They were often stimulated by the theories of a Marx or a Comte, but when disenchantment set in, historians could, with Burckhardt, withdraw to the ivory tower.

The flexibility of historical inquiry—its tendency to reflect the climate of opinion of an age—has undoubtedly been one of the leading discoveries of modern historical thought. It gives rise to a tendency to talk not about history but about historians, and to be aware of the influences coming from outside the historical profession itself. By way of entry into the rich profusion of this century, so violent, so disturbed, and so brilliant, we may observe that at the turn of the century historians found themselves stimulated by a striking group of social theorists and sociologists, including Emile Durkheim, Max Weber, Vilfredo Pareto, and Thorstein Veblen. It was the great age of sociology. This group considerably refined the crude generalizations of Marx, Comte, and Spencer while retaining large powers of generalization. They were learned as well as analytical. To the sociologists would soon be added the new depth or clinical psychologists, Sigmund Freud and Carl Jung, who have so deeply influenced modern people's vision of themselves and their society. A new kind of political science, influenced by psychology and sociology, appeared in such works as Graham Wallas's *Human Nature in Politics*, in Weber's writings on the modes of political domination, in M. I. Ostrogorski's and Robert Michels's realistic studies of political parties, and in Veblen's analysis of class social psychology. These were exciting years for social theory. It offered the historian conceptual tools and significant insights into human motivations. Sometimes suspicious of sociology because some sociologists tried to dismiss the historical dimension as unimportant, most historians became aware of how much they might benefit from sociological concepts. At any rate, the influence of such concepts, coming from other social or "behavioristic" sciences, is beyond question. Historians such as R. H. Tawney in his *Religion and the Rise of Capitalism* directly followed up suggestions from Max Weber about the "sociology of knowledge." Charles A. Beard was influenced by Achille Loria, the Italian social theorist. The important French school, grouped around Lucien Febvre and Marc Bloch, who founded the journal *Annales d'histoire économique et sociale* in 1929, dedicated itself to a new kind of social history influenced by the other social sciences. These are only examples.

Sociology and Freudian psychology were not the only new dimensions in thought. Friedrich Nietzsche, William James, and Henri Bergson brilliantly ushered in a new era of philosophy, post-Hegelian and post-Darwinist. Then came World War I, which overturned the whole physical and moral universe. In the aftermath of the two world wars, the totalitarian revolutions, the political convulsions resulting from the wars, some historians turned pessimist and inquired into the decline of the West; ideas of progress seemed dead beyond recall. Apocalyptic visions might draw on the Russian version of Marxism, popularized by Lenin's revolution of 1917 and the subsequent Soviet society; or on the German ideology of antimodernism caricatured in Hitler's National Socialism.

Historical writing would bear the marks of all these revolutions in thought and action. It will be as difficult to give a coherent account of it as it is to give an account of the twentieth century itself: the sheer quantity of writing and incredible accumulation of knowledge were far greater than that of any earlier period—beyond all comparison. Writing at the end of the nineteenth century, the American historian Henry Adams, addicted to the view that Western civilization was exploding in fragments at an ever-accelerating rate, calculated that by 1921 it would have ceased to exist. Perhaps he was right. Perhaps it is no longer possible to give an account of an age, a century. Perhaps we have only the particles of a shattered culture. But history has preserved its vitality and its popularity, if not its unity, in this frightening but fascinating contemporary world. Like the age itself, it has shown a constant ability to revolutionize itself.

History on the morrow of its spectacular triumphs in the nineteenth century was troubled by two concerns in particular. (*a*) An increase in the numbers of professional historians brought expertise at the price of scope and unity; a proliferating mound of "monographs" on highly specialized topics seemingly defied synthesis, and also led to complaints that history was being divorced from the general culture and from popular favor. Gone were the days when great historians could write best-sellers and become familiar public figures, as in the time of Michelet and Macaulay. (b) Claims to have achieved "scientific" status, which had fortified history's advance to prominence, became dubious in the face of the breakdown of "objectivity" and single standards of truth. These two areas of concern were linked, since the narrowly focused monographs, by reducing history to a wilderness of particulars, threatened all generalizations or "laws."

At the beginning of the twentieth century a wide-ranging *Methodenstreit,* or debate about methods, began in Germany and spread through the social sciences (psychology and sociology, those new branches of humanistic knowledge, were as much involved as history). The debate raised many questions, among them whether the human or social sciences did not differ basically from the natural and physical sciences. To the debate such eminent thinkers as Max Weber, Karl Jaspers, Wilhelm Dilthey, and Benedetto Croce made contributions. The human sciences sought their independence from the tyranny of physics; "there is a grave error in thinking about society in the same way as about nature," the philosopher Henri Bergson observed. The goal of *Geisteswissenschaften,* as opposed to *Naturwissenschaften,* was not to bring individual cases under general laws but to reveal fully their uniqueness; to do so one used a mode of explanation that Max Weber called *verstehen,* an effort to "understand" a situation by intuitively grasping it (as opposed to finding its "cause" by subsuming it under a law). In a related development, the "pragmatic" or "progressive" school of Americans historians, rebelling against "positivism," found historical writing inevitably a tool of some moral or political purpose.

Both of these trends seemed to lead to what many observers saw as hopeless subjectivism. The verifiability on which any science must rest was at risk. History's reduction to mere propaganda or a kind of mystic intuition threatened its hard-won status as a reasonably exact science.

American historiography in the first two decades of this century went through a revolt aimed primarily at the older Germanic, Rankean school of history, which had powerfully influenced American historiography in its initial stages of professional development (for example, at Johns Hopkins University and Columbia University, important centers of graduate study). The revolt was against the subject matter of this school, which was chiefly political and constitutional; against its hostility to present-mindedness, made into a reproach for not being "relevant" enough; and against its colorless or just-as-it-happened ideals of perfect objectivity. The revolt was mingled with a cry from the West that this historical work looked too much to Europe and was too much a product of an Atlantic Coast culture that no longer represented the center of gravity in the expanding nation. Indeed, Frederick Jackson Turner was, by all accounts, the originator of this complaint when in the 1890s he argued that the western frontier was a more significant factor in the development of American political institutions than the European Middle Ages and that American culture owed little to Europe but was an indigenous product of a unique American experience.

Turner sought to direct attention to broader social and economic factors and also to local or regional history. The frontier was at times more interesting to Turner as sociological process than as historical epic. John B. McMaster, and in England John Richard Green, had earlier protested against the Rankean dictum of E. A. Freeman that "history is past politics."[1] Green announced rhetorically that he intended to spend more time on Chaucer than on Crécy, on Queen Elizabeth's poor laws than on her battles, on the Methodist revival than on the escape of the Young Pretender. But he, like McMaster, was something of an amateur—interesting, but a man who wrote, as Carl L. Becker once wickedly said of someone, "without fear and without research." Turner was a thorough professional, trained in the methods of the Hopkins seminar and eager to apply these skills applied to American themes.

The Turner revolt, which caused a considerable stir in American historical circles, was followed by the Beard and Robinson revolt. James Harvey Robinson became identified with what was called in the United States in the 1910s the New History, a school marked by a strong reaction against political history in favor of social history, with an emphasis on relevance or present-mindedness. Members of this school wanted historical understanding that would help bring about progressive social and political change. This approach did not prove very productive, and Robinson could be accused of a good deal of superficiality. But the effort to escape from the clutches of a historiographical tradition considered to be both narrow and arid was strong. Charles A. Beard's wide-ranging mind received influences from European economists and socialists. His much-discussed *Economic Interpretation of the Constitution* (1913) called attention to economic and class aspects of the political process in a way Americans found quite exciting, and his many other writings revealed a gifted pen and a restless, curious intellect. Beard subsequently wrote some essays—"That Noble Dream" and "Written History as an Act of Faith" have been reprinted often—colorful and persuasive in style if somewhat loose in logic, attacking the idea of Rankean objectivity as he conceived it. These writings probably acquainted most Americans for the first time with that growing feeling of the subjectivity and relativity of historical writing which we have mentioned. Faced with an inadequacy of evidence (we can never know anything like *all* of the past) and the inability to deal with this evidence in certain scientific ways (it cannot be manipulated or experimented with), and aware also of one's own position as an observer stationed at a certain time and place, the historian must know that she has dated interests and that tomorrow another work will replace hers. Each generation must rewrite history, making its own terms with the past. "The pallor of waning time, if not of death," Beard wrote in his picturesque style, "rests upon the latest volume of history, fresh from the roaring press." History, one may say, is a tool we use each generation or each year to help us get along in the world, discarding old versions for new ones whenever necessary. The message had an exhilarating flavor of Darwinian or Marxian modernity; only later was it seen in a more sinister, Orwellian context, when totalitarian dictators controlled society by systematically recreating the past.

The similarity of such ideas to those of the great American philosophers of this generation, William James and John Dewey, has caused them to be seen as part of a "pragmatic revolt in American history," a label that very loosely puts Turner, Beard, and the new history in a single category. The influential American historian Carl L. Becker, who wrote a good deal on the nature of history itself, also was fond of pointing to climates of opinion, to the relativity of all historical thought, to the need for frank acceptance of the proposition that "every generation . . . must inevitably play on the dead whatever tricks it finds necessary for its own peace of mind." Perhaps this doctrine enabled such men as Beard and Robinson, who openly took the progressive side in the political controversies of the day, to indulge their bias with less sense of professional guilt. In Britain, Socialist historians, not only the Webbs but also such distinguished professionals as Tawney and the husband-and-wife team of J. L. and Barbara Hammond, managed to combine academic respectability with a frank commitment to a left-wing political cause. (Not that the Hammonds' account of the Industrial Revolution escaped severe criticism from other economic historians.) Since then, some historians have shown a tendency to present themselves unblushingly as political partisans. Did not the allegedly unbiased ones actually conceal a partisan position?

These somewhat novel approaches to history commanded widespread acceptance, yet also aroused considerable opposition and a certain uncomfortable feeling. It has come to seem too obvious to require much debate that the historian *does* bring to his work a mental framework that in part determines the structure of his books. As the French historian H. I. Marrou has put it, "the past cannot be isolated in a pure state and grasped in any isolated manner; it is fused into an insoluble mixture into which enters the reality of the past, its 'objective' reality, but also the present reality of the active thought of the historian who is seeking to recreate the past." Ferdinand Schevill described the situation well:

> Not only in legend but also in veritable history as well there is unmistakably something personal or subjective which is woven into the events described and is recognized by the intelligent reader as a prejudice or a point of view or a supporting mental substructure. Even when history is composed with the most wholehearted submission to the evidence, aspiring, according to the demands of some of its most recent hierophants, to a coldly scientific attitude toward its material, the ideal is never realized. For, when the mastery of the evidence has been effected, it must, in order to be converted into a history, be shaped in the mind of the investigator; and in that process it will inevitably acquire something of the form and color of the vessel in which it was prepared. Moreover, this personal contribution is not personal in the sense of being wholly original with the chronicler or historian under consideration. As an ephemeral and, let us add, an eminently social creature, he is the child of his environment and exhibits innumerable earmarks indicative of his particular time and place. It is for this reason we are obliged to inquire with regard to every history that comes into our hands: Who wrote it? When and where did the writer live? With what particular outlook or religion or philosophy did he face the problems of history and of life? And we shall invariably find that the answers to these questions defining the historian's individuality enter, though not regularly in the same degree, into works passing as histories. They may have been composed with the most devoted attention to the facts, but the facts on getting themselves ordered in a logical and chronological series have had something extraneous imposed on them, something that is not native to them as mere facts. Call this addition form, mind, interpretation—there it is! He who lacks the skill or penetration to detect this often hidden agent with its quiet manipulation and directive comment, he who reads history, any history, as if it were something impersonal communicating an absolute and final truth has never reflected on the necessary limitations of this department of literature and is likely in the end to take from it more injury than profit.[2]

The point that Schevill makes so beautifully has almost become a truism among historians, though it still comes as a revelation to some neophytes approaching history for the first time. But many historians posed persuasive objections to such an extreme relativism. They felt that such relativism reduces the historian to a propagandist pretentiously crusading for any cause that is momentarily popular, and that such present-mindedness is, after all, an obstacle to the proper understanding of the past. A fuller discussion of these issues must be post-

poned to the latter part of this book (see Chapter 11). Here we record
the presence of such debates as a significant aspect of twentieth-century
historiography.

Communicated to the English world by the brilliant philosopher-his-
torian R. G. Collingwood (*The Idea of History*, 1946), the thought of
Dilthey and Croce tended to support most of the relativist argument.
They explained that history is present knowledge, which must and does
spring from current interests; it is "contemporary thought about the
past." Also, we do not find just one truth about the past; there are
innumerable truths—as many as there are perspectives. We do not, as
Ranke thought, apprehend *the* past "exactly as it was"; we see different
pasts at different times, and what we see depends on our present situation. For positivist history, which Collingwood held to be the sort
practiced by historians who seek "facts" about the past and then try to
arrange these facts in a way that will yield generalizations, he entertained
much scorn. Leaning on Vico, whose views Croce as a fellow Neapolitan
was in a good position to expound, and which indeed he recovered
from obscurity for most non-Italians, this school stressed the knowability
of the past by means of the historical imagination: because those who
lived in the past were people like ourselves, with minds basically similar
to our own, we can infer their situation and rethink their thoughts. We
can do so only with the aid of careful research; the Croceans would
agree with Burckhardt that only after long, careful study of the sources
and much critical reflection can one's historical imagination be brought
into play. But essentially the goal is to enable ourselves as historians to
get inside past minds so that we can virtually experience their thoughts.
The tag of idealist or neo-idealist has been attached to this school because of its stress on historical knowledge as knowledge of past mental
states. Some might object to this idealism, though it means no more
than historians normally take for granted when they try to answer questions about motives, as they often do (what was in Hitler's mind when
he threatened Czechoslovakia?) or seek to convey the feeling of some
former age (what was it like to be a medieval monk?).[3]

It seems clear that Collingwood was not an idealist in the sense of
holding that historical reality is mental. If we must in some sense get
inside the mind of Hitler, for example, to know why he attacked the
Soviet Union in 1941, this is not to say that his reasons were of an
ideological or even, by some standard, a rational sort. He may have
been thinking chiefly or exclusively of material gains, or of power to
feed his ravening ego, or of a way out of some very practical political
problems. As historians we must infer his motives from the evidence
we have; that is not to prejudge what those motives were. The focus of
a history is human actions, and actions require an acting and deciding

subject. Criticism of Collingwood comes from those who deny that deliberate human actions shaped the past (as some structuralists appear to do) and from those who claim that Collingwood assumed too much rationality or individuality ("social processes" or collective mentalities may decide the course of events.)

The Croce-Collingwood influence has been helpful to historians because of its stress on the autonomy and worth of historical studies and because of its clarification of the scientist-versus-nonscientist issue. History is a science because it relies on the systematic collection of evidence and on rigorous analysis of that evidence. It is not at all a science in the same mold as the physical sciences. It is the science of the particular; its practitioners seek to understand some one subject in all its inwardness and uniqueness. The natural scientist usually seeks to draw general laws or principles from the external observation of many particulars. The historical scientist seeks knowledge of the particular by getting *inside* it. (A zoologist who engaged in this practice would try to learn what it is like to be an animal, that is, how it feels to be that animal.) History is a special kind of science. As such, it has dignity and importance. It is not a failed attempt at a science on the model of physical science; neither is it a branch of literature. It is the science that investigates the past, by its own special methods, in order to illuminate the present.

Croce's school tied this conception of history to a general philosophy that amounted to a new kind of historicism. (Some times his conception is taken to be the definitive meaning of the elusive term "historicism," a term that has caused some confusion.)[4] For Croce, there is no "final philosophy"; all thought is relative to its time and place. Every intellectual construction is "sufficient for the day . . . but not sufficient for tomorrow, when it must be refreshed or reformed." All thought takes place in a historical context. The ultimate reality is only history; in the last analysis we can say of any idea only that it came to light at such-and-such a time under such-and-such conditions. If history must be rewritten by each generation, so must all other branches of thought. There is no ultimate standard of validity, at least for political and social and esthetic judgments. A thought "escaping history" would be like a man climbing out of his own skin. Thought, like skin, is the matrix in which humankind lives. If a movement arose to denounce history as dangerous and false and banish it from intellectual life, this movement too would be a historical fact that historians would record and explain as a characteristic of the period. The reaction against history is a part of history! A god or some absolute intelligence, seeing the whole stupendous unity of things, might be able to render final judgment, but people never can. So the study of thought becomes the study of the history of thought. Croce's historicism differed from Hegel's in that he found more freedom and less determinism in history and was far less dogmatic; but he agreed that philosophy is history, if not that history is philosophy in Hegel's sense.

Persisting Older Views

By no means all historians yielded up their positivism to the neo-idealist onslaught. In general, historians (at least until quite recent times) have not been a very theoretical or philosophically minded group. Collingwood was a rare example of a practicing historian who was also an accomplished philosopher. Indeed, until about 1950 he was virtually the only British philosopher to take a serious and sustained interest in the theory of history. His theoretical speculations were remote from the average historian's intellectual world for a long time. Historians are inclined to be robust and active-minded rather than subtle; as Marc Bloch commented in *The Historian's Craft*, they love life and like to be involved in it. More sensitive, introspective, and intellectual types are likely to be attracted by literature; intensely analytical minds will gravitate toward philosophy or the more theoretical sciences. Historians do not usually feel comfortable when they theorize about their work; they prefer simply to *do* it, to plunge in with energy, determination, and a rough-and-ready empiricism. And so most historians remained prisoners of the scientism they inherited from the last century.

In his 1923 presidential address to the American Historical Association, Edward P. Cheyney reaffirmed his belief that historians are scientists engaged like other scientists in finding laws. The first three volumes of Arnold J. Toynbee's vast *Study of History*, a work he began in the 1920s, were published in 1934; one of the century's most remarkable achievements, it rested on his conviction that he could isolate specific "societies" or "civilizations" like so many botanical specimens, compare them as to their birth, maturation, and death, and discover the laws that govern this process. With all his breadth of knowledge, Toynbee had little interest in the kind of history that aims only at understanding unique particular situations.

The years after the 1914–1918 catastrophe spawned another major inquiry into the past by the famous writer H. G. Wells. His *Outline of History* was destined to great popularity if little professional approval. (Though millions of copies were sold, Wells himself thought that few were really read; they were "bought and stowed away," like many a modern masterpiece.) Wells's opus, though less vast than Toynbee's, resembled it in featuring the theme of humankind's unification; he found the goal of history to be a world state that would eliminate war and establish a universal utopia. Wells's scope was global, and he joined Toynbee in denigrating history that was nationalistic or narrowly political. His *Outline* might be described as impressionistic and didactic; it was also sociological, dealing with large, impersonal social processes. With his scientific, positivist mind, Wells had no interest in getting inside the minds of former ages and appreciating them for their own beauty or brilliance; to him as to Voltaire, most of the past was simply ignorant or wicked. World history was to educate the coming citizens of the world state, and so to release them from their parochial prejudices. Wells added to *An Outline of History* two other monumental tracts, *The Science of Life*, written in partnership with Julian Huxley, and *The Work, Wealth, and Happiness of Mankind*, a survey of the contemporary world. Toynbee meanwhile wrote annually a superb *Survey of International Relations* (1925–1939). The energy of these amazing Edwardians astonishes us. One could add Bertrand Russell; the philosopher-mathematician turned educator and popular writer wrote much about history, and of his scores of books, the one that brought him his greatest success was probably his *History of Western Philosophy*. Such writers refuted the claim that history no longer had popular appeal. The specialists, however, were frequently appalled by them.

That history should associate itself with the other "social sciences" was the opinion of the influential and quite professional *Annales* school. Even before the first issue of that famous journal in 1929, French historical study had betrayed its Comtean heritage with a figure such as Henri Berr, editor of the *Revue de synthèse historique* and of a mammoth series of books on "the evolution of humanity." It was the latest riposte of the French in their rivalry with the Germans: in the hands of the Teutonic masters of the sources, history had bogged down in a morass of detail from which Gallic synthesizing lucidity would rescue it. Led by Marc Bloch and Lucien Febvre, the historical school loosely grouped around the journal *Annales d'histoire économique et sociale* (later *Annales: Économies, societés, civilizations*) proclaimed the demise of "historicism" in favor of history as past sociology: history should disclose the long "durations" rather than mere "events," deal in social processes rather than the study of great men, in popular rather than elite culture, and above all discover the *structures* of societies at any given time. The goal was an *histoire totale*, embracing the full life of humanity. To this long-heralded but seldom achieved goal the *Annalistes* eventually brought a new kind of expertise, combining multidisciplinary methods with statistical analysis and fresh archival sources at the local level. We will refer again to this new social history, for it has continued into the most recent era of historical studies. Whether in the end it succeeded in finding a wholly new "paradigm" of structural analysis beyond "historicism" may be doubted. But the new social history eventually made its mark in a spectacular way.

Social history of this sort has sometimes been associated with left-wing politics and with the Marxism emanating from the Soviet Union. The new social historians boasted of bringing history down from the corridors of upper-class culture to mingle with the common folk, and showed a strong interest in economic history.

History and Twentieth Century Events

Such dramatic events as the revolutions, wars, and depressions of the twentieth century have obviously influenced historians' choice of subject matter. How many thousands of volumes have been written on the two world wars, the development of the Soviet Union, the rise and fall of the Third Reich! But these events have also affected the general outlook on history. Belief in the objectivity or reliability of historical accounts suffered from the 1914–1918 experience. Historians accepted the war, supported their side with their pens, in many cases participated eagerly in it. A special irony, William R. Keylor points out in his study of the French historical community, was that the most austerely "scientific" historians proved to be the most hysterically chauvinist. In this regard the historians joined virtually the entire intellectual community, but it is hard to avoid the conclusion that they were even more than ordinarily patriotic. Historiography had utterly failed to predict the conflagration: the multivolumed Cambridge Modern History, completed on the eve of 1914 as a triumph of modern historical methods, concluded with an optimistic forecast of stability and peace. When the war suddenly exploded, it swept the historians along in its powerful wake. Then came sharp disillusionment and many cries of *mea culpa*. Toynbee himself wrote war propaganda, later regretted it, and threw himself into his *Study of History* in an attempt to compensate for having been spared in a war that claimed the lives of so many of his fellow scholars.

A long inquest into the origins or causes or "responsibility" for the 1914 tragedy occupied the center of the historical stage for some years after 1919. The results of this vast inquiry were in general an about-face: each side was absolved of the charge of deliberate aggression in 1914, in a reversal of the virtually unanimous view during the war; war propaganda was exposed and the historians who engaged in it were accused of betraying the canons of their profession. To some extent historical research played the role of peacemaker in the 1920s and early 1930s; but when World War II again ranged an aggressive Germany against the Western democracies and the Soviet Union, some historians reversed themselves again and decided that since the Germans were guilty in 1939, they also must have been guilty in 1914. It is hard to claim that history came out of all this commotion with much credit, though many learned and interesting books were written, immense labors of research performed.

Marxist historians who worked for the cause of the USSR after 1917 and German historians who stayed in Nazi Germany after 1933 (to the honor of the profession, many preferred exile, and their contributions enriched and often much changed Anglo-American intellectual life)[5] freely accepted the state's guidance of historical inquiry. History was frankly a form of propaganda; it was to serve the purposes of the Soviet or Nazi state. Needless to say, historians were not alone in their subservience. "Even for the scientist," declared Nobel Prize winner Johannes Stark, "the duty to the nation stands above any and all other obligations. . . . In his work he must serve the nation first and foremost." He approved a National Socialist science, to be distinguished from Jewish and international science, and it was on this basis that German scientists rejected Einstein's theories. On the same basis the Soviets revised their history textbooks from year to year to accord with the tactical needs of the moment, such as removing Trotsky from the account of the Russian Revolution, speaking more favorably of the Nazis from 1939 to 1941, or playing up patriotism throughout the war. They were quite candid about what they were doing, believing that, in Lenin's formula, whatever serves the cause of the Revolution (the Communist party; the Soviet Union) is justified—a principle derived from Marx's view that all knowledge serves either one side or the other in the class struggle.

Soviet historians, with a crude literal-mindedness, carried to an extreme the tendentiousness of history. Let Stalin decree a change in the party line and industrious Communist scholars immediately hastened to change perceptions of the past. In the 1940s, for example, the line was patriotic and "anticosmopolitan." It became the duty of Soviet historians to "unmask," among other things, the "fascist" view that Scandinavians and Germans had first brought political organization to Russia in the Middle Ages. That most historians accepted such a view, on the basis of what seemed plain evidence, without thought (so it seemed) of a reactionary motive, counted for nothing. They were fascists even if they did not realize it. As such, they must be distorters of history. For it did not suit the present perceptions or interests of the Soviet Union, in the view of its rulers, to have it known that foreigners from the West had founded the Russian state. To some extent this never had been a welcome thought; Russian historians argued about it in the eighteenth century, and some among them evinced a nationalist bias.[6] But now the bias was elevated to the level of principle and made compulsory. Historic truth was what the Politburo decreed. And truth was subject to abrupt change; tomorrow, if friendly relations with the West became expedient, yesterday's revisionists might find themselves not only in error but in prison (as antifascists were from September 1939 to June 1941). George Orwell satirized this grim application of historical presentism in *1984*: the Ministry of Truth employs civil servants to change the records of the past to make them correspond with the present situation. If the Party says two and two are five, the Thought Police force Winston to declare that it is so. *1984* hardly exaggerated the worst abuses of history by Nazi and Communist regimes in the 1930s and 1940s.

Amid these depressing twentieth-century developments—frightful wars, totalitarian dictatorships, mass murder—the idea of general progress expired. In John T. Marcus's phrase, one witnessed "the collapse of redemptive historicity." It was no longer possible for thinking persons to believe that humankind gained redemption in time. The years after 1919 rang with a chorus of formal renunciations of such beliefs, which had been so firmly held before 1914. The Russian philosopher-theologian Nikolai Berdyaev wrote in 1923, in *The Meaning of History*, that "man's historical experience has been one of steady failure, and there are no grounds for supposing that it will ever be anything else." According to the new versions of Judaism and Christianity, the old "liberal" theology, which had almost fully accepted Hegel's view of redemption through history, was an illusion and an abomination. It is an illusion, Reinhold Niebuhr wrote, that "growth fulfilled the meaning of life, and redeemed it of its ills and errors."[7] The new "crisis" or "dialectical" theology, dominant in Germany and widely influential throughout the West after 1920 (Karl Barth, Rudolf Bultmann, Emil Brunner, Reinhold Niebuhr, Paul Tillich), made the point that no clear meaning is discernible in history, for humans cannot read God's purposes, which may require evil and destruction at any time, and so the historical record must often appear to us to be broken and terrible. A significant number of historians professed to see no sense or order whatever in the past. This return to Voltaire's view parallels the depiction of blind, cruel chance in the novels of Thomas Hardy, Émile Zola, and Theodore Dreiser.

"Men wiser and more learned than I have discerned in history a plot, a rhythm, a predetermined pattern," wrote H. A. L. Fisher, in words Arnold Toynbee took as a challenge. "These harmonies are concealed from me. I can see only one emergency following upon another as wave follows upon wave . . . ; the play of the contingent and the unforeseen."

Michael Oakeshott declared that the historian loves Clio precisely because she is so capricious, "a mistress of whom he never tires, and whom he never expects to talk sense."[8] The brightly colored past, as Apollinaire called it, more real than the dull present, can be a source of amusement and amazement, a refuge from the present, an astounding spectacle; it can fascinate, even if one gives up the idea that it has meaning and purpose. But can such a justification for history really promote it to the top rank in the realm of knowledge? Can the golden age of history survive the destruction of the idea of progress?

Perhaps the most ambitious answer to this challenge to the worth of history was provided by those historians who accepted the decline of civilization as fact and sought to account for it. Perhaps they hoped that by examining the histories of other great declines they might learn how to check this one. It may be significant that this ambitious project was undertaken less by the academic professionals than by some semi-amateurs on the fringe of the profession. One such writer, who emerged temporarily into great popularity right after the war, was Oswald Spengler.[9] Spengler was an obscure German Gymnasium (high school) teacher before his book *The Decline of the West (Der Untergang des Abendlandes)* launched him into fame immediately after World War I. He had an amateur's cavalier disregard for facts that did not fit his thesis; he was opinionated, conceited, even without intellectual integrity; yet he presented a dazzling thesis with dramatic power as he sought to explain the life cycle of civilizations. The twilight of the gods broods over Spengler's great book; all civilizations are born in barbarism and must return to it. All was pessimism among the intellectuals in the 1920s; Spengler's book suited the mood. His view of civilizations as having life cycles rather in the manner of individuals was open to all kinds of criticism, but it afforded some explanation, perhaps even some consolation, for what seemed to be the collapse of Western civilization. Polybius long ago had noted the curious power of history to console: "The memory of other people's calamities is the clearest and indeed the only source from which we learn to bear the vicissitudes of Fortune with courage." The Stoics and Epicureans knew that we are helped when we see the inevitability of things. In a long prose poem, Spengler told us that we are no different from the rest; we too are mortal. Spengler was not without learning, and his attempt to show that cultures are organic, having styles of life and art which represent their personalities, was often brilliant. Underlying his view, it may be noted, was a profound relativism of thought. He held that what determines the intellectual activity of a civilization at any particular time is the state of life in which that civilization finds itself. Western science was born in the age of Galileo because Western civilization had reached a certain state of growth—just as a boy's thoughts change when he reaches puberty. No one can escape being a product of her times. Spengler, like Marx, did not explain how he alone could escape this all-pervading determinism to view matters objectively.

Pessimism about the Western social order appeared in other historical works of the post–World War I era. (No survey such as ours can hope to include more than a fraction of these works. The teeming productivity of modern scholarship had a long way to go before it reached the proportions of the 1970s and 1980s, but it was still far greater than it had been earlier.) One example: in the 1920s the latest in the series of historians who followed Gibbon's path was the Russian émigré Michael Rostovtzeff, whose *Social and Economic History of the Roman Empire* (1926) promised fashionably to dig deeper than the superficia of politics. Writing in an era disillusioned with democracy, he found the leading cause of the decline and fall to be a plebeian erosion of high aristocratic standards. As the poet W. B. Yeats put it,

> Base drove out the better blood,
> And mind and body shrank.

Preoccupied with declines and falls (consider Evelyn Waugh's first novel), readers in the 1920s paid Rostovtzeff's work a good deal of attention.

Toynbee's study of the rise and fall of all civilizations was conceived on a far grander scale. The 1934 volumes were followed by three more in 1939 and by another four in 1954 (to which was appended in 1961 a volume called *Reconsiderations* in which Toynbee did battle with his numerous critics). A more careful and better historian than Wells or Spengler, Toynbee eventually earned wide fame by this almost incredible feat of erudition. As director of the Royal Institute of International Affairs in London, Toynbee simultaneously produced those annual surveys that were themselves remarkable feats of condensation and commentary. A highly distinctive style—allusive, meditative, poetic—lent further interest to *A Study of History*; many readers found it incongruous that he declared his at times almost mystic vision to be nothing less than an exact science. Toynbee was a positivist, searching for laws of growth and decay in the pattern of human societies; he was also a deeply religious seeker.

A Study of History was abridged for popular consumption, and Toynbee wrote and lectured all over the world, becoming a household name in the 1950s. No other contemporary historian was then so widely known or so much discussed. But critics increasingly accused him of playing fast and loose with the facts of history and of being more a seer than a historian. The *Study* approached metahistory, and in its obvious intrusion of a personal vision it ran counter to professional canons. Other very serious questions about the ability of comparative history on so vast a scale to disclose laws of the development of whole civilizations drove Toynbee to withdraw or modify a considerable number of his conclusions in *Reconsiderations*. It is generally agreed that this remarkable work is a modern classic by one of the twentieth century's most extraordinary scholars. But because he had ranged so widely, Toynbee exposed himself to the criticisms of countless specialists and soon became the most attacked historian in history. The great majority of professional historians remained unconvinced of his work's validity, and it had little influence in most of their areas of study. Pieter Geyl's criticism, that Toynbee's conclusions "are not based on the facts of history . . . they are imposed upon it," was very widely accepted. Toynbee, who declared that professional historiography had become too narrowly specialized as well as too "parochial" to satisfy a human need for bold and broad historical generalizing, evidently failed in his audacious effort to write such history convincingly.

The temporary success of Toynbee's work testified to a potentially large public interest in such broad-gauged history. Like Spengler and Wells, he had in fact offered a version of historicism, in that he claimed that history has a plan and a goal. He saw in the rise and fall of civilizations a long-term progress. They die, to be sure, but in dying each gives birth to a higher religion, which is passed on to the next generation of civilizations. In Toynbee's metaphor, the wheel goes around but the wagon goes forward. In the end, there will be unity in a single global civilization under a world state with a single world religion that represents the best qualities of all religions. We find a little here of Wells's vision of a material paradise presided over by science, though most of the time Toynbee seemed to scorn modern Western civilization, in a Spenglerian way, because of its "Faustian" or power-conscious culture. Toynbee was a kind of combination of Spengler and Wells, at times seeming to decree the almost inevitable death of every civilization, at other times asserting that we can prevent the death of our civilization if we will. But on the whole, the salvation he envisioned differed from the scientific utopia of H. G. Wells. Toynbee placed his hope in religion, which was for him "the serious business of the human race." His call was for a spiritual renewal based on a synthesis of the major world faiths.

In a curious way Toynbee seemed to recapitulate almost all the phases of Western historiography. He was a positivist seeking scientific laws; he was a historicist finding a plan and pattern in the past, with an appointed destiny at the end of the road. He was also an exemplarist finding in history lessons that might be applied to the solution of current problems. His vast system of history contains every type of historical thought known. But none carried conviction. In a torrent of censure, some of it devastating, critics refuted his laws and disparaged his providential view. Great as his work is, it seems unlikely that anyone will want to follow in Toynbee's footsteps.[10] It is as much a dead end as *Finnegans Wake*.

A Crisis in Historiography?

James Joyce's amazing novel was itself a kind of world history; in its dream language he would incorporate all of humankind's myths and archetypes, as well as many of its events (Saint Patrick, Parnell, the Crimean War, and Wellington are among recurring motifs). But this human comedy by the modern Dante has no goal or terminus; Joyce's theoretical model was Vico's endlessly repetitive cycle. The only point of telling it is a Nietzschean affirmation of life for its own sake; knowing it has no meaning, we embrace it anyway.

Most historians seem implicitly to agree with this model. The great majority of them rejected metahistorical schemes in the grand manner, such as Toynbee's and Wells's; neither popular Marxism nor Gobineau-Chamberlain racism nor any other scheme that claimed to reveal the secrets of the human experience found much favor. Most historians agreed with E. L. Woodward (Sir Llewellyn Woodward), to whom most philosophies of history appeared "to be grounded on an arbitrary and oversimplified selection of facts."

Herbert Butterfield, in his *Whig Interpretation of History*, said that Clio is a complaisant lady who will do whatever we ask of her—in effect, a prostitute: "History is all things to all men. She is at the services of good causes and bad. In other words she a harlot and a hireling. . . . We must beware even of saying 'History says . . . ' or 'History proves . . . ,' as though she herself were the oracle." In a celebrated outburst, the outstanding modern writer and thinker Paul Valéry declared that "history will justify anything. It teaches precisely nothing, for it contains everything and furnishes examples of everything." He added the further reproach, identical with Karl Popper's, that history is "the most dangerous product distilled by the chemistry of the intellect," for its myths delude whole peoples, teaching them to hate other peoples.[11] Popper dedicated his book *The Poverty of Historicism* (1957) to the millions who had been led to slaughter by dictators who had imposed mythical laws of historical destiny.

There seems in fact to be no general plan or order to the past; people struggled and created, sometimes succeeding and sometimes failing, in ways that we can describe and evaluate but that reveal no one rhythm or direction, far less any invariable laws. If any final goal exists, it is hidden and must remain hidden from human vision. It may be worth stressing that most modern historians are sure that the future is unpredictable. The more we know about the human situation, the more we see the infinite number of variables and the utter impossibility of any meaningful prediction. "The historian who tries to forecast the future," Collingwood wrote, "is like a tracker anxiously peering at a muddy road in order to descry the footsteps of the next person who is going to pass that way."[12]

Historians nevertheless usually find smaller-scale historical patterns that seem plausible. They spend most of their time arguing about some "thesis" that arises in their own area of expertise, which others attack and usually discredit, leaving the way open for some other, equally vulnerable hypothesis. Historians have plunged into such famous storm centers as Frederick Jackson Turner's "frontier thesis" in American history; Henri Pirenne's theory of the origin of medieval cities (the "Pirenne thesis"); the Weber-Tawney "religion and the rise of capitalism" debate; Tawney's claim, challenged by Hugh Trevor-Roper, that the decline of the gentry class precipitated the Puritan Revolution; Georges Lefebvre's formulation of the origins of the French Revolution in terms of a rising bourgeoisie. The literature of revision, refinement, and restatement generated by each of these hypotheses gave employment and enjoyment to generations of historians. (The "gentry question" initiated by Tawney a half century ago led to the notable researches of Lawrence Stone and J. H. Hexter in the 1960s and still smolders though now almost extinct.)

There are countless others, some less sweeping; the few we have mentioned rank as middle-range theories, far more modest than the totalist conceptions of a Marx or Toynbee but with considerable scope. Virtually every professional historian operates within the purview of some reigning thesis or interpretation in his area; these hypotheses may now be so specialized that few historians in other areas of study have even heard of them. While historians reject the large, holistic theories, they seem to accept many modest ones, provisionally. But the usual life history of such a controversy shows the theory undergoing steady modification and in the end disappearing with or without honor; if it escapes being discredited, it comes to be seen, as the great twentieth century philosopher Ludwig Wittgenstein said of most apparent intellectual problems, to have been a nonquestion, based on a terminological confusion. The debate among American diplomatic historians about the origins of the Cold War supplies an example: reigning interpretation, sensational "revision" of the established view, then compromise, ending after much microresearch in a sophisticated, highly nuanced interpretation that really agrees with neither of the original positions (and is much less exciting). In the end the suspicion grows that all significant patterns ascribed to the past, in small matters as in large, are myths. The cynic concludes that no "interpretation" holds, that there are as many explanations as there are historians, and that each is as true or as false as another. Perhaps, as some have argued, the whole of our alleged past is a myth. Nothing new ever appears under the sun, only a random combination of the same basic components. The elaborate game of pretending that truth is being advanced by the researches and writings of historians is just that, a game—played, perhaps, for the self-serving reason of providing professional employment to people who have earned it by undergoing the arduous apprenticeship of a Ph.D. program (The sociological process by which universities recruit faculty members puts a premium on novelty and trendiness; the selection of one bright young person over another may be decided on grounds of this sort.)

The reviews of historical works by other historians in the professional journals suggest something of the uneasy state of scholarship. The grounds of criticism seem to be contradictory. The work may be faulted for being too modest and narrow, confined to some tiny issue and offering little more than an exhaustively detailed catalog of the evidence. This sort of work is likely to be dismissed as trivial because it raises no large issues and presents no "thesis." The author who attempts to avoid this condemnation, however, will be criticized for going beyond her evidence to state a thesis she cannot prove. The book therefore will fail either for irrelevance and triviality on the one hand, or for mythmaking, "vehement sidetaking," or inability to prove its thesis on the other. "Impressionism" is one devastating indictment; another is dullness. Occasionally, by extreme dialectical skill, an author may manage to write a book that is both "challenging" and thoroughly sound. The chances are, though, that eventually criticism will penetrate his defenses.[13] Historians fear to risk any generalizations, aware that some specialist will prove them faulty. Or they rush in to achieve a momentary sensation at the cost of an ultimate scandal.

The various battles historians wage over the right "interpretation" of some great historic event or process—a war, a revolution, an institutional crisis, perhaps—reveal something of the same indeterminate quality. Such controversies, it is often noted, tend to go around in circles. "Twentieth-century historians often merely go back to interpretations advanced by partisans while the [Civil War] was still in progress," Kenneth M. Stampp observed. The same is manifestly true of many other historiographical debates. A history of the interpretations shows a cycle, emphasis shifting from economic to intellectual to the political-constitutional factors and back to the economy. Oscar Handlin remarked with characteristic pungency that the appropriate figure of speech for one long debate among historians was not a development but a treadmill. Novelties of the hour invariably turn out, on analysis, to be very old wine poured into bottles that look new, perhaps given different labels. The historian Fritz Fischer, for example, created a furor in the post-1945 era by reverting, with massive documentation including some new sources, to the position on German war guilt held by the Allies in 1914–1918; the novelty lay in the fact that it was a German who now presented the evidence. And in the 1970s an enormous controversy was touched off by Robert E. Fogel and Stanley L. Engerman's study of the economic system of the Old South, *Time on the Cross*. To the chagrin of many readers, Fogel and Engerman used impressive techniques of data processing to reach conclusions that seemed to demolish several arguments long advanced to indict the system of slavery as it was practiced in the South.

The usual reason for a fresh look is ideological. When the mood turns left, or perhaps right, or pacifist, or naturalist, some once-rejected explanations take on a more appealing look. It is a mistake to say that these resuscitations of older interpretations are no more than that, that they contribute nothing new. At the same time it is hard not to see at their foundations an element of value judgment that subverts any claim to complete objectivity, in any possible sense of that term (see Chapter 11).

To many historians, the practical failure of historiography was revealed in its loss of all cohesiveness and unity in a wilderness of ever smaller and more specialized subjects. The nineteenth-century pioneers had been content to wait for the expected synthesis while calling for careful preliminary work on details. Only when each county had been surveyed would it be possible to draw the great map of the whole land with any accuracy. They were confident that when all the little questions had been answered, the big ones could be. It seemed, however, that little questions led on to littler ones virtually ad infinitum, each one further away from any conceivable synthesis. The inexhaustibility of empirical reality appeared to be established: if we aim at something like total coverage, we can go on forever investigating the past and never complete the job. Total coverage is an illusion. Yet historians went on grinding out ever more microscopic pieces of research. It is difficult to deny that such research is potentially worthwhile. Can we have too much knowledge? Yet complaints multiplied about the triviality of much historical research, about the absence of any coherent overall program of research (one dug wherever one happened to find a supply of evidence), about the absence of meaningful generalization and synthesis, and about the failure of contemporary specialists in history to serve the public need for knowledge and guidance.[14] José Ortega y Gasset thought that perhaps "God would not forgive" the historians for making so little of their matchless opportunities.

"If history is falling into disrepute, if for many people it seems to be lost in unessentials instead of guiding us . . . ," Geoffrey Barraclough wrote, "the reason is not far to seek: what it needs is a larger vision, a breakthrough to new dimensions." Barraclough defined the crisis as one of historicism, or "the underlying assumption that the whole of reality is one vast historical process, [and] that the nature of everything which exists is comprehended in its historical development."[15] The process no longer seems to have any rational order. As even the youthful Karl Marx had known, history is nothing but the actions of people pursuing their goals. No metaphysical foundation ensures that in all this striving there is a larger purpose, an overriding order. History is not one process but an almost infinite number of separate, sometimes countervailing processes and principles at work in human affairs. Critics and philosophers in recent decades have shown the contradictions and fallacies in every system; the age of systems seems to be over. Such unifying and totalizing creeds as Marxism are now seen to be myths. This erosive skepticism, to be sure, has not deprived past events of their interest, but it has reduced them to dramas, happenings, outbursts of activity and rhetoric. The profession of history had risen to importance in the nineteenth century on the foundation of historicism; could it maintain itself without this support? The "Western Civilization" or "American History" survey courses long successfully taught to freshmen "were comprehensible and vital enterprises because and only so long as they told the once believable story of how liberty and reason progressively triumphed," as William McNeill put it.

"It is now generally agreed that there is a crisis in historical writing," a reviewer of a book on the subject wrote. A 1960 survey found that only about 20 percent of professional historians, compared to more than 60 percent of physicists, thought that the state of their profession was eminently satisfactory[16]—a fact that probably reflected much more than the amount of public subsidies flowing in the two directions. "Future histories of English historical writing," a young historian wrote in a special issue of the London *Times Literary Supplement* dedicated to "New Ways in History" (April 7, 1966), "are likely to reveal the first half of the 20th century as a time when most historians temporarily lost their bearings." These young historians tended to blame this loss of direction on the habit of "grubbing away in the old empirical tradition" and to believe that salvation lay in doses of sociology, of statistics, of computers, or of almost anything rather than what historians had been accustomed to do in the past. Perhaps they were as confused as their elders; but of their dissatisfaction there was little doubt.

Exactly the opposite reason for the crisis was advanced by others; Oscar Handlin found the chief cause for complaint to be a loss of standards resulting partly from increasing numbers (more is worse) as well as from politicization and the new subject matter: historians "have allowed their subjects to slip into the hands of propagandists, politicians, dramatists, novelists, journalists, and social engineers."[17] Handlin echoed Geoffrey Elton's complaint that the university curriculum had become "an historical supermarket, full of goodies in penny packets."[18] He took issue with J. H. Plumb's view, in *Death of the Past* (1970), that what had died was all sense of time or tradition, consumed by the galloping now-ism of a society given to cultural amnesia. Glance at any novel and you find an appetite for the past; the trouble is that historians have turned the task of satisfying it over to others, as their own standards erode. Careerism and trendiness come in for their share of blame in this rather confused but heartfelt indictment from a distinguished older (and Ivy League) scholar, which seems to have been rather typical of the views of his generation. With this group "sixtyish history" became a byword not for freshening vistas but for a sad erosion of standards.

Of course such a crisis was not confined to history. A 1964 symposium whose proceedings were published as *The Crisis in the Humanities* (edited by a historian, J. H. Plumb) registered complaints from almost every discipline. The modern intellectual world suffers from indigestion brought on by too much knowledge. The knowledge explosion is related to the university explosion, which finds ever more scholars writing ever more books and articles, as governments and universities subsidize re-search as never before. In such cognate fields as anthropology, soci-ology, and psychology, the old nineteenth-century syntheses also broke down into an array of miscellaneous small-scale studies with no adequate overarching structure of theory. The output of the more exact sciences, such as organic chemistry, multiplies every few years. This anarchy in the world of knowledge is an aspect of modern culture's centrifugal tendencies, of the bigness of everything, of the immense accumulation of knowledge in constantly multiplying ratios. The result has been a shrinkage of the domains over which scholars can claim mastery: the bulk of material is so great that no one can hope to keep up with the advances in more than one small area of knowledge. "We are all con-fined to our own antheap, which is generally dusty, small, and low," an eminent British scholar sighed in the 1960s.[19]

It would be hard to deny that in a larger sense the twentieth century has taken an antihistorical direction. In the nineteenth century all the signs pointed toward historicism, as we have noted. But in the twentieth, as an intellectual historian claims, "the major intellectual movements and fashions . . . have all been non-historical in their orientation," and "there has been a dramatic shrinkage in the historical branches of disciplines such as philosophy and literary criticism."[20] For a long season, at least, literary critics and artists proclaimed their "emancipation from history." Twentieth-century modernist artists rejected the burden of tradition, seeking a music or painting or architecture of pure forms divorced from consciousness, development, beginnings, and ends. The significant intellectual movement designated as structuralism identified historicism as a "modern malady" whose victims ignored the timeless and metaphysical dimensions of human experience. Human culture is in fact, Roland Barthes has said, an "untiring repetition"; of the things that matter there is in fact no history at all. The "new" literary criticism scorned social background or historical context. Even the Marxists adopted structuralism in the 1970s: the notion that people make their own history, Louis Althusser thought, is a myth of the historians, really a "bourgeois" prejudice. People are puppets moved by laws of language and behavior that essentially do not change. Even the historians of the fashionable *Annales* persuasion shed the optimistic historical illusions of the past.

A generation of young historians responded energetically to these challenges. Despite recent setbacks, the number of historians, as of all university faculty members, is of course far larger now than at any previous time. Ten thousand historians scramble for position and promotion in the United States alone. In an effort to survive the challenges they face, they have looked for new methods and new subject matter. Self-proclaimed "new" histories have multiplied: the new economic history, the new urban history, quantitative history, interdisciplinary history, psychohistory, social science history, each with its own professional journal and dedicated disciples (quarreling with each other). Armed with the higher statistics, computers, and theories borrowed from psychology and the social sciences, historians have invaded allegedly fresh fields of inquiry to study the family, childhood, old age, diet, disease, death, crime, violence, madness (a certain morbidity is evident, suitable no doubt to the age), popular culture, technology, magic, sex, sports, education. If history is dying, it is doing so not with a whimper but a bang. To be sure, signs of panic may be discerned in this frantic pursuit of novelty, as well as a tendency to dissociate from the integrity of their own discipline and to lean on anthropology, sociology, psychology, economics, or some other intellectual neighbor. But hundreds of young historians have believed they were rescuing a tired old Clio and renewing her youth with massive injections of fresh and juicy substance. Most of those who have complained about gimmickry and even quackery (as Jacques Barzun did in *Clio and the Doctors*) were senior citizens. Their younger colleagues have been undeterred by such mutterings in their eagerness to develop a "new" history.

Notes

[1] The call for social history is much older than recent social historians often imagine; it goes back as far as Voltaire. In 1830 Thomas Carlyle gave it vivid expression in *On History*: "The time seems coming when . . . he who sees no world but that of courts and camps . . . will pass for a more or less instructive Gazetteer, but will no longer be called Historian."

[2] Ferdinand Schevill, *History of Florence* (New York: Harcourt, Brace, 1936), pp. xiv–xv. Quoted by permission of James Schevill.

[3] It is undoubtedly true that historians had in fact aimed at such goals long before Dilthey and Collingwood told them they should. For example, a letter of Hippolyte Taine to Alexandre Dumas, dated May 23, 1878, speaks of the "applied psychology" with which he sought in his history of the French Revolution to get at the mental state of a Jacobin. And Taine is often thought of as a positivist. In an article in *Journal of the History of Ideas*, April–June 1983, on J. G. Droysen's lectures of 1857–1883, Felix Gilbert notes anticipations of the Dilthey outlook in this older German historian: the need to emancipate history from natural science as well as from mere philosophical speculation.

[4] See Dwight E. Lee and R. N. Beck, "The Meaning of Historicism," *American Historical Review*, April 1954, and Calvin G. Rand, "Two Meanings of Historicism," *Journal of the History of Ideas*, October–December 1964.

[5] The extent of this debt may be judged by a sampling of names of refugees from Nazi Germany and Austria: Karl Popper, Karl Mannheim, Werner Jaeger, Hans Baron, Paul Kristeller, Leo Strauss, Erwin Panofsky, Rudolf Carnap, Eric Auerbach.

[6] See Hans J. Rogger, *National Consciousness in Eighteenth-Century Russia* (Cambridge: Harvard University Press, 1960), pp. 210–211.

[7] Reinhold Niebuhr, *Faith and History: A Comparison of Christian and Modern Views of History* (New York: Scribner's, 1949), p. 69.

[8] Michael Oakeshott, "The Activity of Being an Historian," in *Historical Studies: Papers Read before the Second Irish Conference of Historians* (London: Bowes & Bowed, 1958).

[9] See J. H. Huizinga's able essay "Two Wrestlers with an Angel," in his *Dutch Civilization in the Seventeenth Century and Other Essays* (London: Collins, 1968). The "two wrestlers" are Wells and Spengler.

[10] O. F. Anderle, a Dutch historian, tried to establish a school of historical research under Toynbee's plan, correcting his errors but following his basic procedure. "Comparative history" has attracted some interest, usually on a more modest scale; and there have been other attempts to write "world history."

[11]See "On History," in vol. 10 of Valéry's *Collected Works*, ed. D. Folliot and J. Mathews (London: Routledge & Kegan Paul, 1963). This essay was written in 1931.

[12]The *Annales* follower T. Stoianovich did decide that there are exactly 16,777,316 variables in history: *French Historical Method: The Annales Paradigm* (Ithaca: Cornell University Press, 1976), pp. 97–100. Popper and Carl Hempel tried to save "scientific" history by arguing that though history does not find laws, it *applies* them; whereas most other sciences use particulars to arrive at generalizations, history uses generalizations to explain particulars. (See the discussion of "Covering-law" theory in Part II.) In any case, these neopositivists agreed that history has no predictive functions, and Popper was most severe with those who claimed to have discovered inexorable laws of historical destiny.

[13]An example is provided by Fernand Braudel, the celebrated historian of the *Annales* school. Braudel was long praised for his works on early modern Mediterranean society, which seemed to combine immense research with broad synthesis, and was considered possibly the most outstanding historian of the post-1945 era; lately, however, he has received severe criticism for factual inaccuracy.

[14]For an article of a very common type, see Theodore H. Von Laue, "Is There a Crisis in the Writing of History?" *Bucknell Review*, 14 (1966), 1–15.

[15]Geoffrey Barraclough, "Universal History," in H. P. R. Finberg, ed., *Approaches to History* (Toronto: University of Toronto Press, 1962), p. 109.

[16]Bernard Berelson, *Graduate Education in the United States* (New York: McGraw-Hill, 1960), p. 212.

[17]Oscar Handlin, "A Discipline in Crisis," in his *Truth in History* (Cambridge: Harvard University Press, 1979), p. 21.

[18]Geoffrey Elton, "Second Thoughts on History at the Universities," *History*, 54 (February 1969), 60–67.

[19]H. R. Trevor-Roper, in *The Spectator*, October 25, 1968.

[20]A. Magill, "Foucault, Structuralism, and the Ends of History," in *Journal of Modern History*, 5, no. 51 (September 1979), 501.

CHAPTER 7
RECENT TRENDS

ONE of the perennial, perhaps consoling claims of professional historians is that they have moved up to a new level of methodological rigor or theoretical sophistication. Or they claim that they are the first to have explored a brand-new field or have taken a novel approach to fields already explored. Thus claims of a "new" history abound in each generation. The claim usually mixes pretension with real achievement. Few of the new histories are quite so new or so novel as their advocates claim, but each usually gives evidence of the changing interest of historians or of a notable enhancement of their skills.

The claim of newness goes back a long way. Many past historians expressed discontent with traditional modes and called for and sometimes achieved a fresh approach. Usually the fresh approach took the form of a broadening of subject matter. Voltaire, then Carlyle and Michelet, then later such Victorian historians as John R. Green ardently championed what they saw as a novelty—less political "court" history of kings and wars and more about the lives of the people; fewer descriptive details and more generalizations about the causes of social change; and more on literature, the arts, and popular culture. James Harvey Robinson launched a so-called new American history in the early twentieth century, and tried to imprint his conception of it on the prestigious multivolumed *New American Nation* series (most observers thought the results not a huge success). Meanwhile, the immensely influential French school associated with the journal *Annales*, edited by Bloch and Febvre, built on earlier foundations when it began another new history in 1929.

Social History and Its Offspring

If anything was common to all earlier "new" departures, or even tied them to more recent trends dating from the 1960s, it was an emphasis on what we now loosely designate as "social" history. Clearly, various types of social history boomed in the sixties and seventies, in Europe as well as America. As usual, definitions tended to be loose. Historians with widely varied subjects and methods all laid claim to the label "social history." In the absence of clear semantic conventions, one has no alternative but to stipulate a definition. The most useful definition is keyed to the subject matter, not to any specific area of human concern. In this sense, a social historian, whatever the area of his or her primary concern, must focus not on leaders or elites but on whole populations. If possible, such historians broaden their search to encompass all the people in a community, and they try to characterize or to trace changes in that society. So defined, social history is not a label equivalent to economic, intellectual, or political history, since these terms designate areas of human interest or activity, not the totality of the community investigated.[1] And even these stabs at definition point up the multiplicity of ways in which historians cut up their discipline—not only by varieties of human interest and activity and by the breadth of the universe studied, but by chronology, by geography, even by methods.

Such a broadly defined social history requires a range of sources, of potential data, not easily available in earlier centuries. In the past ordinary people, with rare exceptions, did not record and preserve the records of their lives, and thus left few readily accessible sources. Also, the broad goals of social historians have invited complexity. It was easy to find unity or a theme in the role of a political leader, but how is one to draw together in a meaningful, readable synthesis the diverse materials that make up everyday life? Ambitious theories such as Marxism invited an exciting totalization, but such theories were highly speculative. Moreover, despite what critics of political or elite history have said, the story of state-building and government, of diplomacy and wars, of elections and parties, is by no means insignificant; on the contrary, it long seemed to be the very stuff of a nation's life. In declaring that "history is past politics" E. A. Freeman was not misreading the story for his nineteenth-century British readers, nor were Bancroft and Adams when they wrote about Jefferson and Jackson for American audiences. And the assertion that the twentieth century no longer is so concerned with wars and politics and "great men" is an odd judgment in a century that suffered two world wars and produced Lenin, Stalin, and Hitler.

In the nineteenth century, by a sort of tacit agreement, the sphere of ordinary private lives fell largely to the writers of fiction. The novel in the age of Dickens, Eliot, Trollope, and Hardy, of Balzac and Zola, of Turgenev and Tolstoy, was mimetic, picturing the realities of personal and social life often with a marvelous skill. As such it was a kind of social history. Novelists did not cite their sources, nor were they held to rigorous standards of factual exactitude; they had the privileges of artists and made no cognitive claims, although sometimes their descriptions (the battle in *War and Peace*, the strike in *Germinal*) were vividly true. In the twentieth century the ablest novelists, bored with mere mimesis or reportage and estranged from normal society, have ventured into subjectivity and fantasy. It may be that this switch in fictional strategies left the realm of social life open to the historian. Historians in any case were now able to find and use sources that permitted them for the first time to get at many of the daily realities of life, from love and marriage and childbearing to diet and health care.

The repudiation of "elite" history, the efforts to tell the story of the broad masses of people, coalesced with the political mood of many young historians of the sixties and early seventies. They essayed to do history from the bottom up, and in the process hoped to gain a new understanding of the masses, to help them gain a sense of pride, or to motivate them to political action, perhaps to revolution. Such political purposes established another label, "radical" history—one uniquely tied to the political uses of the final product. Such "radical" history usually, but not always or by necessity, overlapped with social history, although nothing in social history, as defined here, necessitated any one political or ideological outlook.

Since anything close to an inclusive history of ordinary people is so difficult and involves so many types of data, about the only practical focus of such studies had to be geographically and culturally restricted communities. Thus sophisticated local or village or town histories proliferated. The alternative was geographically more extensive but topically less inclusive histories of ordinary people. From this impulse came a spectrum of "new" histories in most traditional fields and in some relatively recent ones. Labor historians switched their interest from labor unions or labor leaders to the working class; intellectual historians from coherent belief systems to popular mentalities; economic historians from economic policy issues to changes in technology and production; political historians from leaders to the led; religious historians from doctrine to worship and other forms of religious behavior; diplomatic historians from government officials to popular pressures that shape foreign policy; military historians from battles and generals to the life of the enlisted men. Both political goals and new methods helped reinvigorate the history of minority groups and the largely excluded majority made up of women. Most historians who took up residence in the booming fields of black and women's history took a social approach; that is, they focused less on elites than on groups. The desire for geographical breadth, along with social inclusiveness, encouraged very specialized and narrowly focused histories of fertility and mortality (demographic history) or, in the tradition of Braudel, a new historical approach to climate and environment. Only at such a level of generality, and at the very borders of culturally determined behavior, could historians prepare rigorous accounts encompassing great masses of people.

In the last generation, the most encompassing and in all likelihood the most durable change among historians has been a new consciousness of gender. This upsurge of interest not only reflects the proliferation of histories dealing specifically with women, that largely neglected half of the human story, but the long-deferred, increasingly generalized awareness of the role of gender in all areas of human concern. An awareness of the role and status of women has necessarily changed historians' perspective on the role of men. Women's movements, the increased number of women historians, the political awareness and effective agitation by women scholars, all have encouraged these changes. Almost any histories written as recently as a decade ago, even some written by women, almost inevitably seem antiquated today, if for no other reason than an unselfconscious use of exclusively male pronouns. The effort by scholars, mostly women, to right the balance, to retrieve a forgotten past, led to a dramatic growth of women's history and new, interdisciplinary women's studies programs. The women historians who first mined this rich but often elusive vein went at their task with such vigor and with so many political goals that their work assumed the aspect of a disciplinary crusade. One was needed. But the lasting significance of this new awareness will be not the strength of a now maturing and sophisticated field of women's history but the greater inclusiveness of all historical writing.

The emergence of women's history came surprisingly late. American historians, at least, are inclined to date its rise from the post-1945 era, beginning dimly with such pioneer works as Mary Beard's *Women as Force in History* of 1946 and Simone de Beauvoir's *Second Sex,* published in 1949. The women's movement, even in its later incarnation (some historians see it as immemorial), can be traced to the later nineteenth century. Its most violent and heroic moment came just before 1914 with the exploits of the British "suffragettes" and other embattled feminists. Classics of the female declaration of independence, reprinted in every collection of manifestos, range from Mary Wollstonecraft's *Vindication of the Rights of Women* in 1792 to Virginia Woolf's *A Room of One's Own* in 1929. Women's history lagged well behind the events and the ideas that ultimately propelled it. Historians, it may seem, are glacially slow to pick up a dominant idea, but when they do . . . !

We have already referred to the boom in "social history" and its borrowings from the social sciences. The work of historians inevitably overlaps with that of social scientists when they aspire to produce histories that encompass groups, crowds, or total societies. Characterizations of groups of people tend, almost by necessity, to smooth out many local or idiosyncratic particularities and to highlight average or general features. The available data often permit no greater detail, even as one's purpose may indicate such generality. At this level of description, cultural patterns or uniformities often stand out, hinting at highly probable or even established social structures and suggesting a high degree of predictability. Insofar as the historian tries to describe the human community on which she focuses and to trace its evolution through time, her focus remains particularistic, for her story necessarily encompasses many characteristics that are not found in other societies. The economist or sociologist is not likely to focus so narrowly on a particular society, but will try to identify structures that are found in many societies, and may use these uniformities to develop usable models. Models of this type, including the most significant one ever developed by Western social scientists (that of a free market economy), may be almost indispensable to historians, as a comparative reference for careful description, as a yardstick with which to gauge the characteristics of a particular society at a particular time. The purposes of the disciplines thus vary, but the points of convergence are greatest when historians focus on large numbers of people and describe those often abstracted characteristics that are most widely shared within a population.

Of course, some historians may share certain goals with social scientists. Historians may seek not only to understand events in a particular past but to exploit the possibilities of more general knowledge applicable to a whole class of societies (modern industrial societies, for instance). Thus, even as they tell their story of economic development in the United States in the nineteenth century, and one hopes they tell it truly, they may be searching for and frequently remarking similarities to economic development in western Europe. They may even, at some peril, hazard some guesses about developmental patterns or causal factors that help explain that elusive class of events so often referred to as an industrial revolution. If they become so fascinated by such general explanations that they stop trying to tell multifaceted stories about particular past societies, one may argue that they have crossed that vague boundary between history and the social sciences. Histories have ceased to be of primary importance for them; recurring social patterns are most important.[2] But a perfect division of labor is rare. The understanding of a particular history invites knowledge of the various classes of phenomena that a single history may imperfectly exemplify, while it may be difficult for even the most abstract economist to work entirely with completely general models without at times noting their relevance to real, historical societies. Once again, a disciplinary distinction based on form and purpose need not preclude a rich and continuous interaction.

Unfortunately, the areas of overlap have led to pretentious claims and all manner of methodological confusion. In the United States, for example, a group of historians formed a Social Science History Association. Apparently this semantic nightmare seemed quite plausible to them. Of course, if one defines history as a social science, then "social science history" is as redundant as "economic economics." If, on the other hand, one so defines history as to differentiate it from the social sciences, by either its subject, form, methods, or use, then no history can be social-scientific, although a history may be about a social science. Unfortunately, the near nonsense of the title was often eclipsed by the extravagance of the claim that social science history was better, more rigorous, more precise, more useful than other kinds of history. But what "other kinds" could there be? Usually such cheerleaders of a new era point to either formal or methodological differences. Thus one heard vague references to social science theories, or to such dualities as analytical versus narrative history, or quantitative versus impressionistic history. Yet on close analysis (note the word) such dualities are found to involve as much nonsense as the label "social science history."

Not only is the word "theory" very ambiguous, but it is not clear what a social science theory could be, save perhaps any "theory" developed and applied by people called social scientists. A theory may be a hypothesis, with more or less supporting evidence; or an imaginative model, with or without intended empirical relevance; or purported laws either exemplified in actual human events or merely present in abstract models. Today, laws, hypotheses, generalizations, theories, and models float in and out of discourse, and no one tries very hard to make any of them very precise. But the semantic difficulties aside, still it is clear that economists work with increasingly complex models, most expressed in mathematical form. It is their task to develop, extend, or clarify such models (a purely intellectual game in itself) and, more difficult, to establish the relationship of such models to real human societies, and thus their usefulness for descriptive purposes or as guides to policy. Such models, to some extent, shape almost everyone's understanding of economic events. It would be difficult for economic historians to avoid some such theoretical models, or the concepts that fit within them, and one can wonder why they would want to avoid them. Why not use them, to help clarify issues or as tools for measuring economic changes in real societies? In almost any field of history, historians need to learn the intellectual conventions, the jargon, the models used by scholars in related disciplines. Such borrowings are useful for description and com parison; they enable historians to communicate with other scholars, and in some cases may help make historical writing more precise. But analogous, at times useful ideal types, models, theories, and formal conventions are present in almost all disciplines, not just the social sciences.

None of this useful interaction with other disciplines leads to any new type of history. The economic historian still has the same old task—to tell the truth about a past economy. If newly refined concepts, ideal types, or models help make the story clearer, then so much the better. It is absurd, because redundant, to talk of narrative history. A history is a story of past events, and thus a narrative, a coherent account, a bringing together or synthesis of great complexity. Of course, one may tell a story well or poorly, eloquently or dully. And almost any story told by a historian will be internally complex. It will include not just a chronicle of events but efforts to account for them or to show relationships. At times any historian may take a rather long analytical detour in order to identify various types of causes that were preconditions of an event or state of affairs. The word "analysis" simply means the breaking of wholes into parts. It is only by such a breakdown of gross events, such an attempt to distinguish various parts or aspects of events, that historians can gain an understanding of causes. Thus any history whatsoever is a narrative, and any significant history will involve analysis (a cutting apart) as well as synthesis (a putting of pieces back together). The two are completely complementary. Of course, analytical essays abound in historical journals, and much of the time, even most of the time, historians may be involved in work that contributes to histories but that in itself may not involve the actual writing of stories.

But at the very least, one may argue, most of the vaunted new histories are distinctive in one aspect: they are "quantitative." They involve new methods, methods that radically distinguish the newer social histories from all the old histories that preceded them. The claim has a small kernel of truth and a lot of confusion. All historians try to infer from present artifacts what happened in the human past and why it happened. When surviving artifacts support inferences and help validate a historical hypothesis, they become data or evidence. The artifacts, and thus the data, may be variously classified. Almost any conceivable type of object, so long as it has human relevance, may serve as a datum to support or refute some historical claim. Some artifacts—a thousand-page diary, say—are packed with potential data, and may allow a wide range of inferences about almost every aspect of an individual life. Such an artifact is comparatively rich, thick with meaning. Other artifacts, such as one line of information about an individual written down by a nineteenth-century census taker, may be very thin by comparison, but the total census record contains roughly similar details about millions of people. For a biographer the census report will be of minimal use, the diary indispensable. For a social historian who wants to characterize a whole population, the diary will be suggestive but in itself will be all but useless, for nothing in it certifies shared characteristics; the census, though, will be invaluable, since its coverage of the information it supplies is all but complete. It is the quality and range of information that distinguishes these two potential historical sources, and not a quantitative distinction. Each is one artifact; in the context of various hypotheses, of questions posed, each has numerous bits of needed information. Either source permits either loose or exact counting; the information in each is quantifiable. All data are. Thus it makes absolutely no sense to talk of quantifiable data. It does make sense to talk about possible statistical tests that one may use to ensure the richest harvest of inferences from a body of data.

The misleading label "quantitative history," if it makes sense at all, refers not to a type of history but to certain methods a historian may use to count, sort, or manipulate data. In social history, in most contemporary economic and political history, historians confront immense piles of potential sources, such as ballooning public records. Use of such records requires statistical skills, from beginning sampling techniques to various types of correlations. In loose ways, historians have always counted data and estimated proportions and ratios and relationships—all quantifying techniques. But only in the last twenty years have great numbers of historians, and by necessity almost all economic and social historians, turned to refined statistical tools. Their subject and the type of data available require such tools. Statistical methods are as important to a historian faced with massed data as are critical and semantic tools to one who analyzes a medieval document. And for the storage of many types of data, for quick retrieval, sorting, or complicated calculations, the computer has become all but indispensable. It allows analysis that would have been so time-consuming as to be unthinkable in an earlier age. These innovations and new types of training have indeed marked a major, irreversible shift in the kinds of tools and skills now valued within the historical profession. A critical undergraduate subject, for one who would become a social historian, is now calculus.

By the 1980s, the boom in social history seemed to be over. Historical fashions always change quickly. (They change even more quickly in the even more competitive discipline of literary criticism.) In Western countries, the political mood has also shifted dramatically from the equalitarian concerns of the late sixties. In the late eighties, older, more elite subjects—political leadership, diplomatic history—came back in vogue; and intellectual history, with a few new fads of its own, staged a strong comeback. Even in the philosophy of history, the dominating concerns have shifted from epistemological issues, from the explanatory value of historical assertions, to issues of form and artistry, with the word "narrative" once more central to attempts to define or understand history. Even in graduate seminars, now that statistical techniques are commonplace and everyone depends on computers, the emphasis has shifted, once again, back to problems of meaning and effective writing. Historical subjects and data of various kinds have always required very technical skills. One has no alternative but to learn those that are necessary to write the history one wants to write. But, while almost anyone can learn how to set up a research project or how to process various types of data, few historians ever learn how to tell a story clearly and effectively. This is, after all, the most intimidating intellectual challenge faced by historians. It always has been and it always will be.

Psychohistory

The word "psychology" has an almost disjunctive set of meanings. On the one hand it refers to an experimental science grounded in physiology and entrenched in most psychology departments; on the other, it refers to the concepts and theories that undergird clinical counseling or therapy, and particularly a complex of theories in a field often denoted as "depth psychology." The two types of psychology seem to have little in common these days. Of the two, the more clinically oriented theories have had a greater impact on historians, for obvious reasons. Historians, in our fragmented, Hellenistic age, have continued to focus on problems of individual identity, and on the aspects of personality shaped by language and culture. The more scientific forms of psychology are too general, too physiological or behavioral, and thus too reductionist to offer insights useful to historians. The lessons of modern learning theory, for example, apply to all higher animals, not just to humans. But depth psychology, from its first masters—Freud, Jung—to later neo-Freudians and anti-Freudians, has offered theories that claim to illuminate almost all aspects of human personality development.

The label "psychohistory" is now applied not to the work of all those historians who use one or another psychological theory in their research but rather to the efforts of a cohesive, intensely self-conscious group of historians who use psychoanalytical theories in order to understand individuals or groups. The prefix "psycho" thus refers, most correctly, to the broad psychoanalytical tradition, to Freud and his later disciples and adapters, and not to the academic discipline of psychology. At best it refers to only one theoretical perspective barely within this academic discipline or on its outskirts. But, in the United States at least, these psychohistorians demonstrate the hazards and the possibilities of historical writing closely tied to broad, encompassing, but still purportedly empirical or scientific theories. In Europe the Freudian theoretical tradition has often competed, or blended in fascinating ways, with an even more sweeping, more controverted and variously elaborated, but still purportedly scientific theoretical system—Marxism.

Almost from its birth, psychoanalysis seemed to be a potent tool for biographers, even as popularized versions of it became favored tools of novelists. In fact, Freud himself, with some rather disastrous results, wrote some of the earliest psychohistory. By the 1920s, a scattering of historians endorsed the new psychoanalytical gospel, tried to apply it, or recommended it to the historical profession. But in the United States, at least, a school of psychohistory flowered only after the horrors of Nazism and World War II, and was most influenced by the neo-Freudian ego-identity and life-crisis theories and the controversial biographical studies (Luther, Gandhi) of Erik Erikson. By the 1980s, psychohistory had become a widely recognized, somewhat sectarian, often resented specialty, with its own recognized masters and its own journal. Once again prophets claimed to have found a new and inspired approach to history, and at times they could sound as arrogant and as esoteric as their very different but equally competent brethren who were now armed with all manner of coefficients.

That at times the psychological approach seemed to shed new light on historical issues can hardly be denied. Psychohistorians have produced a host of provocative reinterpretations, injecting new interest in old subjects. Rather like the insights of the feminists, the view from the psychoanalyst's couch was sharply and interestingly different from what most historians were accustomed to see. Can World War I be attributed in part to antagonism between German and British diplomats who had been conditioned to contrasting patterns of behavior and response in childhood? Did Hitler's anti-Semitism owe less to his reading of Houston Stewart Chamberlain than to a projected self-hatred connected to his own Jewish ancestry? One might argue about such propositions but, presented in appropriate scholarly manner, they were at least stimulating. A large number of such interpretations, varying in quality, flowed from the presses in the 1970s and 1980s, enhancing no little the interest in history. They also elicited very divergent reactions from historians. David Stannard, in *Shrinking History* (1980), declared that all psychohistorians

> share, in varying degrees, the problem of making much of matters that
> are notable only for their lack of singular importance once they are placed

in their cultural context. . . . All build complex arguments on virtually non-existent evidence; all violate elementary rules of logic in developing these arguments; and all analyze data using theories that fail to withstand empirical examination and experimental testing. [Pp. 29–30]

But Peter Loewenberg wrote in his *Decoding the Past* (1985):

Psychohistory provides a new tool for historians with which to analyze their data and interpret the complex configurations of human behavior in the past. Historians have applied it both crudely and well. . . . To the historians of the next decades falls the task of moving beyond these beginnings to explain mankind's past and current behavior with greater sophistication and certainty. [P. 34]

Psychoanalytical theory poses special problems for historians. Of all purported scientific theories, it focuses most specifically on acculturated humankind. It is the modern science of the mind, not just of the brain. Freud, its chief progenitor, not only worked out a theoretical scheme encompassing the development of the individual personality but in his later years moved to some highly speculative theories about the motives underlying the development of civilization, or to one type of speculative philosophy of history. Freud, like most of his disciples, believed that psychoanalytical theory correlated with physiological structures. But the theory was not, could not, then be derived from such structures, and it is still impossible to demonstrate exact correlations. Thus the theory had to rest largely on clinical observations, not on physical observations or experiments. This, as events quickly proved, seemed to be a critical weakness. Critics of Freud, beginning with his former friend, Carl Jung, made basic changes in the theory without clearly distorting the clinical data. Thus as we wend our way from Freud's earliest formulations through his revisions to those of apostates and on to a proliferation of alternative theories and theorists after World War II (Sartre, Frankl, Rogers), we find ourselves in a maze of competing theories. Internal confusion is only part of the story; the main body of academic psychologists have denied all along that such clinically based "speculation" has any claim to scientific status. The more hardheaded behaviorists have continued to view Freud and his quarreling offspring as no more than modern magicians or mythmakers. They argue that the speculative, literary nature of Freud's formulations (he did draw many insights from literature) are too imprecise for definitive testing, just as it is difficult to prove the effectiveness of psychoanalysis as a therapy.

The perils of psychoanalytical theory for historians are only one dramatic example of the problems inherent in all general theory that purports to explain human motives and action. To the extent that such a theory shapes or guides inferences drawn from data, the historian who relies on it has to take responsibility for its empirical validity. If the theory is ill founded or unclear, then so will be the resulting history. Fortunately, historians confront a high degree of unanimity among specialists in most areas of knowledge, from physics to physiology, and so they appeal without hesitation to such knowledge, which in most cases provides only a background for human events. It is widely held that historians have no alternative but to use one or another theory of human motivation, either one drawn from common sense or one devised by experts. Any theory one chooses rests on a debatable assumption about some fixed human nature. Actually, it can be argued that no general theory applies to human action, and that the only needed guidelines for a historian are the habits, customs, and norms of a given society at a specific time. An experienced historian may be the best-informed expert on these things. But no doubt a more general knowledge that could be applied to the phenomena under consideration would be helpful. If, for example, some hidden dynamic, some deeply rooted instincts, control personality development, then a biographer can infer several parts of a story not supported by direct evidence (in a now famous case, this is what Erikson did for the young Luther). Freudian theory is heady stuff, and in many contexts it is wonderfully beguiling to historians. It helps us make sense of so much that is otherwise confusing. But the final question has to be: Is it true? In the case of psychoanalysis, the pitfalls are unusually great—the experts disagree, the theory is less precise and operational than those in use in most other disciplines, and the whole approach is challenged by a majority of academic psychologists.

These hazards make psychohistorians a special breed. They assume the validity of certain psychoanalytical theories. As believers, they spend their time justifying not the theory but only the historical judgments shaped in part by such theory. Thus as a group they take on the characteristics of a cult. If one happens to be a rigorous behaviorist in psychological outlook, one will never take psychohistory seriously, however careful the research, however consistent and plausible the judgments. A psychohistorian bears comparison with a zealous Christian who explains events as the workings of Providence. He may be right. But the explanation assumes a determinant of all events which is never itself subject to proof or disproof. The interpretation transcends the empirical foreground, and today, whatever the cognitive status of the gods appealed to, it lacks the consensual support that at one time made providential explanation an accepted and normal part of historical writing.

It is both the status of the theory and the occasionally extreme claims of psychohistorians that have left psychohistory at the fringe of the profession. New methods, such as those of sophisticated statistical analysis, may at first create anxiety and doubt among practitioners who lack such skills, and thus trigger hostile rejection. But as they are only tools, almost all such innovations sooner or later take their place among the others in the professional's kit, for despite the differences that for a time seemed to separate the "quantifiers" and their detractors into two warring camps, no really substantive issues divided them. But psychohistory has not been assimilated in this way, and it probably will not be, unless or until all clinical psychologists agree on a theoretical approach and gain respect for it among their experimentalist colleagues. By that time, of course, there will be no need for a separate group of psychohistorians or even for the use of the label.

Whether justifiably or not, historians long before Freud accepted generalized theories about what they often called human nature. From religious beliefs, from folk wisdom, and from literary sources they drew their often eclectic and unsystematic insights. Freud himself drew on the imaginative writers (Shakespeare, Goethe, and Dostoevsky, who, he declared, first discovered the unconscious) and from the biblical reading on which he was raised. That a purportedly scientific vocabulary now replaced these older roots of knowledge about humanity may represent as much a retreat as an advance. The replacement may be indicative of a loss of the traditional culture, a body of material drawn from world literature which once was second nature to educated people. The "disinherited mind" in a specialized mass-educated society no longer knows this material, and substitutes for it the mechanical formulas of science or pseudoscience. Where an earlier historian might have used a quotation from Milton or Shakespeare, a phrase from the Bible or a folk proverb, the newer ones may apply some theory advanced by Freud, Jung, or Erikson. Arnold J. Toynbee, the last flower of a humanistic, classical education, bolstered his arguments with lines from Sophocles and Meredith; now we get a "Fairbairnian object-relational model" and a "Reichian psychodynamic model," and some hearts sink.

The Confused Present

Perhaps the present always strikes observers as a welter of confusion. Time and perspective always filter out the ephemera and clarify significant patterns. But it is difficult, as this century nears its end, to suppress the belief that the last half century has witnessed dramatic and enduring changes in the historical profession. New interests, new fields, new methods accompanied a dramatic expansion in the number of historians, and in their racial, ethnic, and sexual diversity. Thus it is no wonder that in the midst of all the specialized inquiry, all the seeming fragmentation, we now hear on all sides cries for more synthesis or for some "new"—note the word—interpretive framework. How can one write a textbook, a general history of anything, even teach a basic course and do justice to all the subgroups?[3] How can one present the perspective of women (or of homosexuals, children, the aged, blacks, native Americans, and other ethnic minorities), fully encompass ordinary people (voters, the working class), pay obeisance to demography and to enduring environmental constraints, incorporate all the returns from highly technical, statistically sophisticated inquiries in economic and social history, be up to date on and able appropriately to borrow theories and models from the related generalizing sciences, and still somehow create a unified and eloquent story? The task seems all but impossible.

Once again we confront the obvious fact that the golden age of history in the Western world rested on a silent consensus about most values. Everyone who counted broadly agreed about what was important, and about who merited inclusion in histories, and from what perspective. It is pointless to lament the demise of this consensus, but without it we may well lose the rationale of history as a unified discipline. Clearly departments of history today are at risk of becoming battlefields, where a variety of subject matters backed by dedicated proponents compete for scarce places in the curriculum. The cost is a degree of chaos.

But there are compensations. Much more historical writing, and in many ways much more rigorous writing, takes place today than ever before. The output is huge—huge at least in the number of books and articles published, the amount of research done, the time and money expended on it. If all this activity has resulted in chaos, the outcome only places history very much in the current swim of things, makes it quite "postmodern." Having given up the obsessive search for unity, we can wallow in life's plenty without worrying about unifying systems or common interpretations. After all, unifying systems tend to break down. Macroeconomics, like macrosociology, is a disaster area. The scene is not significantly different in physics, where scientists labor in vain to find some principle of order in the two hundred or more subatomic particles they have identified and whose curious habits they attempt to chart. The new literary criticism finds no solid core of meaning in works of fiction, only innumerable and shifting meanings as individual readers meet protean texts.

Such chaos does, however, contrast with what history once stood for, and may threaten its status. According to David Cannadine, the downward trend of history as measured by the proportion of secondary students and college undergraduates studying it has continued beyond the sixties and seventies; he attributes this decline largely to "the cult of professionalism" with its fragmentation, its hyperspecialization, its loss of unity and comprehensibility.[4] This process of course affects all branches of knowledge, but history can least withstand it because it has the highest stake in coherence and communicability. C. T. R. Wilson, in the glorious days before Einstein, thought that physics could be made clear even to barmaids; no one now has any such expectation. But nuclear science does not depend for its success on being intellectually accessible to the masses, whereas history to a considerable extent does.

"A belief in the Historical Method is the most widely and strongly entertained philosophical conviction of the present day," the philosopher Henry Sidgwick wrote at the end of the nineteenth century. It seems unlikely that such a statement will be made at the end of our own century. Old Theodor Mommsen was awarded the Nobel Prize for literature in 1902; no historian has won it since, unless we agree to call Winston Churchill a historian. (The blow is somewhat softened by the fact that Joyce, Lawrence, Proust, Kafka—in brief, the century's greatest imaginative writers—also failed to gain the coveted prize.) But rejection by the arbiters of philosophy and literature does not deter countless historians from believing that they are doing important work. A recent poll revealed that of all occupations, teachers of history are happiest in their work. May it always be so.

Notes

[1]Political and intellectual history are not mutually exclusive; one may write both in the same work, insofar as ideas were important to a leading political figure or movement—to Lenin or Woodrow Wilson, say.

[2]"The issues of British politics of a century ago are now dead, and I can muster little enthusiasm for them," a leading quantifying historian has confessed. They are interesting to him only insofar as they "can be used to shed light on certain theoretical problems, the nature of political attitudes and why men hold them." William O. Aydelotte, *Quantification in History* (Reading, Mass.: Addison-Wesley, 1960), p. 160.

[3]In 1988, amid considerable controversy, Stanford University replaced the traditional "Western Civilization" course with a "World Civilization" one to provide equal time for a variety of black, Hispanic, and Asian cultures. Those who welcomed this as a necessary adjustment to the times debated with others who saw it as a surrender to hopeless confusion.

[4]David Cannadine, "The State of British History," *Times Literary Supplement*, October 10, 1986.

PART II
THE CHALLENGE OF HISTORY

CHAPTER 8
WHAT IS HISTORY?

As Part I has demonstrated, self-conscious historians have long grappled with the numerous theoretical and methodological problems suggested by their own discipline. No one has solved the problems to the complete satisfaction of either all historians or all the philosophers who think and write about history. Thus the controversies still rage, and the arguments are ever more subtle and rigorous. Near ignorance of these perplexing issues scarcely becomes a historian. But historians must not become so morbidly involved in theoretical perplexities that they flounder in enervating anxiety. They still need to create histories. The best antidote for either extreme—ignorance or enervation—is a discriminating understanding of the controverted issues in a subject area now generally termed the critical philosophy of history. This and the following chapters should provide some of that understanding.

One must take care to make neither too many nor the wrong claims for the value of philosophical self-consciousness on the part of historians. Above all, one must not expect such self-consciousness automatically to make one a historian. A philosophic genius may develop a clear and precise definition of history, see the exact relationship of history to other disciplines, understand all of its methodological intricacies, and appreciate its various personal and social uses, yet be a poor historian. One has to learn the exacting demands of historical inquiry through practice and then assimilate them as working habits. No shortcut works. An awareness of theoretical issues will at best provide only some important critical guidelines in the learning of such habits. But a critical understanding of history does contribute immensely to appreciation, to an awareness of both the intellectual dilemmas and the intellectual challenges of the discipline. Unless leavened by such an appreciative awareness, a historical apprenticeship can be an intellectually deadening pathway to mere technical proficiency.

Definitions of "History"

The first issue in any discussion of history is how one will use the ambiguous word. No firm semantic conventions control its use, even among
professional historians. For example, many people use the word "history" to designate the past, or at least the human past. Some almost
personify the word, as in such statements as "history will prove her
correct," by which they probably mean that future historians will praise
her actions. But people most often use the word to designate a field of
inquiry, including the distinctive subject matter of such inquiry, the
methods or discipline appropriate to it, its finished product, and the
form assumed by the product. A historian is one who carries out such
inquiries, contributes to such products.

While the generic word "history" usually refers to a field of inquiry,
the singular reference—"a history"—usually designates a product of
such inquiry. And for most people, a history is a story, purportedly true
rather than fictional, about the past, and most often about the human
past. Such a conventional definition—"a history is a true story about
the human past"—works well as the departure point for critical analysis.
Of course, it raises more questions than it answers about almost all the
controverted issues in the philosophy of history, but by that very fact
it opens up a very wide range of issues for clarification. We will thus
stipulate it as our working definition.

The "true" in "true story" suggests that a history is a type of empirical
knowledge. Whatever else it is, a history contains truth claims. In this
it joins with the products of other empirical disciplines, including the
physical and social sciences. Presumably the truth claimed for such
stories rests on methods of inquiry at least comparable, if not similar,
to those in the sciences. In Anglo-American philosophy, from before
World War II until the 1960s, the most debated issues about histories
had to do with epistemology and method. How is it that statements
about the past are in some sense true, and how it is that one can establish
their truth? How does a history differ in form from knowledge claims
in other disciplines? Do historians, or should they, "explain" the events
included in their stories? Do they explain them in the same sense that
"hard" scientists purportedly do? These issues at first seemed rather
simple, but led to an enormously complicated debate over the role of
covering laws in historical explanation.

The "story" in "true story" suggests that a history has close ties to
fictional short stories and novels. It is a type of literature, for it involves
unifying themes or plots, beginnings and endings, and various narrative
devices needed to construct a convincing, entertaining, or instructive
story. It is a truism that conventional, culturally specific, formal ele-

ments are present in all knowledge claims. The physical sciences are creative human products, refined arts. But a history, because of the unique properties of a story, seems to offer more leeway to an inquirer, to permit more imaginative construction, than do the hypotheses and models that physical and social scientists develop and submit to verification procedures. Thus since the 1960s philosophers have directed an increasing amount of attention to the distinctive properties of narratives, and to the linguistic and formal conventions that may exert more control over the final content of a history than do the more limited truth claims. In fact, advocates of extreme "subjectivist" views of historical narratives almost ignore the problem of truth and either deny any basis for establishing exclusive and objective knowledge or reduce such cognitive issues to a minor role. To a large extent, the more skeptical and subjectivist views of history have drawn on continental European philosophy, linguistic theories, or canons of literary criticism.

The first critics of our working definition of a history as a story are likely to be people who call themselves historians. As a matter of fact, many such historians are not busy constructing stories at all, and some may even resent any implication that they should tell stories. Nor are they particularly concerned that their work extend or revise already well known stories, although in fact this is one almost inevitable outcome of their work, however narrowly focused or analytical it may be. Whatever their self-image, they do contribute to stories, and have, at least indirectly, gained their title as historians by this fact.

Many stories about nations, cultures, or individuals are in their main outlines and dominant themes already a part of general knowledge. But no story is perfect. Such stories invite new insight and additional elaboration. Thus a historian may seek out new causes, more carefully describe some pattern of culture or personality, or introduce some new theory that makes sense of heretofore mysterious events. Viewed in isolation, apart from the tentative story that originally suggested this area of inquiry, such products of historians hardly seem historical at all. Their assertions may be in the past tense, but collectively they may reveal no development in time and suggest nothing remotely resembling a coherent story. Thus it is at least verbally confusing to describe an analysis of the causes of the French Revolution as a history, but it is quite plausible to cite it as a possibly important contribution to a history of the revolution.

As a unified story, any history may reflect the earlier research findings of many individuals, even though only one author has constructed it in its present form. Those who carry out the detailed research, even though some of them by inclination or ability never come to tell such stories, may make as critical a contribution to a story as the storyteller. They may even demonstrate more demanding skills; in any case, their skills differ from those of the storyteller. But only because someone has, or eventually will, construct the stories can the nonstorytellers earn the title of historians. In this sense, their role, however critical, is contributory. Clearly the word "story" and its more pretentious twin, "narrative," stand for inescapable elements in any history. For example, a history always relates events separated in time. Some events must come before others. Thus it is possible to locate beginnings and endings. And given some relationship between events, one may emphasize patterns and themes. These characteristics—beginnings and endings, development in time, continuity or thematic unity—are all properties of stories.

History, as the telling of stories about the past, was undoubtedly an ancient activity, although few early storytellers sought "truth" in the sense of severely factual accuracy. We have none of the early product. Surely soon after humans developed a language they began to recount memorable past events and to construct sagas and epics. But people's earliest conceptual products, as well as many of their later ones, did not develop in pure form. Our remote ancestors probably did not distinguish true from purely imaginative stories or their stories from early theories about the universe. Early humans, like most people today, easily merged many forms of linguistic activity—purely imaginative (fantasy, poetry, numbers); imaginative, cognitive, particularistic (history, common-sense wisdom); and imaginative, cognitive, and general (cosmology, early forms of empirical science). Such complex human constructs as religion often made use of all human arts, including expressive forms in its rituals, and linguistic structures in its epics and in its theories about gods and nature.

The construction of stories about the human past is a distinctive conceptual activity. Like all conceptual arts, it requires imagination. As a literary art, it not only involves conventional rules of grammar but has to meet the formal requirements of a story (theme, development). Since the telling of a story requires many inferences, historians as storytellers must observe conventional rules of logic. Since they try to tell true stories, they must adhere to accepted rules of evidence. And whenever history attains the level of a demanding art, it requires contributory nonstorytellers who, in highly specialized inquiries, rigorously attend to problems of inference and evidence. These inferential and evidential requirements decisively separate history from other forms of literature. Almost incidentally, the final narrative form, and much more crucially the necessary incorporation of particular, nonrecurring, qualitatively unique, humanly significant aspects of events as well as the narrowly abstract and general features, separate it from the generalizing sciences.

We shall give more detailed attention to these distinctions in later chapters.

The Human Dimension

All references to humanly significant aspects of the past implicate another part of our working definition—that a history is a story about the human past. Why restrict the unqualified word "history" to the human past? Before answering this question, one must respond to another question. What is the human past? Surely we now see many events, remote from and unknown to persons in the past, as vitally related to them, and so we typically and correctly incorporate the events into a history. Even though the people who lived at the time they occurred knew nothing about them, these events were very significant. (A rumor about my private life prevented me from obtaining an important position. The rumor never reached my ears, but my biographer may find out about it.) Thus the historian of humankind often has to use a criterion of relativity which his historical subjects could not have shared. And because of vast chains of possible relationships, almost any non-human event, such as an event in the solar system, may have some vital relationship to particular people—to their survival or their suffering or their fulfillment. Thus the human past, so expanded, seems to have no clear limits. It can, by one perspective or another, include almost any conceivable event.

In order to draw a distinction between the human past and the non-human past, between human history and natural history, one has to select one's criteria carefully, for much of the evidence is common to both. The historian of humankind selects only events as they relate to human purposes, whether the persons involved understood these relationships or not. Natural historians select from among some of the same events and may even on occasion combine them in a similar temporal order, but they select events for reasons other than their direct relationship to human purposes. That many of the events they investigate did relate to human purposes is completely incidental to natural historians, for such relationships are outside of their frame of reference and play no role in their selection or ordering of events. Moreover, an intrusion of human purposes and values as selective criteria would be distorting and confusing to them. Of course, they may well expect their natural histories to be of some use to someone, to serve some human purpose. Some conception of use must have guided them in their selection of the natural histories they wanted to write and even of the way they chose to construct them. Thus the creation of natural histories, as an example of purposeful and significant human endeavor, becomes a prime subject for the future historian of humankind.

In a sense, the use of the word "history" exclusively for stories about the human past is a mere semantic convention. But the convention seems to rest on an apprehension of a major difference between the subject (not the form) of human as compared to natural histories. If the difference is great—if in fact, as the more partisan proponents of human history have argued, the two are worlds apart, as qualitatively different as any two subjects could ever be—then the word "history" should be the exclusive property of only one of two quite different disciplines. When put this way, the question opens up a real can of worms and is an entrée into some of the most basic issues concerning knowledge about the human past. What is at stake is nothing less than human beings themselves and their assumed or asserted uniqueness. After all, humans talk, conceptualize, evaluate, enlist in causes. Rocks and plants and dogs do not. Therefore, one can argue, the human past is qualitatively different from the past of inanimate objects and even of non-conceptualizing (or mindless, unspiritual, amoral) animals. This is the case even if people are also animals and are constituted of chemical compounds and thus in some sense, under certain descriptions, are appropriate subjects for natural histories or (to implicate another issue) for general types of explanation. Unless humans have a special status as so different from animals in either substance or function that they must be seen as different in kind, then any special claim for the distinctiveness of human history evaporates. It becomes not only a mere subclass of natural history but, in the same sense as natural history, an early and more primitive form of science, a preface to more lawful, universal, timeless, and thus useful ways of dealing with phenomena.

Four interrelated issues help distinguish one empirical discipline from another: subject matter, methods of inquiry, the form taken by the acquired knowledge, and the possible uses of such knowledge. By defining a history as a story, we have already tried to establish a formal difference, since in no other empirical discipline is the telling of stories such an essential or defining goal. Not that stories about the past are thereby excluded from other disciplines; in several contexts, in all the physical and social sciences, stories may be appropriate, and in fact appear more frequently than they are often imagined to do, as anyone in such a field as geology will point out. But they do not define the normal form of such disciplines, and usually are incidental to efforts to construct general theories or models.

At first glance, it would seem that a history does not involve a distinctive subject matter. Social scientists, for example, also make humanity their subject. But most modern social scientists, as their label suggests, have tried to adopt the methods and the goals of the physical sciences. How well do these methods and goals fit the human subject? This is the question. In the nineteenth century, particularly in Germany, it was customary to distinguish the physical and cultural sciences. The distinction often drew upon metaphysical claims no longer in fashion, particularly forms of objective or absolute idealism that posited mind as the only, or highest, reality. But involved in the distinction was an assumption—that cultural phenomena are so basically, substantially different from physical and organic phenomena as to require quite different concepts and possibly even different research methods, leading to a very different type of knowledge, with different uses, than those of the physical sciences. This claim is challengeable at each point, but remains central to any effort to defend history as a distinctive discipline.

The broader claim is that humans differ in substance from even the higher animals. Such a claim usually rests on a metaphysical position, on either idealism (mind alone is real) or some form of dualism (mind and matter are both irreducible substances). A more modest claim is that humans, because they command language, are distinct from other animals in function, though not in substance. This position at least allows historians, who may not be up to heavy philosophical speculation, to defend their discipline and to distinguish it from the physical and social sciences. It also exempts them from the hazards that attend all attempts to fashion a conceptual ontology, to reduce to human terms the contours of ultimate reality. Not that it is easy to escape ontological assumptions. The ghosts of traditional ontologies—of reductionist idealisms and materialisms and unbridgeable dualisms—always lurk in the wings. And however many times the old mind-body problem is laid to rest in its now well-marked philosophic grave, it still lurks all too often in the interstices and ambiguities of our language, ever ready to exact its due in confusion and perplexity.

The metaphysical traps suggest that, for the historian at least, the most fruitful way of seeking out or vindicating human uniqueness is not in ontological excursions but in the humble analysis of distinctive modes of behavior. The following pages will involve such an analysis and offer at least a preliminary sketch of certain unique features present in human societies. These features will then serve, in subsequent chapters, to advance the possibility that historical thinking constitutes a distinctive discipline that deals in a distinctive way with distinctive phenomena and makes a distinctive contribution to human aspirations.

Language and Conceptualization

Humans talk, both aloud and to themselves. This is their most distinctive behavior. It is quite enough. In all of the universe that we have as yet experienced, only people have developed a symbolic language. Through human intervention and careful conditioning, the higher primates seem to be capable of learning a symbolic language and of passing at least some of it on to their offspring, but no other primates have yet developed a language of their own. A language both facilitates and conditions learning. Thus humans have either entirely or in large part replaced instincts by elaborate acquired patterns of behavior. In fact, such learned behavior includes learning to talk and to think, or to manipulate symbolic meanings. And almost all other human behavior is interactive with and conditioned by this linguistic behavior. One can use the word "culture," if a bit too loosely for some scientists, to designate not only a body of shared, evolving meanings, encoded in and expressed by the conventional symbols of a human society, but also for all aspects of nonlinguistic behavior displaying the influence of such symbolic meanings. In such a general sense, culture is as broad as humankind.

Linguistic tools are surely as important a component of human behavior as either inherited dispositions or the aspects of behavior learned without the direct or indirect aid of language. In fact, the most distinguishing human behavior—that for which we feel justified in using the term "human"—is culturally determined, for it is either the use of symbols or behavior closely related to symbols. Thus the use of symbolic language radically separates humans in function but not in structure from other organisms. By use of conventional symbols a person is able not only to think and communicate but to project alternatives of action and to unite with other people in common projects made possible by shared meanings. A person is thus part of a communicative universe, or a community, that displays some organic unity of its own, and that has, in its organization and reciprocal relationships, characteristics that are not the mere sum of its separable individual parts. In fact, if completely separated from a communicative universe, an individual never becomes human, for he or she cannot learn to talk.

Historians in constructing and perfecting their stories about the human past may, among other things, endlessly recount the developments of new meanings in a given human society. They may focus on the meanings themselves, or on broader and more encompassing bodies or systems of meanings (ideologies, religions, sciences), or on the behavior variously conditioned by culture, on habits, institutions, and stylistic forms. But no historian can grasp all facets of culture; a complete cultural history is impossible. Moreover, any historian is a participant in some human society, more than likely the one he writes about, and thus is always captive to some of its most basic assumptions. Yet, in a curious sense, the historian is also master of these assumptions. For any belief or cultural form, if it rises into the historian's awareness, may become a subject in a narrative.

When emerging humans learned to talk (it might be less confusing if the word "human" referred only to talking and thinking animals rather than to a certain biological species), they became veritable gods. They now had, at least potentially, a tremendous power to control events, and in their symbolic creations they also possessed new objects of great esthetic value. But like all new tools, these creations came at a price. Even the earliest symbols (expressed either as words or as gestures), loose and rich as they must have been, were still selective and abstract. No symbol could be as rich as the perceptual image that it stood for. A person usually encoded only the more arresting and striking features of an experience. Possibly the first symbols were like proper names and thus were least abstract. They stood for specific, individual things, not for classes of things. But symbols did not have great utility until they were even more narrowly selective, encoding only the more general features of an experience. Only then did they become class terms or concepts. Only then could a word or gesture warn of danger from bears rather than from "Bruin," only then could a broad community of meanings develop, stretching far beyond the particular objects encountered by individuals. But greater generality, apart from adding to usefulness, forced symbols ever further away from the richness of perception and toward quite abstract and narrow regularity and similarity. The elusive, vague, rich, discontinuous nuances of experience remained largely uncoded and uncommunicable.

To reduce the content of any experience to a concept, to give it a class name, it is to narrow it to the elements or features also present in other unique but somewhat similar experiences. Some persons, remarking this aspect of language, glorying in existential experience, have berated symbols and concepts. But in all ages overintellectualized persons have loved regularity and order and have glorified the generalizable features of experience. To them, what was common in various experiences was the archetypal form, the real essence, of the object; all particularizing features, those not subsumable under the essence, were accidental or scarcely real at all. It has been equally inviting to ontologize these essences (Platonism), to see reality as being composed of them or of a divine mind that thought them into being and sustained them. Here in the realm of essence was an ideal order, logically prior to any experiencable object and possibly the creative source of such objects. One could write much of Western history around this infatuation with concepts or essences or pure meanings and the inverse disillusionment with the existential richness of immediate perception. Finally, in the late twentieth century, the evaluation has shifted until essences have never been less loved.

By use of precise concepts, early humans were able to make all types of distinctions and either discover or create all types of order. They came to believe that one basic distinction was between themselves as conceptualizers and the experienced world, which, by concepts, they slowly transformed into a world of conventional and discrete objects. And indeed, self and world, ego and nonego, mind and matter were key concepts, as they still are. They were also sophisticated concepts, for they required inference as well as symbolic invention. Systematic concepts about a human as in some sense a mind or spirit and about a world as in some sense material or physical are twice removed from experience, first by the selective generality of class concepts and then by inferences made from certain conceptualized experiences to the idea of a unified self and some cohering world. These basic conceptions not only abetted religious and scientific mythmaking but supported such fundamental metaphysical positions as idealism and materialism. Soon humans had their pet pictures of reality—their luxuriant conceptual ontologies—and they too easily ignored the selective and abstractive character of all concepts.

By such a genetic perspective on concepts, it is rather simple to distinguish at least the major forms that human conceptualization could, and eventually would, take. But such formal distinctions rarely fit ordinary discourse. Almost no one fits into one conceptual niche. We are all, at least at times, metaphysicians, theologians, historians, scientists, and dreamers. We rarely consider how these roles interact. It was the classic Greeks who first distinguished professional scientists, philosophers, and historians in any clear, self-conscious way,. And with this first professionalization of thinking came both intellectual rigor and intellectual myopia. Before long the most prestigious conceptual systems, in whatever specialty, became coercive world views—distinctive ways of conceiving reality—and during their ascendancy they successfully camouflaged the selective bias that characterizes all such views. Today we are still influenced by a world view that we inherited, along with much else, from the very successful post-Renaissance physical sciences—a view that may now be passing from ascendancy.

Historians must ever emphasize what becomes so evident to them, that all conceptual systems are products of human art. People construct them, guided by some formal selective criteria, however much they also continuously tie them to perception and thus to some nonconceptual reality. Growing up in a world of concepts (a cultural environment), a child learns the symbols that, by the conventions of her society and its particular language, go with various experiences. She learns to talk and think. Her world is quickly an objectified one, for she transforms raw perception into various classes of things, into intellectual furniture. To a child this is all given, as are also the more complex conceptual systems that relate these various objects. But individuals continuously alter old meanings and develop new ones; people come to accept some of the new meanings, and all children then learn them. Our dictionaries grow in testimony to humankind's conceptual inventiveness, or in some cases by almost accidental accretion. It is almost impossible to think about a subject without adding some new nuance of meaning to our concept of it. Every vast intellectual system, such as a particular religion or science, develops by such gradual steps that it is impossible to distinguish all of its key moments or all of its key individuals. But any conceptual system is still a human contrivance. The necessary raw materials for it are always cultural. These cultural materials are a developed language, a body of conventional symbols, awaiting some new arrangement according to some formal criteria. And insofar as we intend a conceptual construct about the directly encountered world to be true, it must also refer to a second raw material—perception.

One type of conceptual activity—one that has been pregnant with suggestions for historians—occupies a special status. This is the attempt to use concepts to picture or explain reality itself, either fully or in its most essential features. This is the ontological enterprise. Here experiential piety serves well as an antidote to any form of metaphysical arrogance. If one accepts the directly experienced world, or the world of perception, as real, and recognizes the selective aspect and the human origin of all concepts, then no conceptual product can ever encompass reality. All conceptual structure is abstract; perception is concrete. There is absolutely no way to bridge the gap so as to make the two identical. Our inability to equate them does not prevent us from tying selected concepts to perception in a rigorous, unambiguous, and reliable way. To do so is to threaten neither objectivity nor existential truth, unless one limits these terms to some copy theory of knowledge.

To accept our inability to do other than selectively and partially conceptualize reality is not to give up all hope of knowledge. In fact, such humility may be a necessary prelude to defining knowledge. Valid knowing, in any area, is just a selective conceptualization of some experiences, even when we claim knowledge that extends beyond the focal experience that supports it. The nature of some hidden reality does not determine the cognitive validity of our chosen concepts; rather, this validity depends upon a relationship that we establish with our experience according to well-defined methods and that reliably leads to some desired human good. A person's inability to frame a completely adequate conceptual ontology in no wise threatens his ability to construct valid cognitive systems either in history or in the generalizing sciences. The lack of any determinable one-to-one relationship between reality and concept does not mean that all valid relationships are impossible between the two or that all concepts are thereby rendered totally subjective or even without any ontological status. In the poetic language of George Santayana, we can learn much about how the wind wisps without discovering its source or nature. To want more than this is to want something other than knowledge—intuitive insight, certainty, or some carbon copy of a reality totally apart from and in no wise shaped by human concepts.

The very conditions of knowing mean that all cognitive inventions have a human stamp upon them, just as do all other arts. Being products of human imagination, our propositions about experience are always less than the experience even when they are in some sense faithful to it. By brilliant conceptual invention, one may validly interrelate all of one's experiences, but in doing so one has to ignore almost all the striking features of each experience. To relate more and more, one must exclude and ignore more and more. Although in one sense a universal science is inconceivable, a universal science of some selected aspects of experience is possible, and is in fact a goal of the physical sciences. Limited as we are to the varied accounts we compose about reality, and as fruitful as experience is in providing new revelations, only a peculiar type of vanity could lead anyone to affirm a finished ontology, an exact model of human nature, a complete science, or a universal history.

The most basic distinctions in our word games is that between cognitive and noncognitive intent, between those verbal constructs that claim to be about matters of fact and those that do not. Much linguistic effort does not even lead to any sensible statements, for such statements require some formal criterion, some ordering, some art, whereas much of the time we are absorbed in spontaneous and unstructured thought, in reverie, dreams, or idle imagination. And in artful conceptualizing, the noncognitive probably exceeds the cognitive and often provides more satisfaction. Intent, not form, separates the cognitive and noncognitive. Imagination plays the same crucial role in both. And in this particular form of imagination, the image developed is one of ordered words, with an awareness of their meaning but a nearly complete suppression of the object images suggested by them. Humans share imagination with other animals. Dogs probably relish images as much as we do, although they do not have our ability to induce images by symbolic stimuli. Since a dog does not have a symbolic language and thus never has the direct experience of talking and thinking, it cannot possibly image patterns of words and, with them, related patterns of meaning. As soon as a child learns a language, she can do just this and open to her fanciful or creative imagination a world closed to any other animal.

In imagination we variously, purposefully, artfully associate words and the concepts they symbolize, forming various patterns. One pattern, and not another, may be thought to parallel or imitate a pattern that holds for objects open to direct experience. When we intend concepts to reveal something about such an existential realm, they are cognitive. Very often we do not assume the indicated pattern to be existent, but believe that by certain efforts we may make it so. Here the concepts designate possibilities. When we try to designate possible relationships that may come into existence, because of a present structure that makes them possible if we manipulate it in a certain way, we have an unverified scientific hypothesis that leads not so much to discovery as to creative induction. One can produce noncognitive conceptual constructs with great freedom. But the avoidance of evidential limitations does not excuse inferential sloppiness.

One form of conceptual invention is loose and only in part cognitive. In this case, the concepts are those that express the particular nuances of experience. Here the language of passion and emotion, ambiguous as it may be, alone seems adequate. The conceptual patterns have to do full justice to experience as a human possession and not to the object experienced. Then our conceptual imagination focuses on the distinguishing aspects of experience and thus on what always seems a peculiarly subjective perspective simply because of the admission of the whole range of qualitative uniqueness, of unrepeatable and unrecoverable feelings, and thus of the very aspects of an experience that are personal and often also of most value to us. Here, in a literary form of imagination, one pushes abstractions as far from conceptual art as is possible, and accepts only the necessary generality of concepts, of class names. Often in such rich construction, as in some poetry, the artist tries to wring from language even more than these concepts can ever bear; he does so by metaphoric suggestion and through expressive and rhythmic effects. He sees not the ambiguity of a word but its expressive poverty. He constructs a conceptual product that is a great deal more than conceptual, in concert with other nonlinguistic arts. From time to time we all resent the abstractness of any concept, even or especially one that tries to represent intense emotion. At these moments we stop talking and seek more direct, more overtly sensual forms of expression. We dance in our delight or roll in our torment.

In contrast to such expressive, concrete, and imaginative constructs are even more free but completely abstract creations. In themselves they are not cognitive at all, although they have cognitive uses. Mathematics is a prime example. Any perceptual moment may have features common to other such moments; some minimal similarity of this sort permits experience-relevant class names. But the ultimate in generality, in universal usefulness, is numerical identity. A tree and a unicorn are equivalent in one respect—their oneness. Quantitative relationships are abstract. They denote none of the perceptual qualities present in existential objects and often display an order never duplicated in events. With no direct homage to perception, one can work out all types of numerical and geometrical patterns and all variety of manipulative rules, using unambiguous but perceptually barren symbols. Insofar as one can discover in the perceived world any constant and widely distributed features, one can correlate them with such abstract imaginative systems. By such abstraction one can unify quite diverse objects and discover certain invariant relationships that hold between them. One can, in other words, bring the precision and inferential exactness of mathematical reasoning into a description of existence. If one is selective enough, one can rationalize the world. This is the work of the scientist.

In our cognitive creations some of these same distinctions apply. On one hand, one can seek the most detailed and qualitatively exact description of an object or event and thus encompass not only the aspects that are widely present and often repeated but also its most particular and unique features—those that make it differ from all other events. On the other hand, one can search out and describe the common features of experiences—those that are the most general and recurrent. If one seeks such generality, one will have to be quite selective. In a world of ordinary discourse, we almost always merge qualitative uniqueness and selective abstraction. Only with the modern sciences did some people, at certain times, reliably unify far reaches of experience and thus construct the broadest possible classifications of phenomena. But, except possibly for physics in its broadest definition, no existential science has a universal subject matter; in fact, all make use of descriptions that are less than fully general. Yet however restricted the universe of inquiry, the scientist usually looks for the most general, the most unifying, and the most instrumentally or predictively useful features of experience.

Thus far, the analysis might suggest that a history stands not only as a formal twin to literature but as a cognitive opposite to the products of the generalizing sciences. Such is not quite the case. Most stories about the human past, for the best of reasons, are conceptually one with ordinary discourse and occupy a treacherous middle ground between descriptions of concrete particulars and of abstract relationships. Being a true story, a history has a literary form that includes much that is particular, nongeneralizable. In fact, the distinctive content of history—the humanly significant, culturally conditional aspects of the past—never allows any time-neutral or open generalizations. But significant events do have many aspects that are recurrent, widely shared, and, within a limited time frame, regular and predictable. The criteria a historian selects may lead her to be most concerned with these recurrent and enduring aspects of the past, so that her focus is quite narrow and somewhat abstract. In fact, historians rarely join the novelist and poet in trying to communicate the full, qualitative richness of an event. If they did attempt to do so very often, they would dwell endlessly on a few events. In certain contexts, a historian may emphasize or even try to describe the human feelings, the pain and suffering, the joys and elation, that were part of or a result of certain past events. Some histories are quite evocative. A true account of the past that, by selective choice, focused primarily on feeling, even over a very short but thematically unified period of time, would be a history. But such a history would be narrowly selective, and it does not represent the norm for historians. The presentation of exact nuances of feeling, even when it is possible (rarely indeed), is at best only one permissible emphasis in historical construction.

Because a history is a story of the human past, it must at least relate to feeling and value. And here a parallel exists between a historian's use of quantity and quality. Only some historians choose to recount the history of a particular science or often remark the more general and repetitious features of humanly significant events, but all historians assume some regularity, some abstract structure in things, and at least continuities or enduring patterns in human communities. In an at least partially ordered world, the historian plots out certain sequences of gross events that involve many types of ordered relationships. These events make up a story, for they are related chronologically and reflect some pattern or unity. Against an assumed background of more or less generalizable order, which one may not look for, emphasize, or try to explain, the historian performs her art.

Likewise, a historian assumes feeling, or a qualitative dimension, in all the human events selected for a narrative. Each historical event must relate, even though at a distance, and by way of many causal connections, to some human experience, which is never qualitatively neutral. Pain and bliss, even as structure and law, are always involved. In fact, quality or value is a key criterion for locating the domain of the human as against the natural historian. This backdrop of qualitative experience does not mean that historians must dwell endlessly, or even at all, on the way something is experienced. They may, and most often do, recount what people have experienced and in what ways they have reacted to experience. Since structure and value are a part of human experience, both are implicit in history. In a selected context, either may become explicit in a historical narrative, but neither need be explicit and neither usually is. As a subject for historical treatment, generality, or law, is a subject only because of its relation to human value. The history of a science is the history of a human art, never a history of impersonal forces; a history of people seeking and finding ordered relationships, never the tracing out of such relationships.

Historians face few specific limits on their subject matter. The human past is immense. Within it the historian selects according to some purpose. He tells the particular story he wants to tell. His story will be an imaginative product, necessarily formed from concepts and sharing their abstractness and generality. But being about the human past, it cannot exclude all the qualitative and concrete aspects of human experience. In many contexts, the historian must report the gross, particular events that people suffer or effect. He cannot escape the world of common sense and of ordinary experience. His concepts must never be so abstract as to lose their contextual coloration, their ability to suggest the nuances that people often find most important. The historian must relinquish to generalizing social scientists any exclusive concern with narrowly selective, recurrent, quantitatively regular features of human experience. It is not the historian's primary task to isolate these more abstract aspects of human experience (he may indeed tell about the imaginative, value-pregnant, artful isolating of these abstractions by scientists), for in doing so he would not only be leaving the world of ordinary experience, he would also be turning away from a time-conditioned past. The more abstract conceptual objects of a physicist are barely open to experience, and then only after long inferential journeys and through elaborate technical aids to the senses. The world of electrons is not the world of most human experience but a very special conceptual rendition of such a world. Yet increasing numbers of people are physicists and do experience such abstractions; and these particular abstractions have enabled people to change the world, drastically altering all manner of ordinary human experiences. The development of modern physics is an excellent subject for historical treatment, for it is a fascinating as well as a vital story. It is a story resplendent with value, with joys and frustrations in the effort as well as in the results. But it is a story of a deliberate attempt by humans, for their own ends, to formulate very precise concepts that necessarily exclude all reference to value.

Time, Pastness, and Value

Other aspects of our definition of history raise many questions, but none more basic than the one suggested by the word "human." Even the "pastness" of events described in a historical account raises crucial questions about generality and causality. A historically significant event is not only unique (all events are) but time-conditioned. It has a significance because of its temporal context and, usually but not always, because of some of its particular and unique features. Thus two events quite similar in many respects but occurring at different times often have greatly disproportionate historical significance. Where an event fits into a series of events and how it relates to other events are important in a history (as they are in natural histories). To the historian seeking some causal relationship between two events separated in time, the most particular and exceptional aspects of an event may be crucial. A historian who wants to tell a particular story about the American War for Independence may not be concerned with the episodes that clearly fit some accepted definition of a revolution or that conform to known behavioral uniformities. The key events for her may be quite particular and exceptional. On the other hand, a social scientist trying to develop an analytical model of a revolution or looking for enduring uniformities in human behavior would discount these historically significant episodes. Social scientists look for aspects least conditioned by time and least burdened by momentary accidents and eccentricities. However much they use human and value-laden data from a past age, their selective interest may not allow time or value to play any role in their conceptual constructs. Theirs is then a nonhistorical discipline.

At the level of immediate, relatively indiscriminate perception and of the loose concepts by which we ordinarily objectify or name it, every object is almost overwhelmingly individual, unique, and wayward. The only obvious relationships are temporal and spatial, and these relationships are rooted in aspects of immediate experience and not in some type of analysis or inference. But aided by quite precise and discriminate concepts and guided by accepted generalizations, we can analytically dissect much of our gross experience and slice perceived objects into such uniform and general descriptive constituents as elements, cells, atoms, and electrons. As experienced entities (one can "see" an atom indirectly), they have the specificity—the temporal and spatial context—of any other perceived objects. Each atom is different from every other atom, at the very least in its spatial and temporal coordinates; it is always a potential character in some natural history.

Even the indirect perception of an atom is a value-laden human happening; it is an episode in some human history. In theory, one could trace the movements of an individual electron (granted some limit conditions set by quantum theory) and tell its history over a period of time. But as a highly analytical, barely experienceable entity, an electron usually has significance not in its individual peculiarity but in its formal,

abstract, invariant qualities and in the regularities of behavior it displays.
Even when an electron is crucial in an experiment, no one cares about
its remote past history or about its idiosyncratic career. Unlike humans,
it does not gain its identity from its past. It makes sense to speak of
the French Revolution of 1789 but not much sense to talk of the "Smith
electron of 1946." The word "revolution" denotes a connected series
of roughly unified, partly classifiable, but always contextually variable
events and cries out for contextual or historical qualification—for the
when and the where. This is true of most complex wholes, for as complexity increases, generality and behavioral order almost inevitably de-
crease. But one can view any conceptualized experience, any object, as
an individual surviving through time and thus as part of some history,
natural or human. And one can view even as complex an event as the
French Revolution as exemplifying some discrete class characteristics
or some behavioral patterns. Ultimately, purpose determines the way
we conceptualize each event.

Even granting that every thing has a temporal (or spatiotemporal)
context and that where value is also present there is subject matter for
human history, one can still view the telling of true stories about the
past as an inferior conceptual activity. It may be a secondary path to
understanding, and at best an interim substitute for general knowledge
or lawlike forms of explanation. Just as it is usually foolish to view an
electron historically, just as natural history is often a poor substitute
for theoretical synthesis, so it may be foolish and archaic to view humans
historically. Why not, in all cases, move away from history to a true
science of humanity, to an unambiguous human nature, and to the
universal and necessary laws that such a nature obeys? Such a challenge,
at the very least, requires a historian to justify his storytelling by pointing
to uses demonstrably not served, or not served so well, by the generalizing sciences. Can anyone fully comprehend cultural phenomena—
the distinctively human world of symbolic communication, of purposes,
ideals, and final causes—by general types of description and explanation? Or have we here a subject matter that permits only a genetic or
historical treatment, whatever one may mean by the term?

If one could fully describe all culturally conditioned events by their
more elemental and universal constituents and explain them by unchanging laws, then the temporal coordinates of human events would
seem to have little intellectual significance. In principle, if not in fact,
one could transform any history into empirically valid generalizations
and laws with no cognitive loss and much gain in precision and scope
of understanding. Most historians feel compelled to reject this view and
to present reasons for rejecting it. But they must not overextend their
claims. They do just that if they suggest that any event, even a culturally

conditioned event, ever fails, under some possible narrowed description, to conform to one or more empirically verifiable generalizations or precise probability statements. If one observes carefully, any perceived object has features that are also present in other objects, possibly in all others. If one looks for similarities, again guided by general knowledge, one can always find them at some level of abstractness. But if one wants, and without all the intellectual effort, one can also find the particular and the unique, and between these poles all manner of limited sameness and rare but not unique particulars. Not all experienced objects are electronlike (almost none are); not all involve inexpressible floodtides of feeling.

There remains an unremarked alternative. Could not a history be as lawlike and as predictive as a hypothesis in physics? Why not seek out in the past the invariant and universal laws that govern the human journey through time? In the clear light of such a universal history, one could dissipate the apparent particularity, the contextual relativity, of human events—not by a deliberate and selective abstraction, as in the present-day empirical sciences, but by making each and every particular event a necessary part of a grand scheme, governed by universal laws. Then our histories, now unfinished and partial, could yield to a universal view, one equally relevant to past and future. We could finish all our accounts and tell the story of the future. The past would then serve us well by revealing heretofore hidden patterns. Our former fumbling stories, so laboriously constructed, would then seem only prefatory and henceforth inferior to the vast design that now unfolds before our eyes. Is there such a schema awaiting discovery? Few working historians believe there is. Past speculative philosophers of history, from Isaiah to Hegel to Toynbee, have lacked both precision and persuasive evidence and have relied on both logical and methodological illusions. This, of course, does not prove that all future attempts have to fail. But the wide gulf between past aspirations and almost complete failures in execution, plus the diversity and the complexity of cultural phenomena, nourishes a profound doubt both that such an overarching pattern exists and that such a pattern, even if in some sense it were meaningful to say that it might exist, could ever be open to human understanding.

A more critical objection is that such grand schemes threaten or even doom prosaic historical inquiry as it is now practiced. Such schemes render pathetic the laborious work of historians, which now seems so very humble beside laws that determine all that has happened and all that will happen not only in appropriate areas of selective abstraction but everywhere. The specialized, empirical sciences pose no real threat to history. Often, in more direct and dramatic ways than history, they serve humanity. Their very abstractness, their selective bias, removes any possible conflict, for what they select in no wise threatens the temporal contextuality or the genetic determinants of all individual human events. Some speculative philosophies of history are quite imaginative; many represent great and challenging products of the human mind. But they, in all their formal completeness, and not our hesitant, unsure, ever partial, and quite selective stories about the human past, are speculative and in a sense subjective. No historian dare tell such grandiose but fictional stories. Our poetry has a more demanding discipline and can never break into such wanton and impious excesses.

CHAPTER 9
HISTORY AND THE GENERALIZING SCIENCES

IT is almost impossible to clarify the distinctive aspects of historical knowledge without making comparisons with knowledge claims in other empirical disciplines. Since the physical sciences play such an intellectually intimidating role in our present intellectual life, they often serve as a model for other disciplines. Even the social sciences have drawn upon them for form and methods. Thus to get a clear sense of what is unique about history, one has to note points of overlap and divergence from the generalizing sciences.

Long before humans developed any of their present sciences, they were already telling at least crude stories about the past. The devising of histories was thus a prescientific activity. But a storyteller must often make references to conventional conceptions of order and structure in nonhuman phenomena; otherwise, he can scarcely construct plausible narratives. In fact, historians have usually relied on accepted knowledge, in rare cases on the most recent and innovative understanding of the world. At times scientific knowledge has seemed threatening to the historian. General knowledge, when turned into fashionable ontologies, has seemed to deny a place for humanity, and has left no humanistic subject matter for the historian. Unfortunately, in overly defensive retaliation, historians have too often minimized the success of the generalizing sciences or have tried to elevate historical knowledge to an especially privileged position that it hardly deserves.

Contemporary conceptions of scientific inquiry scarcely predate the Renaissance. Only then were such scientists as Kepler and Galileo able successfully to tie nonteleological mathematical forms to experience. They used internally consistent, precise theories to relate formerly diverse phenomena. Descartes grasped the implications of such ordered and lawful relationships and gloried in a great, impersonal world machine. The fully lawful and determinate world of matter encompassed every phenomenon except mind, a noncorporeal and ghostly substance that usually inhabited the fully material bodies of people. Except for this ego-salvaging concession to humans, Descartes finally and completely deanthropomorphized the universe. Soon it was at least possible to suggest that persons also be deanthropomorphized (incongruous as this seems) and conceived as fully part of a single, physical continuum.

Newtonian mechanics made up a fully mature science of great scope and value. Surely here was the ideal explanatory system, an ideal to be sought in all empirical sciences, including those concerned with humans. David Hume tempered the early enthusiasm engendered by such a system. He stressed the empirical foundations of all scientific laws and challenged the legitimacy of any a priori certainty or ontological revelation imported into existential propositions. Kant, standing at the crossroads of so much of modern thought, accepted at least a part of Hume's skepticism. He also denied any metaphysical reach for the existential sciences. But to him the formal aspects of scientific explanation (primarily mathematics) were analytical elaborations of given constituents of mind. By emphasizing the rational side of science, he tried to minimize a skeptical empiricism. In a path followed by later analytical philosophers of science, he also clarified a logical model of explanation, a model that stressed universal and necessary laws.

Both historical knowledge and immediate experience provide antidotes for conceptual myopia. Looking back, we cannot miss the variety of and continuous changes in both metaphysical and empirical claims. Whether on structural or functional grounds, the generalizing sciences have fragmented into many diverse subject areas, each with a distinct body of concepts and theories. Each makes use of quite distinctive patterns of thought, as witness the quite different intellectual styles of physicists and experimental psychologists. Even the common methods shared by different sciences do not, as logical formalists too easily assume, rest on a priori grounds. Methods of inquiry and forms of explanation are cultural products; they developed through time and through successful use. Logicians can, belatedly, analyze them. In a different way, a close inspection of immediate experience discloses the selective nature of all generalizations with empirical relevance and the particular features of experience on which the various sciences focus. Since selective abstraction is clearly present in all cases, any explanatory system, however complete and determinate, still unifies only a fraction of the richness directly presented to us. No empirically validated explanatory theory can ever be all-inclusive, for each relates only the selectively described aspects of experience to which we adapt them. Even a unified field theory in physics would encompass only the quite narrowly abstract and restricted world of matter.

Since no empirical laws seem to govern the total historical process, historians cannot appeal to a tight, coherent conceptual system. They do not apply historical laws to individual cases or show how one can deduce individual historical events from such laws. Even at the less general level of class terms, it is hard to find any classifications that are peculiarly historical, with the possible exception of chronological periodizations. The concepts and the words used by historians are usually those of prescientific common sense. Thus historians discipline their constructs by esthetic criteria and by evidential requirements, but by no arbitrary and precise symbols (no jargon), by no clear, defined manipulative system, by no master explanatory concepts or models. This approach both invites sloppiness and encourages breadth. Historians often lack even simple precision in their terms or rudimentary inferential rigor in their causal statements; yet they almost never display the narrowed, experientially selective, overly abstracted outlook of many scientists, who too easily assume that reality is simply a further projection, in form and content, of their own conceptual tools. It is easy for a historian to assume that all cognitive propositions are rooted in experience and that one must never claim more for them than experience justifies. Conversant with many conceptual schemes, historians easily view experienced reality as multidimensional. They thus accommodate their thinking to diverse categorizations of phenomena.

Generalization and the Material Universe

For anyone who loves order and symmetry, the most intellectually satisfying knowledge, and in many contexts also the most useful, is the most general. Kant stressed universal and necessary laws and in so doing set the goal for any empirical science. But the very goal determines the conditions. Only those aspects of the perceived world that are ever present, that are ever similar in form, that always reveal invariant, precise relationships, can meet this standard. And it seems, although one can never be sure, that every experience does reveal this regularity, however narrow, selective, and abstract it is. A minimal but ever-present order seems to underlie all events. This pervasive order makes up what we call the material world. In broadest definition, physics is the science that encompasses it. The old word "matter," stripped of all its metaphysical meanings, stands for this structure.

Matter is seemingly present as one feature of every event, although one may not remark or notice it. Only selective interest leads us to look for it. In fact, the material aspect of most experience is so narrow, so small a part of the qualitatively rich whole, that centuries of discriminatory refinement in concepts had to pass before scientists could isolate and characterize matter, and of course the detailed characterization still goes on. But in an age when almost everyone is aware of even some of the details, it is well to remember that matter, basic concept that it is, remains a human invention. It is a characterization of certain irreducible aspects of experience; it is not an ultimate substance finally discovered (or being discovered) in all its ramifications.

Physicists have developed the most discriminating as well as the most general concepts yet attained by humans. But generality has come at the expense of complexity and concreteness. Many conceptualized physical objects are only remotely perceptual, and a few useful ones are not perceptual at all. This abstractness has served a good purpose. Only at this level, it seems, can one find firm, invariable relationships of great scope. Only at such an abstract level can we unify in rational, coordinate systems at least some aspect of every experience (for reasons given later, one need not assume that all physical systems make up one supersystem). And only by such conceptual systems can we develop almost unbelievable power over physical events. And power over the physical aspect of events also gives people some of the control they seek over the occurrence of qualities they value most highly.

A purely physical world, itself a selective conceptual construct, is a world without quality, without feeling, without purpose, and without history. It is a theoretical creation deliberately constructed to exclude everything distinctively human. In such a world, all material objects include simple constituents that observe invariant laws. Subject to the laws of motion, this world reflects continuous transformations but no agency. Given sufficient knowledge, one can trace chains of these transformations endlessly backward or forward, with neither direction having any physical significance. But to talk of such tracing—or even to talk of past and future and so to take a unidirectional perspective—is to leave the conceptualized world of matter and to revert to the godlike creature who invented it and who uses it to make such tracings into the past or to predict some future. By physical concepts alone, one can locate neither life nor cultural phenomena, for they involve other than simple physical aspects of experience and require different concepts. Of course, since physical processes are ever present, and in this sense universal, correlative physical attributes are always present in organic or cultural phenomena. But only by reversion to a form of conceptualization that discriminates life from nonlife, or symbolic mental functioning from organic and physical processes, can we ever isolate the exact physical correlates. When our vision is limited to the abstract, material skeleton, we have no clues as to whether any flesh covers any of the bones, much less any guide to what the flesh is like.

In the expressive as well as the conceptual arts, abstract forms are simple, universal, and difficult to come by. Their discrimination requires great mental discipline or a willingness to exclude those aspects of experience with the most immediate value to people, those nongeneralizable qualities that make one experience more enjoyable than another. Thus rigorous physical concepts, being abstract, are almost all latecomers. Humans only slowly abstracted them out of common-sense conceptions that always had some place for quality and for at least vague concepts of life and mind, to focus on the two other obvious, major characteristics of our experienced world.

A great fallacy can distort understanding of the generalizing sciences. Perhaps because of a rational bias, or an esthetic mystique that favors unifying scope over perceptual richness, one can view the more abstract and general concepts of the physical sciences not only as having more usefulness (a function of precision and explanatory scope) than the loose concepts of common sense but also as closer to reality. But if by "reality" one means that qualitatively varied world directly encountered in perception, then just the opposite is true. Physical concepts are further from experienced reality (and they surely have no power to create some new reality) and also encompass much less of reality than common-sense constructs. But they encompass the very aspects of experienced reality that are most subject to control—the regular, law-conforming, predictable aspects. Historians must use some of the loose, rich concepts of common sense. Because their work lacks precise concepts and predictive theories, it is no less real or even necessarily less valid or true than work in the generalizing sciences. It is, in fact, closer to experienced reality and can be true to broader dimensions of reality. To sacrifice generalizing reach is to open up the possibility of greater reach in other directions. The way we want to reach is, or should be, controlled by our purpose.

Historically, conceptions fitted to more complex, less general relationships, such as conceptions of mind and life, came before precise physical concepts. In fact, early humans conceived all reality as mindlike, as willful and whimsical. But as we try to decipher an evolutionary pattern of development on our earth, we find that simple physical relationships came first, then organisms, and only belatedly culture, or the type of interpersonal unity made possible by shared meanings. Culture is thus a belated and rare phenomenon, for it exists in only a minuscule portion of the universe that we have so carefully objectified in our physical sciences.

One can rigorously define either life or mind, however primitive their origins as concepts, although in their complexity they present great hazards to generalization. It is difficult to find empirical justification for any enduring and universal structure of a distinctively organic or mental type. At least, no generality even in the organic world can have the scope of physical laws, for organic material is quite limited. Without doubt, organic phenomena, such as adaptation, reproduction, and nutrition, allow rigorous classification and organization. Yet rarely in the biological sciences does anyone try to isolate or maintain pure biological theories; instead, as in contemporary genetics, scientists work out composites of biological and physical theory. Thenceforth biological phenomena, discoverable only within the conceptual horizons of biology, are always open to purely physical analysis. In many cases today (if not in most), about the only role played by biological concepts is the isolation of phenomena for physical investigation. The end products of biophysical or biochemical inquiry are physical uniformities correlative to biological universes and not properly biological objects at all. Yet without a biological conceptual perspective, one could never isolate such physical problems. Reproduction is not simply a chemical or physical process. Despite some recent, quite complex speculation by physicists, no one has successfully reduced such biological concepts to physical terms without some loss of meaning.

Mind and Culture

For the historian, the all-important characteristic of experience is mind, the concept that best stands for functional traits that people do not share with other animals. The human past is always in part the past of people as creatures of culture, as developers and users of symbolic meanings, as products of existing cultural forms. Only their possession and use of such symbols allows people to be historically as well as organically and physically conditioned. This emphasis on culture, or on mind as a transpersonal and enduring body of meanings, does not require an idealistic form of reductionism. Mind, as so defined, is only a fit characterization of some aspects of experienced reality. Such a position is fully consistent with some forms of naturalism.

Although cultural phenomena lend themselves to analysis, classification, and comparison, it is difficult to conceive of any empirically valid, transcultural generalizations about humans as products of culture. If the word "generalization" denotes not only universality (propositions of the form "all X is Y") but also temporal and spatial openness ("always, everywhere, all X is Y"), then cultural phenomena can never be the proper subject of general statements. But this does not preclude intracultural patterns or norms or rules that endure over long periods of time and allow valid, reliably predictive, though time-limited judgments

("In the modern era, all members of the tribe have participated in the initiation ritual"). Such judgments, at the risk of linguistic confusion, may be called closed generalizations, for they require temporal or spatial qualifications. One may assert such closed generalizations about the most restricted universes, including ones that encompass only one individual and for only a brief period of time. Possibly the organic and behavioral sciences are also limited to time-conditioned and thus closed generalizations, closely tied as they often are to correlative physical structures. This would suggest that all empirically valid generalizations are physical statements.

Even the acceptance of valid generalizations in the physical sciences raises some complex issues. Physical scientists do generalize. Their statements have this formal property. But the form of their statements is not necessarily the form of things. Thus the structure in physical concepts is only a structure in the language used. To assert more than this is to make an ontological leap of some sort. By an analysis of concepts, the logician can enjoy a nice, agnostic retreat; she need affirm nothing about reality. But neither does the scientist. Practically, the concepts and laws of the physicist serve people very well. And even if metaphysically unanchored, these generalizations do unify experienced phenomena and enable people to predict and control events. They work.

With all the perils of generalization even in the physical sciences, it is as much a relief as a threat to find that cultural phenomena do not lend themselves to such general statements. Open generalizations about humankind as a cultural entity (people assert them all the time) never seem to stand up to rigorous tests. In other words, and despite all the possible (and usually exaggerated) methodological implications of quantum theory, one can vindicate general statements of the strongest type in physics (they work) but not in any cultural study. Of course, as one must continually stress, matter is omnipresent, and thus cultural phenomena always parallel generalizable physical events, including physiological events.

Many historians and social scientists have been unhappy with these conclusions and have sought some general structure or framework present in all cultural phenomena. Ernst Cassirer sought a science of symbolic forms to provide the same backdrop to cultural studies that Kant's transcendental esthetic (or mathematics) provided for the physical sciences. Claude Lévi-Strauss sought necessary patterns or structures in all languages, and thus in social relationships. Linguistic and semantic inquiry may reveal some formal boundaries for all symbolic communication and thus provide a transcultural perspective on culture. So far, such efforts have not been unambiguously successful; they have produced only the most vague formal schemes. Even a successful analysis of the necessary formal properties of language, and thus of all cultures, would only set certain broad limits within which one could look for cultural phenomena. It would be a science of possibilities comparable to mathematics and not to physics. Such a formal system would in no wise determine any specific cultural patterns or serve as a structure of laws from which one could deduce any specific cultural phenomenon. Even given such a formal backdrop, one would still have to seek the particular ideals and purposes that give some unity and distinctive character to a given society. One cannot deduce them from or transform them into any universal order. All attempts to do so involve an unnoticed move from focal and authentic cultural phenomena to some organic or physical correlates, a procedure often quite useful but one that we must recognize for what it is.

Then how does one explain or understand human phenomena? The question requires great precision in the use of such words as "explain." If to explain is to subsume distinctively human phenomena under some deterministic structure, under general laws, then humans, as creatures of culture, are beyond explanation. One simply cannot understand them in some of the ways we understand physical objects. And this is not even remarkable, since any physical object is a conceptual product, as are all the laws by which we put it in its correct place. But a person is not just a product of conceptualizing (although people do continuously define themselves and try to put themselves in some correct place); he is also a conceptualizer. Is it really surprising to suggest that, even though a person can grab his own tail in his conceptual teeth and endlessly gnaw away at it, he really will never quite succeed in swallowing himself? Could he consummate this awesome task, he would kill himself. Reduced to a physical object, firmly and fixedly in its place, a person would be only a thing and no longer human at all, for he would no longer be conceptualizer, master of symbols, creator of words, ever open to new definitions as he creates new cultural forms.

But the fact that humans, as products and creators of culture, do not fit within any system of open generalizations does not preclude such an explanation of all regularities of physique and behavior that they exemplify. All such regularities are correlates of culture, for they reflect simpler characteristics of experience than mind. But they are indeed correlates, and this we must not forget or deny. We isolate them by reference to culture; but henceforth we can, and in fact must, investigate them in accordance with the conditions set by physical and behavioral concepts. But no such delimited inquiry is possible without some conception of such a distinguishable phenomenon as thought.

Reductionism

How can one relate conceptually to (we will temporarily dispense with such loaded words as "explain") the world of culture? In an age when the generalizing sciences are in the ascendant, the normal response is to seek some way of generalizing about people—to find their nature and the laws of behavior such a nature obeys (an excellent tactic for all the subhuman attributes of *Homo sapiens*, none of which we lose by learning to talk). But this approach stops short at the cultural threshold, where one has to be satisfied with comparison, description, or time-limited, never fully determinant norms and rules. One can best describe a given society (and by implication the individuals who share its meanings, beliefs, or culturally conditioned habits) by the purposes, the ideal ends, and the established valuations that give it some distinctive unity. But one who offers such comparison and description, if pressed for some larger scale on which to view a society, has to turn in one direction—to history—and not to the generalizing sciences. The only way to clear up any puzzlement about people, to determine why they believe and value the way they do, and not as small chunks of the physical world, is to produce a genetic perspective, to tell a story about the past. What a person has been, rather than some coercive structure of laws, conditions what he is and what he will be insofar as he is a participant in culture. Thus history, as a discipline, is uniquely tied to the rarest phenomenon in our experienced world—to mind or culture as a body of ever-expanding symbolic meanings. Telling a story of the human past offers the most comprehensive conceptual tool we have for understanding people as products of culture. This remains so despite the fact that historical knowledge is not fully general, not rigorously predictive, and does not have the same type of utility as general knowledge.

One can still be dissatisfied and seek a more determinate and universal knowledge of humans. If one does so, however, one has to leave the highly abstractive, generalizing sciences, whose reach is simply not sufficient for the problem. Too often, people then turn to some intuitive insight or revelation not given to ordinary people. Even in theory, such determinate knowledge of humankind is suspect; being more than a temporally limited, historically conditioned characterization, it violates what is distinctive of humans—conceptual fertility and unending cultural elaboration guided by ideals or final causes. Those who want determinate knowledge of people are really, in some way, dissatisfied with humanity. Using terms drawn from a literary and nonscientific psychology, they reflect a type a cultural death wish. They want to be exempt from history.

Such a reductionist outlook is quite prevalent today. Some students have great difficulty grasping a multicharactered perceptual world and therefore the possibility of quite varied conceptual systems. Note the following example: A woman raises her hand in a gesture of greeting. By the gesture she roughly communicates the following verbal message: "Hello, I am very glad to see you." Surely here the gesture has a wealth of symbolic content; it is clearly a cultural phenomenon. It is not merely a signal that triggers some instinctive learned response, although it could also be that and a psychologist might so explain it. In fact, the arm movement exemplifies not only aspects of modern learning theory but quite determinate physical laws. But physical laws explain only the mechanical motions, isolated from the vast world of such motions only by an organic concept: arm. Such mechanical laws do not explain the gesture, with its symbolic content, or even arm movements as a form of organic or animal behavior. Likewise, theories about behavioral conditioning, which may account for the animal behavior, the perhaps habitual arm-raising when a certain positive reinforcement is present (the glimpse of a friend), are also only correlative to the gesture, for they do not explain the symbolic content that turns a signal, of a type common to many animals, into a gesture. In fact, the symbolic content, being subtle, expressive, qualitatively rich, and particularistic (in a slightly altered cultural environment, the gesture might express extreme distaste), does not belong in any true, highly general science of behavior.

Both the physical and psychological explanations may be true. They may explain muscular tensions or habitual arm motions in accordance with physical and psychological laws. But how move from either explanation to the fact of a gesture? The only way to answer the question— Why the gesture? Why did the arm movement mean what it did?—is to show how such an arm movement developed such a symbolic meaning in a given society—to turn to history or anthropology. And even then one can never show why such a cultural form had to develop just as it did. In fact, many quite similar arm motions, even in the same society, are not gestures (symbolic acts). Some may be involuntarily flexing of muscles; some, well-conditioned responses to nonsymbolic stimuli. The only way to isolate arm motions that are truly gestures is to establish on other than physical grounds what is quite clearly a gesture. This task requires cultural knowledge. The operative physical laws explain why the arm rose and, given a gesture, they supply a complete physical correlate of it. In some cases, puzzlement about a gesture, and what we want to know about it, may be entirely at such a correlative level. Then we might, with some imprecision, assume that we explain the gesture by the physical uniformities present in it. Note that one can always move from the level of broader, more complex relationships (from mind and life) to simpler, more universal relationships (matter). But one cannot go in the other direction. One cannot locate motions that constitute gestures within a purely physical frame of reference. This is only to demonstrate that cultural knowledge is not an elliptical form of physical knowledge awaiting reduction to physical terms.

This position does not necessitate or even necessarily imply some notion of free will or vitalism. In fact, the classic battle between free will and determinism, like that between body and mind, is only another example of the operationally meaningless (but experientially vital) antinomies that ever develop from ontologizing selective, conceptualized bits of experience. Many hard determinists (there are at least three levels of determinism), in their intellectualistic myopia, try to compress all experience in the narrow, mechanical mode of an often outdated physics. The traditional advocates of free will, impressed by the expressive and qualitative aspects of experience, seek a similar impossibility—a modicum of agency, a rare phenomenon exempt from any law or even any cause, and thus under the control of either pure chance or some strangely demonic, esoteric entity called, by an atavistic psychology, a free will.

Some types of determinism are quite consistent with choice, responsibility, and a kind of freedom. Such determinism does not threaten cultural phenomena and true final causes. And one does not have to view such causes as unscientific renditions of transformative laws, which a rigorous materialistic reductionism would require. Although deanthropomorphizing was a sine qua non for the development of the generalizing sciences, it cannot be a requirement in the nongeneralizable world of culture. Anthropomorphic concepts are necessary when one talks about humanity, but we cannot then conclude that even the social sciences should return to Greek essences. Just the opposite. But people still talk in terms of such essences; in all their teleological glory they defy exclusion from the human temple.

From a material perspective, culture is additive. The gesture could or could not be present in the arm movement. Without any distortion or exemptive escape from the conceptualized world of the physicist, any conceivable elaboration of cultural phenomena is possible (of course the concepts of the physicist are one such phenomenon). The physical correlates ever present in a cultural event in no wise determine the event. The world of meaning, here and there complexly and partially relating large numbers of people, does not require for its existence some loopholes in the physical world, some random events, some miraculous spontaneity.

One difficulty remains, and is at the heart of the old mind-body problem. The world of culture, it seems, has directive power over the physical world, not only in the sense that it gave birth to the very physical concepts concerned but in the sense that human choice, made possible by teleologically pregnant symbols, seems to guide physical processes. Few historians, or few other people, ever doubt some efficacy in choice, even when they view choices as necessary expressions of some ultimate metaphysical design, whether the laws of a god or of some universal history. But even if there were no physical efficacy in choice and thus in cultural phenomena (and here there are extremely subtle issues involving the tie between choice, conceived phenomenologically, and the ever-present physical correlates of choice, viewed in a stark behavioral perspective), culture could still exist in (or on) a physical world. But then final causes would operate not in redirecting natural energies but only in reshaping human affections, in changing tastes; the world of culture would be a strangely aloof, detached world, despite its inescapable ties to biological and physical correlates.

Thus, if final causes do somehow govern physical objects (and thus culture is effective rather than merely affective), such causes cannot be fully correlative with a certain physical construct, that of one world machine in which all parts are related to all others according to completely determining laws. Final causes are quite consistent with an all-pervasive materiality and with unexceptional physical laws of a transformative type. But they conflict with a single, all-pervasive structure. Of course, a phenomenological insistence on the selective aspects of physical laws ensures only a partial, if universal, order. But here the universality, even though selective, cannot be determinate in any absolute sense. Only interactive, intramurally determinate transformative series are consistent with human choice, not one total, coimplicative whole. Now, as a matter of fact, the machine metaphor, and with it a form of hard determinism, is always speculative, for no one can trace more than limited systems. And such are the subtleties in modern physics that neither the machine nor classic concepts of law are very useful even for explaining limited physical universes; in quantum mechanics, they can be distorting and irrelevant. Except for this one qualification on a correlative view of culture and matter, the two worlds, representing conceptualizations of two quite different characteristics of our experience, make no compromising demands of any sort upon each other.

The "Science" of Mind

The example of the gesture helps differentiate the logical form taken by all general explanation from the genetic approach so congenial to historians. But the references to psychology suggest one further qualification. Is not psychology the science of mind? Can we not find here generalizations proper to a person as a thinker, as a product of culture? Assuredly not. No scientific psychology, distinguished from loose speculative psychology, can in any sense be a science of mind. No legitimate, empirically verifiable generalizations can include "mind." Such culturally linked concepts as mind do not fit a psychology that would attain the status of a generalizing science, with rigorous, predictive knowledge. But behavioral psychologists establish their limited universes of inquiry by necessary reference to nonpsychological concepts determined by cultural phenomena, such as the common-sense word "mind." Such ordinary words as "mind," "human," and "social" imply culture and lose almost all their meaning when they are made to fit some generalizable conceptual system. They are descriptive only in qualitative contexts. But except for their role in isolating a subject matter, one cannot tie any truly scientific (generalizable) psychology to the historically conditioned world of culture. Thus valid psychological generalizations that are related to culture (usually at the level of animal behavior) reach far beyond the most distinctive forms of behavior exhibited by humans.

The social sciences, insofar as they reflect either physical or behavioral laws or uniformities that encompass acculturated humankind, are also correlative to culture. They are narrowed branches of physical science (climate correlates with aspects of culture) or, more often, of a general behavioral science or psychology. But they too must establish their narrowed universes of inquiry by use of cultural and value-laden concepts, even though they may try to exclude any such concepts from their generalizations. If they do not exclude them, they can never create any clear, verifiable generalizations at all. Of course, much of the work done in disciplines now modishly defined as "social sciences" is not scientific at all, in the sense that social scientists aspire to rigorous, open generalizations. Some of their work is clearly intracultural and primarily comparative and descriptive, but they use statistical tools and explicative models that are much more rigorous and revealing than simple reportage. Many so-called social scientists still seek time-conditioned, culturally relative, but enduring regularities in human behavior (closed generalizations) and use them for predictive purposes. These regularities are similar to the enduring cultural patterns so often remarked by historians. If such patterns are the goal, then a social scientist should acknowledge a historical backdrop for their work rather than a system of "laws." Finally, some moral philosophers still exist. They continue to work out ideal constructs and often try to alter the culture by modifying taste and purpose rather than by creating predictive or manipulative tools.

All of this is not to argue that some people, and possibly even some self-professed psychologists and social scientists, do not try to generalize about acculturated humanity. Clearly, some psychologists have worked out what they profess to be the laws of mind or psyche. But such attempts have either been plagued by imprecision and nonverifiable speculation or have been confused and unremarked misuses of related generalizations about the workings of the brain or about uniformities in animal behavior. Therapists of various schools of depth psychology, beginning with Freud's, have attempted to isolate the general structure of the psyche, importing at least the form of physical concepts into these murky waters. But their terms have been elusive, their affirmed structures too imprecise and too speculative for unambiguous testing, and their concepts too metaphorical, too literary, and too phenomenological for other than loose clinical or suggestive speculative uses. Thus any rigorous psychological science will be physiological or behavioral in subject matter. In a similar way, professed social scientists have at times combined history, related generalizations of a physical or behavioral type, and loose assertions about human nature which are always culturally conditioned, even if they do not recognize them as such. Many of the generalizations of the nineteenth-century economists were of this sort. But note that these generalizations about human nature or even about the psyche are formally similar to those in the physical sciences. One can easily assert such generalizations; one cannot so easily test them, even if in rare cases they are precise enough for testing.

Although historians tell the story of the human past, their subject matter is not limited to the narrow world of mind or culture. It is, indeed, restricted to culturally related objects—to those things that have had some significance, some value, to humans in a given cultural context. But anything may be or may become affected with value. At a given time, any river or mountain may be a boon or an obstacle to people and figure prominently in a history of human progress. Almost any generalizable characteristic of the experienced world can be of human significance. In any case, it may enable people to develop some extremely useful science. And the generalizable structure that, by our most rigorous methods of inquiry, seems to be present in our world also provides an ordered backdrop against which one can relate human events.

A historian seeks no open generalizations, simply because none are available within his special subject matter. And although a historian is not concerned with the verification of such generalizations, he is very much concerned with their verity, for he makes use of such generalizations all of the time. He consumes scientific products, not in the usual manner of putting them to work in order to control events, but as aids to his storytelling or his causal analysis. He may use the latest hypothesis about hurricanes to make clear some otherwise inexplicable complex of weather that was a determining condition in a major historical event.

Perhaps some historians still dream about some elusive class of phenomena which is both distinctively historical and fully generalizable, and which only the historian has a license to deal with. But this dream is empty unless some fully determinate laws govern the development of societies and the course of human history. The historian may attend to any conceivable class of phenomena, so long as it relates to a cultural context. But these phenomena, apart from the cultural and valuative context, are never in any distinctive sense historical. They are always potential subject matter for one or another of the generalizing sciences.

The Covering-Law Model

These distinctions are directly related to the most prolonged and complex recent controversy concerning history. It began in 1942 with an article in which Carl G. Hempel stressed the applicability of a well-developed model of scientific explanation to history. By Hempel's model, one can explain a single event in a history or anywhere else only when one can deduce its occurrence from one or more empirically verified laws, joined with certain prior conditions. Only by showing how an event, in one or more of its possible descriptions, exemplifies one or more universal laws can one show why it had to occur. Anything less, such as showing some necessary conditions for its occurrence, does not constitute a satisfactory or full explanation. This model, in all of its detailed logical development and as supplemented by a less satisfactory but often required probability model, has not been fully accepted by all philosophers of science. Its detailed development was one of the most complex and critical issues for philosophers of science in the World War II period. However, the issue for the historian is not the exact logical adequacy of any such model but the relationship of such scientific explanation to the historian's task.

When Hempel first published his article, he in effect issued a positivist manifesto against certain lingering forms of idealism and historicism. Even as he tried to demolish any idea of a special type of historical explanation, other logicians tried to overturn the related idea that historians have a distinctive method of inquiry or a unique road to truth. Given the entrenched strength of idealistic motifs in European historiography, the devastating arguments against some of its more extreme positions seemed in order. In retrospect, Hempel's 1942 article seems both truistic and dated.

Surely, if one wants to explain why something had to happen, one must try to demonstrate that it exemplifies one or more empirical laws. But two questions are always in order. Can one so "explain" a particular event? Even more important, in what contexts does one generally want so to "explain" it? But if one does attempt such a task, clearly the historian is in no sense exempt from the formal requirements of an adequate explanation. Much of the earlier analysis has indicated that cultural phenomena, as such, are not open to such explanation, because they do not permit valid generalizations of the strongest type. Yet in accounting for human action historians often appeal to a much looser form of order, to the norms and rules that people learn in a society and that most people follow. At best, these norms allow only highly probable predictions. But every culturally conditioned phenomenon has its organic and physical correlates. One may be able to explain some of them by an appeal to complete regularity. To repeat, one cannot show why a gesture had to occur, but in principle at least one can show why the arm had to move.

The problem for the historian is not a logical one but a functional one. When should a historian incorporate an accepted scientific generalization or a probability equation into a historical narrative or into more restricted causal analysis? Obviously, one should do so when the physical or behavioral aspects of a historical event or series of events seem implausible or mysterious according to the conventional wisdom but quite clear by a better scientific understanding. Historians, at points of puzzlement or incredibility, work a skein of overt or implied general knowledge into their stories. But in most cases the events recorded by historians do not require such explanation. Both the historian and her audience assume an underlying organic and physical order. They assume the "explainability" of the physical and behavioral aspects of events. Any historian who spent pages detailing the mechanical equations of an arm movement would rightly be dismissed as a fool.

A special form of myopia can afflict even the more discriminating philosophers of science, particularly if they are most conversant with the physical sciences. Here Hempel was not immune. If one refuses to deal seriously with the problem of culture, and if one fails to distinguish correlate forms of conceptualization, one almost inevitably falls into a vicious methodological reductionism (or even by implication an ontological reductionism). Such a reductionist assumes that one can explain all phenomena, in principle if not in fact, by subsuming them under covering laws. This position permits little respect for the nonlawlike causal relationships, the social norms and customs, that historians so often appeal to. Historical narration then is a mere sketch, a way of ordering events that still await proper "explanation." Historical inquiry, if directed only toward such narratives, has value and intellectual stature only as it provides either subject matter or data for the true scientist. (I will analyze these issues in more detail in Chapter 10.)

Methodological reductionism often feeds on a simple failure to distinguish between formal and substantive issues. Obviously, since one can make assertions in the form of general laws about any phenomena, one can make them about humans as cultural products. In loose ways, all of us make such assertions all the time. Here the problem is not formal but cognitive. Can we verify our assertions? If not, they remain suspect. Even if some such assertions are verifiable in principle, they must have explanatory scope to be of much practical use. Under some description, one can fit any event to some general statement, but often for no good reason except, possibly, for the purpose of logical analysis. "John Jones raised his hand in greeting to a young lady" can seemingly be made the deductive consequence of some general law and thus of some asserted social structure. One could assert that "all normal Americans greet ladies by raising their hands." Such a statement may be both revealing and useful, but as a valid generalization or law it is suspect on several counts.

The word "normal" is vague and imprecise. What specific class of phenomena, what specific social structure, does it refer to? More critical from the standpoint of culture and history, unless such an asserted law governing John's behavior is qualified by a reference to time, it either may be demonstrably false (colonial Americans never used such a greeting) or may become false in the near future. But if it is limited in time, it ceases to be a proper or open generalization and loses its predictive value in any rigorous sense. It may or may not apply tomorrow, for it depends not on universal physical laws or on universal behavioral patterns but on a changing cultural pattern. Being circumscribed by time, it cannot show the necessity, or even the specific probability, of any gesture at any time in the future. Of course, any generalization may not hold in the future. But in the context of recognized cultural change, one must qualify all such statements by reference to time, and must understand them in a historical context. Our experience, at least, does not suggest such changes in physical behavior. This is why, with great confidence, we explain physical phenomena by general, nonhistorical laws.

The Uses of Scientific Generalizations

Both in their numerous contacts with the generalizing sciences and in their frequent references to general knowledge, historians gain much more than helpful devices for navigating serious gaps in their narrative. Often they learn from scientists how to use words with greater precision and the value of quantitative exactitude. In other cases, subtle relationships that historians may have missed become visible in the light of some hypothesis or model. In other words, the best scientific knowledge variously fixes historians' attention and improves their vision. But the relationship should not be overemphasized. In topically and chronologically narrowed histories and in much contributory causal or structural analysis, the historians may develop a very close tie to a peculiarly relevant science. In broad, sweeping narratives the tie may scarcely exist at all, since the historian will then most likely rely on the conventional wisdom on most issues.

Always the historian's subject matter is broader than the generalizable aspects of it. Hence it includes much that one cannot relate to any science. Even if one could, by stipulation, make a class term such as "revolution" completely rigorous and exact and could formulate some determinant behavioral laws that would hold true for all revolutions (whether any ever occurs is beside the point), the historian would still write the history of the American Revolution very much as before. He would still look to the distinctive, nongeneralizable features that made it an American event and that made it of particular significance to Americans. If the rigorous term became accepted and was, as it would almost inevitably be, too restrictive for his subject, he would blandly write his history of "the American War for Independence." If the term, despite the monumental odds against it, did fit, then he might economize a bit in his description, allowing the class term to suggest to his audience many of the now analytically transparent details.

Generalizations, whether rigorously scientific (a methodological as well as a formal criterion) or loosely commonsensical, present certain problems to historians. Since historians use and endlessly implicate borrowed or commonly accepted generalizations, their first problem, theoretically simple but practically difficult, is to determine which generalizations to use. It is easy to assert that historians should use only the best ones, those that are the most rigorous and most scrupulously verified. But this demand requires of most historians, in most areas, much greater critical ability in many specialized sciences than they can ever hope to gain. Thus all too often the historian falls into a superficial modishness, into an infatuation with new, popularized, or striking theories, particularly in such scientific borderlands as clinical psychology, economics, and sociology. Our recent historical literature is full of metaphorical Freudianisms, loose psychological labels, and imprecise class and status concepts. Rather than offering naïveté advertised as sophistication, the historian might better remain loyal to common-sense wisdom, parochial and ambiguous as it usually is. Even within these conceptual boundaries, she may tell very suggestive and true stories. Most great works of history have been of such a type. And at least one can meet certain narrative demands easily at the level of conventional understanding. Whenever historians introduce new, unassimilated scientific hypotheses, they must at least spend some time explaining them and may have to sacrifice some of the esthetic unity that they crave for their story.

Historians easily relate to the scientist as students and consumers, but only with great difficulty as critics. They may, from a broader perspective, condemn the myopia of a specialized scientist but they can scarcely make critical judgments about the merit of highly specialized work. Yet even if this is not their intent, historians play a crucial role in disseminating scientific knowledge or, when they remain blind to it, in preventing its wide, popular acceptance. Here they join with journalists and novelists. Ideally, a historian should be well trained at least in the common methodology of the generalizing sciences, be able to detect overt frauds or fuzzy and misleading popularizations, and be cautious in the use of the specific generalizations that allow her to find new, significant meaning in past events, even if such caution requires her to explain them at great length.

Generalizations Produced by Historians

A second problem concerns the historian not as a consumer of generalizations but as a producer of them. Historians quite infrequently but almost without exception do make general assertions of their own invention, or at least assertions that do not fit into any of the developed, generalizing sciences. These general statements are often loose and perhaps similar to ones made by nonprofessionals; in many cases, they fulfill a rhetorical rather than a cognitive function. Historians are rarely aware of making such generalizations. What can be said about them?

First, the greatest peril lies in generalizing about the whole course of human history. Universal historians who try to do so are in a class by themselves. Most historians content themselves with more limited generalizations. Save for a tendency to looseness, these generalizations are of the same type as those developed by scientists. Many seem to be allegations about a purported human nature. But here "human" variously stands for physical regularities, behavioral patterns, and assumed invariant cultural forms. The first two are legitimate, but the historian rarely is competent to offer worthy generalization about either; the last is illegitimate. As a functional distinction, one might classify such generalizing as a nonhistorical activity occasionally and often incidentally indulged in by historians in the manner of amateur scientists. They can tell true stories about the human past without recourse to new, ad hoc generalizations, and probably tell them better. Obviously a historian who casually asserts some new generalization will rarely attend to it to the extent of clarifying it analytically and indicating the kind of evidence necessary to prove it, much less go to the trouble of seeking inductive support for it. If historians were classed as scientists on the basis of their typical generalizations, they would surely be considered among the world's worst. If a historian falls in love with some new generalization and spends his time trying to verify it, he becomes a practicing and possibly able scientist; certainly one individual may be both historian and scientist. In fact, such is the relaxed maturity of history as a professional discipline that few historians are methodological puritans. Most historians quite unselfconsciously do other things than tell or perfect true stories. But more often than not this extradisciplinary fun takes the form of moral preachments, not generalizations.

A historian's generalization typically takes the form "Human nature being what it is . . . ," followed by some description of some human act, such as "he fought back." Such statements reduce to such assertions as "It is the nature of humans to defend themselves" or "It is the nature of people always to seek security"—a very prevalent form, for historians are most inclined to generalize about economic motives. Often such statements are only shabby rhetorical devices to hide a lack of empirical evidence. When one lacks any other support, "human nature" is a convenient device for justifying almost anything, but it explains nothing at all. Since a vague conventional wisdom also accepts such sloppy explanations, a historian can get by with them. But the argument that all people seek security, given the vagueness of the word "security," is a near truism in the United States. When a historian makes such an assertion in a history of the New Deal, he probably does not intend it as a scientifically accurate generalization at all. He uses it as a verbally loose but contextually clear way of summarizing some empirical evidence about how most Americans behaved in the 1930s; at best, he intends only a limited generalization. Thus one should rarely take such statements literally. Historians could perfect such general assertions by needed class and temporal qualifications: "All middle-class Americans sought security in the 1930s."

To summarize an involved chapter: History is a nongeneralizing form of knowledge, for its key subject, acculturated humankind, does not display a uniform and invariant structure. Therefore, one cannot apply broad generalizations to understand cultural subjects. Culture, or mind, is a legitimate characterization of a scarce but quite distinctive feature of our directly experienced world. Cultural phenomena always coexist with more extensive biological and ever-present physical phenomena. At least the physical phenomena, including the part related to culture, may allow successful generalization, but any correlative generalization is not an explanation of cultural phenomena. Yet no opposition exists between culture and matter, and one need not seek some nonphysical chinks in reality in order to sneak in culture. Finally, the problem of generalization, to the historian, is the problem of critical choice among the various generalizations that claim verity. It is specialized scientists who develop generalizations with greatest rigor. Their work can be a valuable tool for any historian.

CHAPTER 10
CAUSATION

By present semantic conventions it is easy to link generality and causality as if they were inseparably related. But in the oldest sense of the very ambiguous word "cause"—in the sense in which it is still most often unselfconsciously used by historians—the very opposite is true. Generality excludes causality. Historians assume and often explicitly refer to a general order in events. But they do not often, and never by necessity or by reason of their historical task, invent or try to verify such generalizations. However, historians continuously use causal language. In fact, they are in the only cognitive discipline in which it is correct to emphasize the types of causation present in ordinary, undisciplined, common-sense discourse.

History and Teleology

The concept of causation was, in origin, a simple inference from human volition and action. A person desired something, rearranged some objects, and attained her goal. Her act was the cause of some effect. With great precision, Aristotle first analyzed the full implications of such causation, which is clearly based on human or divine agency. He isolated four distinct aspects of or perspectives on causation, including the efficient cause, or the actual energy that lies behind an effect, and the crucial and determinant final cause, or the end toward which one directs action. In Aristotle's perspective, a person is an agent and not just an isolated complex of mass-energy states in endless transformation. One can view a person as the efficient cause of many effects, but such efficient causes are only the inverse side of operative final causes, of ends that such efficacious acts serve. This view clarifies the complementary relationship of efficient and final causes; they require each other and are only analyzable aspects of a more complex whole.

Thus in origin, as most often still in ordinary language, the idea of causation involved agents and teleology. This usage is best illustrated by the use of "cause" as a synonym for "end" or "ideal" ("she is committed to the cause of peace"). Whenever one can so render causal judgments, one is necessarily using them in a teleological sense. Thus a historian may assert that, among other things, British violations of American naval rights caused the War of 1812. This is another way of indicating that the United States as a collectivity, or the American people as individuals, embraced the cause of neutral rights on the high seas. Very often arguments that include abstract entities or historical forces ("American imperialism caused the war in Vietnam") are clearly teleo-logical statements, but with emphasis on the often unselfconscious na-ture of the commitments (hence the translation: "Whether they rec-ognize it or not, Americans are committed to the cause of imperialism").

When so used, causal language reflects an almost obvious and ines-capable common-sense understanding of ourselves as end-directed agents. In this original and conventional understanding of causation, any causal agent has an enduring identity that is not radically altered by an effect and, above all, never becomes such an effect. John Smith may cause all manner of effects, but he is still John Smith. Imperialism may cause hundreds of wars. Such causal analysis requires of a desig-nated cause (John Smith) that he be not the sole determinant of an effect (he never is) but only a necessary condition of it.

Likewise, one may view any particular event as the effect of a variety of contributing causes. Any of a whole range of such teleologically pregnant causes may start as a proximate necessary condition and range back to broad, sweeping cultural forms that conditioned the proximate act: "The man died because the angered boy shot him, because his father gave him a loaded gun, because the family loved to hunt and had numerous guns, because the society approved of hunting and the use of guns, because it tolerated all kinds of violence, because the eco-nomic system reflected a generalized expression of capitalist aggressive traits," and so on. This causal series does not conflict with other judg-ments that contain causal language in a seemingly nonteleological sense: "The man died because a bullet pierced his heart." This example ex-cludes a direct reference to any purposeful agent but implies a contin-uing identity in the bullet. It is either an elliptical causal statement, with an agent implied but not identified, or else a poorly worded or incom-plete statement of physical transformations. In the latter case, no agent means the absence of ends, and thus no cause in the ordinary teleo-logical sense.

In the development of the modern physical sciences, scientists had to turn away from traditional causal relationships, those imbued with teleology. If they had not rejected such causation, a science with wide scope, reliable prediction, and great utility would have remained impossible. In place of these traditional forms of causation, scientists sought nonteleological, even nondirectional types of transformation in isolated systems. But in a quite new use for an old word, scientists often used "cause" to designate any arbitrarily isolated state in a tranformative series, one that preceded an arbitrarily defined subsequent state, and "effect" to designate the subsequent state. According to this definition, a cause, rather than being an unaltered agent, was a state of affairs that in the next instant became another state of affairs. And without a quite arbitrary, human isolation of points in a continuum, one could never discriminate either a cause or an effect. Any cause was, from a slightly altered perspective, also an effect. Obviously, to call this relationship causal was to invite all kinds of verbal confusion. The confusion has been largely dissipated by perceptive philosophers, but it still haunts the historical profession and renders ambiguous much historical language. This observation leads us to perhaps an unanticipated or even perverse recommendation—that scholars restrict causal language to ordinary discourse and to history and eliminate it from the generalizing sciences. Scientists have nothing to do with causes; historians do.

Causes as Necessary and Sufficient Conditions

These distinctions at least suggest some of the ambiguities and hazards that lurk in the word "cause." Some people today use causal language for, or even want to restrict it to, fully determinate relationships within isolated systems. These relationships, on analysis, always involve law-conforming changes or transformations in systems in which all causes subsequently become effects and never retain any separate identity through time. That is, they have no attributes of agency. In such a transformative series, each cause is both a sufficient and necessary condition for what comes next, for each successive state reflects the working of physical laws. Such series allow prediction and retrodiction so far as one wants to trace transformations. The relationship may be stated as follows: If state A is present at time 1, then state B will necessarily result at time 2. One way of symbolizing such a tight relationship is $A_{t1} \Leftrightarrow B_{t2}$, where the double arrow represents the strongest possible form of implication.

Such a causal model seems to be irrelevant to historical inquiry. Since human history always involves agents and intentional activity, the identified causes of events seem to retain their identity whatever they effect. But a weaker, nondeterministic version of a transformative series does lend itself to historical storytelling. A typical historical subject is a group of people, related to each other by shared beliefs, preferences, and institutions. Such a group has many of the complex interrelationships that make up any system, and historians may trace changes, or transformations, within a continuing social system. A state of affairs in a country at one time yields to a slightly altered state at a later time. This development usually involves some outside intervention, and thus violates the unfolding of an isolated system according to its own rules. But at times the basis of change may seem largely internal, a natural unfolding of a social system. This is, indeed, more of an organic than a physical model, but it is closely related to the physical model. The crucial difference is the lack of full determination. An existing state of affairs in a human society is never both the sufficient and necessary condition of what follows. The form is at best a weak probabilistic alternative to mechanical forms of relating.

In this model of causation, note that both the cause and the effect are cross-sectional states of affairs, not events. "Event," of course, is a muddy and overused word, but here we use it to refer to a distinguishable happening, one with some pattern or theme that sets it off from others, and one that involves changes taking place within a delimited amount of time. Historians, like all other storytellers, freely mix events and states of affairs. A state of affairs (the developed character traits of an individual) may "cause" an event (the assassination of a king). Or an event (the assassination of the archduke) may cause a new state of affairs (a state of war in Europe).

Likewise mixed, and thus often confused, is the exact logical relationship between such causes and effects. Since human affairs (not reductionist descriptions of them at a behavioral and physical level) are never fully determined by laws, and since no human society is ever really isolated, the central subject matter of history precludes tight, mechanistic relationships (any fully sufficient and necessary conditions). Thus the only possible causal links sought by historians are either sufficient or necessary conditions for either events or states of affairs. To explicate all the issues involved in these forms of causation would require a book, and would lead into some of the most fruitful and controverted work in the philosophy of history. A sketch will have to suffice here.

Time is critical in a story. Whether a state of affairs or an event, a historian's cause always precedes an effect. Formally, logically, causal relationships may be time-neutral, but never for the historian. Thus some of the formal logic of causes may seem little more than verbal trickery for a working historian. For example, one may symbolize a sufficient condition for an event or new state of affairs as $C \rightarrow E$. The presence of C ensures the subsequent occurrence of E. An inverse relationship is also present. E is a necessary condition of C, for without the predicated occurrence of E, it would be untrue that C was its sufficient condition. Thus whether a cause is sufficient or necessary depends on the direction in which one traces the relationship. But the historian has only one direction—progressively through time. It seems pointless, therefore, to call a later event the cause of a prior one.

This means that a historian would symbolize a necessary condition as follows: $C \leftarrow E$. This schema keeps the cause first in the order of events. In this case, it is clear that E could not have taken place unless C preceded it. Yet C is not sufficient to produce the event, although C would be part of any set of sufficient conditions, if such existed. It is at least conceivable that some events, or even some classes of events, at certain levels of description, have no sufficient conditions, which is to say they are in no sense inevitable at any time. But to cite merely necessary conditions is not to escape the logic of sufficiency. The inversion still applies. In this case the E is a sufficient condition of C. This may seem a rather trivial point to the historian, but it is a valid point. C cannot stand in a necessary relationship to a subsequent E unless every occurrence of E entails a C. This means that every historical event that historians want to understand is a kind of logical guarantor of all the necessary conditions without which it would never have occurred. Unfortunately, the E does not reveal those necessary conditions. Historians have to search for them.

Such logical distinctions help clarify the argument advanced by Hempel and others about the conditions of an adequate explanation in history. In Hempel's covering-law model, he made the deducibility of an effect from prior conditions, guided by relevant laws, a necessity of explanation. Only this would allow an answer to one type of why—"Why did the war have to begin when it did in fact begin?" If one knew a law, or a group of laws, that determined the occurrence of wars, or of certain traits present in all wars, then one should be able to specify a set, or more than one set, of prior conditions that would be sufficient to make a particular war inevitable. In this sense, the historian who tackles such conundrums as "What caused the Civil War?" must launch a search for one of these predicated sets of conditions. The one found becomes, quite clearly, a cause of the war and, if no other sets are present, even *the* cause of the war.

Hempel, in other words, made sufficient conditions the desired type of cause in human histories. He did not try to reduce human affairs to mechanistic transformations, and never suggested that causes in a history should be both necessary and sufficient, or that the appropriate cause must be one state of affairs that subsequently, by the force of relevant laws of historic change, was transformed into a new state. He assumed human agency. But he hoped that psychologists or social scientists could identify enough fixed or enduring dispositions or motives in human societies to allow explanation by reference to fully sufficient conditions. Without this, one could not explain why a historical event had to occur. He soon acknowledged that such hoped-for regularity was exceedingly rare in human societies, or at least had not yet been identified, and thus admitted that historians would rarely be able to meet the demands of his model. He soon conceded that, in most cases, they would have to be content with probabilities, and thus with citing only the degree of probability for the occurrence of events such as wars. But even here the causal model remained one of "flawed" sufficiency, for the goal remained one of accounting, as far as possible, for the occurrence of an event.

The question that followed, and one almost exhaustively explored since World War II, is whether historians usually seek this kind of sufficiency. In Hempel's terms, do they ever try to explain anything at all? Do they really crave sufficient conditions and the sense of inevitability that such conditions allow? Surprisingly, the question is not easy to answer. Confusion still plagues efforts to answer it. Since the goal is almost never in reach, and thus probabilities always take the place of certainty, historical practice seems to give very ambiguous answers to the question. Of course, some historians do claim sufficient conditions—that at some point conditions were such that the Civil War was inevitable—and presumably no historian would be unhappy with such claims if they could be justified by evidence. But if one reads the work of contemporary historians, one rarely finds such a causal claim, and with it the sense of inevitability. Almost as rare are attempts to cite with precision the exact probabilities of an event, given certain prior conditions and presumably certain assumed frequencies of normal or conventional or sanctioned behavior in a particular society. At least, this would seem to be one possible goal of historians, and for those who have worked most closely with social scientists, it may well be on the way to becoming an articulated goal, one self-consciously taught in graduate schools.

Why is it clearly not the goal of most historians already, and not the achievement of most? One reason, once again, may be the direction in which time flows. The historian is fully aware of the effect. This is where he starts. Unlike the social scientist, he may not be concerned to establish a rule for the occurrence of such effects, given that any rule governs them. He is not interested in predicting the future, or even in finding useful probabilities that would make more precise any predictions about the future. Also, the historian may be too fascinated by the particularities of a very complex event to attend to the class of events with which it may be associated. And it is much less messy to try to account for a class of events, defined as narrowly as possible, than to account for individual events very broadly described. The historian interested in enormously complex events or congeries of events, such as wars and revolutions, is aware of the looseness of labels, and realizes that no label in common use clearly describes any class. The particularities are more important than the essential traits, if such are even present. No generality is then possible and no recognized rules apply. Given the looseness of description, the particularity of events taken as a subject, and the lack of concern for prediction and control, it is not too difficult to *explain* why historians offer so few sufficient conditions. Incidentally, the preceding sentence is a low-probability explanation of the sufficient sort. That is, our goal is to account for certain present characteristics of historians by citing the conditions that most probably account for the fact that they are as they are.

Maybe there are more fundamental reasons why historians cite so few sufficient conditions. Such causes may not be congenial to storytelling. Given the occurrence of certain events, maybe the historian is usually interested not in why the events had to occur but rather in identifying certain prior conditions without which they could not have occurred. If so, then necessary, and not sufficient, conditions are more congenial to historians, and to the tracing out of events through time. This is a position that has numerous defenders, and one that seems to correspond much more closely to the practice of historians than any sufficiency model. Much recommends it logically. Note that the assignment of moral or legal responsibility rests on identified necessary conditions, not sufficient ones. In fact, no human intent will, in itself, ever be sufficient to any outcome, although such might be part of a larger, more inclusive sufficient set. Thus the type of causation that is most consistent with arguments about intent or purpose is of the necessary type. A choice, a human act, is necessary to results of many kinds, but almost never sufficient. Insofar as historians want to assign responsibility—and the responsibility for the outcome adds most of the poignancy to a story—it is natural for them to seek out certain necessary conditions. Insofar as they are unconcerned with predictive knowledge and have no interest in explaining why an event that so obviously did happen had to happen, they easily turn to necessary conditions, and to the elements of human responsibility so identified. Finally, the retrospective perspective itself invites this type of causal interest, a looking backward. In this perspective, necessary conditions have a strength not present in sufficient conditions. They had to be there. The claim is a strong one, but sufficient conditions, unless also necessary and part of a mechanical system, are not exclusive. In looking back, we often realize that any one of a dozen sufficient conditions might have accounted for the event, and thus it is very difficult to make a definitive judgment about which one was operative, if any at all.

Yet necessary conditions have their own problems. In a sense, they are weak causes. They allow no prediction and do not tell why anything had to happen. One addicted to the generalizing sciences is sure to be disappointed with them. And even though they fit well the special characteristics of mind, of intentional behavior, of final causes, it is not clear that many historians self-consciously seek such causes. Even the term may not be familiar to them. But that a historian's causal language is of this form more often than not is easily established: just read a few histories. Such conditions, although well fitted to a genetic perspective, are, when most significant to a story, very hard to identify and verify. In many cases, an event will be preceded by dozens of factors, all of which seem to be linked to the outcome but no one of which is clearly necessary for it. In other cases clearly identifiable necessary conditions will be completely trivial. A thousand conditions, proximate and remote, will be necessary for almost any event. Some of them may rival the shape of Cleopatra's nose as a cause of subsequent world history. For example, if Lincoln had overslept on the fateful morning he decided to reprovision Fort Sumter, the Civil War (the one that started on April 12–15, not a possible later war) would not have occurred. More remotely, if Lincoln had not been born, the war could not have occurred, and so on ad infinitum. The whole line of conditions rests on the prior judgment that Lincoln's decision was essential to the events that immediately followed. When so many seemingly trivial conditions may be identified as necessary for any event or change in a state of affairs, the problem is often not in finding them (there are all too many) but in justifying the ones included in a history.

Final Causes as Necessary Conditions

The necessary conditions of interest to a historian are usually those that are tied to human purposes. The selected necessary condition will be a final cause, or an efficient cause linked to a final cause. Even when efficient causes do not clearly indicate the purposes behind them, the fact that acculturated humans are involved ensures that purposes are present. Of course one may, in a sense, join Aristotle and find purpose even in physical events, for such events may reflect some hidden divine purpose or some cosmic design. But one need not make such an assumption to maintain that all events in any way conditioned by human choice reflect final causation.

Too often the very idea of final causes suggests such an Aristotelian world view, some vast cosmic design, or some prime mover or ultimate good toward which all things converge. Then final causes seem to lurk in every event, whether the event directly relates to human purpose or not. At the other extreme, final causes suggest a narrow, subjective perspective. They seem always to require an exercise of volition, of self-conscious choice by individuals. Then one can appeal to final causes only when acts are quite deliberate. Habitual behavior, and even human acts in which one cannot decipher the thought component, if any, have to be dismissed as mysteries or else explained at a reductive, physical level. Thus on one hand, one can generalize final causes completely and make them the crux of a mindlike account of all reality; on the other, one can push them into a narrow, subjective limbo, scarcely open to objective investigation of any sort.

To push final causes beyond subjective volition is to move very close to the idea of an objective mind or spirit and thus to the central doctrine of objective idealists. And much in the idealist position is valid. Final causes are not solely subjective. If they were, they would be of little cognitive interest. One might then dismiss them as unreal apparitions reared on real, transformative organic and physical processes, which alone would be worthy of serious investigation. But the objectivity of final causes does not justify the idea of some unified higher mind or the extension of final causes to the physical world, which yields no evidence at all of purpose, conscious or unconscious. Final causes are observably present where meaning or mind is present; thus they are now demonstrably present only in humans. One may posit a cosmic mind behind all events and some far-off divine purpose pulling the universe toward some glorious future, but one can adduce no evidence to substantiate the assertion.

Thus true causes (efficient and final) are always distinct from but fully correlative to noncausal, generalizable physical and organic structures. In any context where people need instrumental knowledge, or some new ability to guide events in certain directions, they should seek the general features, even transformative laws, and not efficient and final causes, not agency and purpose. They should deliberately shift their attention from the value-laden features of experience, from the valuations of themselves and their society, to the regular, uniform features that allow generalization and precise prediction. Of course, they do so as end-serving agents, as products of culture, and for culturally conditioned purposes. For this reason, cognition of any sort is necessarily relative to value. But only when, as in a history, final causes furnish the very key for selecting a subject, are always present in the subject matter, and provide some of the unity, the coherence, and the continuity that permit a subject to be traced through time are values at the very heart of a discipline.

Only when one locates final causes in an objective, cultural context and not just in the volition of individuals can one grasp the great breadth of true causal relationships in the human past and see the potential for causal judgments by historians. Any person is a product of some existing culture. She learns to talk within its social groupings, uses its symbols and grammatical forms, and first makes sense of the world by means of its generalizations. In her personal loyalties and institutional ties, she soon reflects her captivity to myriad valuations that have long since ceased to be matters of focal awareness and conscious choice but remain as controlling ends or final causes in her culture.

Of course human thought continuously modifies the meanings that make up any culture. At the point of such modification, of such focal and conscious awareness, meaning is always individual and, in that sense, subjective. Any person may, at times and in a few areas, become aware and critical of existing habits and institutions and of the ideal ends they serve or loosely reflect. Any culture changes, either by circumstance or by design, but such change always takes the form of elaboration. The past sets inescapable conditions for change. Insofar as change is a product of successful criticism rather than of accidental circumstances, it has to be, in its ideal aspects, in its intended purposes, a product of historical knowledge, even as the instrumentalities of change will most likely be the predictive knowledge provided by the generalizing sciences. In fact, the stories people tell of the human past are, whether intended or not, prime determinants of cultural change. What one selects as significant in the past and seriously thinks about in the present surely shapes the direction of change. What one ignores in the past will, by that very neglect, have no impact on the self-conscious and critical selection of new goals, but as an inescapable condition of choice may still exert great influence.

When new meanings, new concepts, new and brilliant hypotheses, or lofty new ideals remain the uncommunicated or uncopied possession of a single individual, they have only a minor and brief cultural impact. Such private intellectual possessions are of vital importance to the owner and would figure large in her autobiography. But from any broader perspective they make up a very tiny, scarcely noticeable episode in any society. Very few historians, save parochial family historians, would ever select these topics as a part of any history that they would want to tell. But just the opposite is true if these new forms of behavior and new ways of thinking and valuing become socialized, if they are widely imitated, if a whole society slowly absorbs them. As the new ways of acting become common and habitual, no one thinks about them. They are scarcely a part of anyone's symbolic experience or anyone's conscious desires and goals. But they will still be an aspect of the implicit belief and unreflective behavior of everyone, awaiting only the interested future historian who will, perhaps to everyone's surprise, so tell the story of that particular past as to make an audience aware of who they are, of the ends they unconsciously serve, and of what in focused self-awareness they may now gladly affirm or scathingly reject.

Such an analysis is in all ways consistent with, but does not require, a radically behavioral perspective. Thinking (or talking to oneself or using symbols) is a type of behavior, and even though it seemingly is unique to humans, it still is open to physiological and behavioral investigation. Such verbal behavior is often an adjunct of other types of habit formation, but in this case the habits are conditioned not only by physical and organic necessities but also by a repertoire of acquired symbols or meanings and, in a larger sense, by a whole environment of such meanings, or by mind in its social or transpersonal sense. Habits formed in part by the aid of a symbolic language are not different as habits, although at one point they accompanied some overt belief, some conscious assessment. And the symbols used, the beliefs present, and the values asserted were at least in large part the bequest of a cultural environment, with its unifying ideals and final causes. In a few cases, children may learn habits by direct conditioning, without symbolic accompaniment, without language. But even here those who direct or control the learning may be conscious believers, directly and intentionally transmitting a cultural inheritance. Finally, even habits formed without any conscious control by the operant and without verbal awareness in the learner may be cultural products. They reflect nonconscious group habits that at some time in the past did develop in part through symbolic reflection. At that point, such habits directly reflected projective goals and purposes that may once again become objects of critical awareness, at least if anthropologists or historians recover them and bring them back to a level of conscious awareness.

Clearly the realm of final causes is almost as broad as human behavior. By correlate generalization one can chart some physical and organic limits to behavior. But only by causal analysis, by looking to efficacious human acts, to human goals as they operate over long periods of time, can one account for the diversity of human behavior and the remarkable variety of cultural elaborations. Without reference to real final causes, the variety of human behaviors—all within limits set by physical and behavioral uniformities and none in their particularity predictable by any generalization—is quite simply a disturbing miracle. It is a miracle that some social scientists, in their fear of teleology, can scarcely acknowledge. Humanity can be a most disturbing phenomenon. People, perversely, will not fit neatly into any generalizable order; they will not submit exactly and completely to any universal or necessary laws. No one can completely objectify humans simply because they do live in a world of causes.

In causal judgments in either history or common sense, one may focus either on an agent as the energizing source of some effect or on efficient causes that implicate but do not necessarily reveal final causes. But when the agent is the focal point of our concern, we are rarely satisfied with efficient causes. Either directly or indirectly, we try to identify the final causes that are present. To say that President Franklin Roosevelt dropped Henry A. Wallace as his vice-president in 1944 may be sufficient in a history of the presidency but not in a biography of Roosevelt. If Roosevelt's purpose were not contextually clear, we would emphatically ask "Why"?

But this example suggests many difficulties. Often, and typically in cases like that of Roosevelt and Wallace, historians do cite immediate, presumably conscious reasons or considerations that led to a particular decision. They introduce conscious purposes into their narrative, although they have to infer the purposes from indirect evidence. But one could always challenge their account. Roosevelt was an experienced politician, with sound political habits acquired over years of political life. He continuously exhibited a quick, almost instinctive pattern of decision-making. Maybe he did not think very much about the Wallace candidacy or consider many of its implications. However reasonable and justifiable the decision, it may have largely reflected nonconscious habits. In any case, only a kind of mind reading could reveal the actual mental processes he followed. Even his retrospective accounts to cronies or to a diary would be misleading, for they would lead to some reflection and the development of conscious and good reasons for the choice. He might even be quite sure that the good reasons dictated the choice. And surely, in a sense, he would be correct, for they were operative in the decision, even if he did not focus on them.

Thus since even a subject's firsthand accounts rarely reveal actual mental operations, the historian, working with no better and usually less reliable information, can rarely do more than suggest possible thought processes. We can know the product of what, at one point or another, must have been a reasoning process, but we are not privy to such a process. When the historian feels it necessary to read his subject's mind, as a biographer often must, he should at least acknowledge the evidential perils even as he exploits the literary opportunities. If he does not see the perils, he may fall into a methodological error that has long afflicted many accounts of historical inquiry—the belief that a historian can substitute insight for the inferences warranted by evidence that

almost always reveals only human behavior and not internal delibera-
tion. Even carefully articulated beliefs are end products of unrecoverable mental operations.

Even though final causes are never, in themselves, sufficient conditions for any event, this does not mean that they have no predictive
power. Given a knowledge of physical circumstances (which make up a
relatively constant state of affairs assumed by most historians) and given
some stability in either a personality or an institution, knowledge of
operative final causes—of ends, purposes, and dispositions—provides a
quite reliable base for predicting certain future events. In the absence
of unanticipated physical obstacles (disease or death) or unlikely cultural
events (a revolution or coup), John will vote Democratic in the next
election. But any sufficient explanation of John's actual vote would have
to go beyond all causal conditions, beyond preferences and established
habits, and encompass all manner of biological and physical conditions.
If one focused on these things, one would have to drop from attention
all distinctive, particular, valuative, time-conditioned aspects of the event.
In other words, to seek sufficient conditions for human events is to seek
ways of dehumanizing events.

True causes are in time and conditioned by it. Being adjuncts of
culture, of human-created worlds of meaning, habits, and institutions,
they come into being, develop, and finally cease to operate. Some endure longer than others. Final causes that, despite a conditioning backdrop of cultural forms, develop almost capriciously and lead to only
slight changes in behavior are most ephemeral. To focus on these causes
and on the spontaneity, unpredictability, or seemingly unconditioned
aspect of human choice is to get an altogether subjective view of causal
phenomena, or of any subject of a teleological sort. Surely in such a
capricious area one can find no prospect for fruitful cognitive efforts,
for any truth. One may then be led to repudiate history as a cognitive
discipline, to flirt with wanton forms of relativism, and to embrace
deliberately subjective, nonevidential, intuitive types of insight.

Emphasis on the stability of culture or on the endurance of culturally
conditioned habits and institutions may lead to a loss of any historical
sense at all; it may even lead to false assumptions of true universality
in human events. In areas of well-established behavioral patterns, where
conscious human purpose seems remote or even inoperative and where
analytical descriptive models have reliable predictive uses, the historian
may join with cognate social scientists in attempting to turn stable patterns of culture into time-neutral scientific generalizations (this happens
most easily in economics). Then the so-called historian will view artifacts
from the past not as cultural monuments of possible value but as evi-

dence for or against some hypothesis of a lawlike form. He may even deplore the lack of rigor or predictability in other areas of history.

Pitfalls of Causal Language

Causes, if understood by their traditional and common-sense meaning, are so intimately related to the human past as to be all but essential to any storytelling. Thus one or more types of causal relating of events and states of affairs are always legitimate. In no extensive history can human agency, and thus causes, be avoided. But some historians are still apprehensive about causal judgments and prefer to use other than causal relationships in structuring their stories. Perhaps they are wise. Causal relationships are difficult to establish. Many causal claims made by historians reveal ambiguities in causal language and confusion about different types or levels of causation.

As a beginning, historians should be aware of, and on occasion distinguish, at least the following five uses of causal language: (1) to identify the conscious purposes and deliberations that guide choice ("He joined the army in order to defend his homeland"); (2) to denote decision-influencing conditions—either physical, organic, or cultural—and thus the grounds for choice ("He halted his troops because they were too tired to attack"); (3) to identify certain nonconscious but fully cultural conditions necessary for an event ("Because of prevalent strategic habits, he always deployed his troops in massed formations"); (4) to identify, among clearly generalizable phenomena, certain necessary but clearly not sufficient conditions for an event ("Because it rained, he lost the battle"); (5) to refer to fully sufficient conditions for an event and thus to identify the generalizable order that necessitates it ("Mustard gas caused the death of his men").

Unfortunately, historians rarely make any distinctions between agent causation (true causes in the traditional usage) and generalizable order. They rightly assume some generalizable order and then use causal language to indicate sufficient conditions for a physical event of human import ("Because of the buildup of pressure, the mine exploded, with great loss of life"). Because of such unanalyzed usage (incidentally, this is a typical causal judgment, couched in the same language as that used above for a necessary condition of a cultural type), historians often confuse the meanings of "cause" or mix two meanings in complex statements. One obvious temptation is to cite necessary but insufficient conditions without proper awareness and then to fall into the modes of thought that fit sufficient conditions (inevitability and a kind of scientism). Sometimes one intermixes physical order and human purpose in causal statements: "Because of his slight stature, John could not scale the wall." Although the statement is full of intent, and even suggests frustration and rage in John, the causal judgment still refers to physical conditions that limit the options open to an agent. Here a physical state B could not occur because a previous state A, containing the sufficient conditions for B, was not present. In a quite different sense, physical or biological limitations influence human choice and lead to the following causal statements: "Because of the driving rain, he disengaged his troops"; "Because of the severe winter in the north, more people than ever before vacationed in Florida, with great impact on its economy." Here the physical conditions are in no sense sufficient conditions for the designated effects. No relationship of a physical, transformative type exists. The physical circumstances are only decision-influencing considerations in human choice. Compare such statements with a true physical statement containing a sufficient condition, such as "Because of the cold, he died."

Subject to a lot of qualifications, historians can make unambiguous causal judgments of an exclusive sort, judgments that they can support by logic as well as by ample evidence. As an example, the following statement is quite clear and, given enough evidential support, also true: "Lee Harvey Oswald shot John F. Kennedy and caused his death." Oswald's act was the direct cause of the death and the indirect cause of many other consequences. But the statement names only a final cause; it does not indicate a sufficient condition for the death. A pathologist might provide such an explanation and even use causal terms, but she would have to use the terms in a quite different way. The shooting by Oswald was not an isolated, unconditioned, or spontaneous event (we have no compelling reason to believe that such events ever take place, although we often know none of the determinants or conditions). His act also was caused. We might cite one of these causes if we knew it, even assert it to be the indirect cause of Kennedy's death. Thus one had best claim only that there are single, exclusive, proximate causes and that an almost limitless number of ever more remote conditions cannot falsify such causal judgments. Typically, the causal judgment about Oswald and Kennedy is not very ambitious. It does not indicate what, if any, conscious reasons lay behind Oswald's act, nor does it reveal any mental operations that preceded or accompanied the act. We may not be able to infer this reasoning with any assurance from the evidence. The judgment does assume that Oswald was an agent, that some external physical force did not jerk the trigger against his wishes, that he was not under hypnotic control and thus acting for someone else, and that he was not insane and thus incapable of responsible behavior. It also assumes the obvious, that there were various cultural determinants stretching back from the act. Further inquiry may disclose some of these remote causes, many of which may become quite significant in a history of wider scope.

Myriad conditions, physical and cultural, contributed directly to Kennedy's death. Why select Oswald's shots from all these necessary conditions? Even if one leaves out all generalizable aspects—all purely physical necessities—there still seems to be no clear reason to select Oswald's act over that of someone else. After all, Oswald would probably not have had the opportunity to kill Kennedy had the President not made the decision to go to Dallas. Could one not correctly state: "Because Kennedy went to Dallas, he was assassinated and the whole nation plunged into grief"? This alternative strikes at the heart of any claim that, even in simple human events, one can establish exclusive causes, for any number of truly causal (not physical) conditions could be cited and, in a certain frame of reference, made the focal or significant cause. Still, there is a rather obvious way of distinguishing Oswald's act from all other culturally conditioned causes.

But first one must concede that the history one writes does set up criteria for selecting causes. If one were writing a history of the tragic career of John Kennedy, showing how innocent, even idealistic choices often led him into totally unforeseeable misfortune, then his choice of the Dallas trip would capture our interest, and in this context it might be cited as *the* cause of his death, in much the same way that one could cite a thunderbolt that struck him down in Dallas. But here the story being told involves Oswald only incidentally. It is a story of misfortunes that afflict a person. This is quite different from a history of the Kennedy administration or a history of recent American history, in either of which the Oswald explanation would most likely be relevant. Extended events grouped under a single label but which have numerous and variously emphasized aspects, such as a war, often reflect a near infinity of necessary conditions. Here a diversity of causal arguments often reflects quite different stories, each told for quite different purposes.

The earlier judgment about Oswald is a proximate causal explanation with some exclusivity to it, for one feature of Oswald's act was not present in any of the other necessary conditions that one can imagine. His was not only an act by an agent (so was Kennedy's choice of the Dallas trip) but an act displaying intent appropriate to the result. At least, his act seemed to display such intent, although almost no conceivable evidence could conclusively prove it (he may have been hypnotized). No causal judgment, particularly when it involves human agency, can ever be certain. But certainty is an issue apart from exclusivity. Such emphasis on intent appropriate to the result parallels the idea of direct legal or criminal responsibility. In the assassination only

Oswald was legally subject to a charge of murder, although such causal judgment in no sense depends on any legal guilt. Oswald's act would still be the cause of Kennedy's death even if no criminal law applied.

From Kennedy's perspective, Oswald's act was an unexpected calamity to be suffered, much like an unexpected thunderbolt. None of Kennedy's choices displayed any intent at all appropriate to the terrible outcome. His contributory acts, such as riding in an open car, had no intentional connection with the murder. But Oswald's intent gives him a distinguishable type of responsibility for what happened. Responsibility attributable to intent does not preclude other types of responsibility. Perhaps some Secret Service agents should have anticipated some such attempt and taken greater precautions. They may have displayed poor judgment, for which they might be expected to suffer some professional punishment. But no such dereliction, in any intentional sense, caused Kennedy's death.

In isolating a special category of necessary conditions or causes through intent (impossible in many situations where such intent is not present), one assumes that such causal acts are volitional or voluntary. But one need not assume that they are, always or even usually, carefully planned or even immediately conscious (surely Oswald's act was both). Again, many final causes become embedded in habit, and in numerous events of lesser moment than Oswald's assassination of Kennedy we all do habitual things for which we take responsibility and are held to be responsible. In fact, we would not like to lose all the praise that comes from such activity. Many of the things we do are truly our acts, voluntary even if unthought, for we have in the past been conscious of such acts even as a structure of habits formed. In other cases, we have formerly been conscious of certain habits and thus in a position to criticize and modify them. Particularly in more complex, group behavior, at a community or national level, intent often lurks, well hidden, in long-established ends now thoroughly embodied in institutions. It will not show up even in polls of citizens, for almost no one is consciously aware of these ends.

Causation and Moral Responsibility

The tie between cause and responsibility (a rather obvious connection when one correctly views all efficient causes as dependent upon final causes) does not necessitate moral judgment. But, by almost any conception of morality, the location of responsibility is a prerequisite for moral judgment. A historian can assert that Lee Harvey Oswald caused the death of Kennedy, that he was legally responsible for the death according to existing criminal laws, but without any desire to place the act against some accepted scale of good and evil. Even if the historian reacts in a moral way to the act, and even if he expresses his admiration or distaste, the causal judgment still stands. Oswald killed Kennedy. The historian knows that such a causal judgment, such fixing of intent and responsibility, invites moral judgment by his audience and that much of the interest and fascination of history lies in this moral dimension. Now, in fact, historians often reveal their own moral verdicts and thus try to guide their readers' reaction. But although such overt moral judgment seems acceptable to the community of historians, and is often valuable in fulfilling noncognitive purposes (interest, relevance, involvement, sympathy), it is still extrinsic to the causal judgment. Thus the historian is always trying to construct correct accounts in areas full of valuative content. In fact, any subject matter completely value neutral to humans is not a historical subject matter at all.

When an event, such as a duel or the outbreak of a war, involves antagonistic intent by two or more agents (and thus two interacting series of causes reflecting intent), the assessment of cause easily becomes, in fact, an assessment of blame; it is a moral judgment of the historian concealed in causal language. Causally considered, a duel almost without exception would be the result not only of an array of conditioning circumstances but of many intentional acts by two people, some of which may be appropriate to the final results, some surely directed at very different results. In a loose, quantitative way, a historian may, with some peril, try to determine the causal weight to be given to the acts of each protagonist ("John's angry statement was the greatest single cause of the conflict"). He may also try to determine to what degree one side misinterpreted the intent of the other and thus seek elements of tragedy in such conflict (without ever desiring such an eventuality, a person may be forced to defend himself or face death).

But too often the historian falls into the moralistic trap not only of evaluating the issues at stake (as a moral person he can scarcely avoid evaluating them and should not try to do so) but of letting the evaluation determine the alleged causes (really, he means blame rather than cause). Thus he turns the evil agent into the asserted cause, and he turns the good agent into a suffering and innocent victim of some causal act. After all, the good person only acted out of self-defense; he did not "cause" the fight. The causal agent was the only aggressor. Such ascriptions of blame, cast in the form of causal judgments, plague all intensely emotional conflicts, such as the American Civil War and the more recent cold war, both much too complex for anything close to exclusive causes based on intent. In neither case can the historian do more than isolate some of the necessary conditions, including varied intentional acts, almost none of which led to intended results. In fact, whenever a historian asks such questions as "Who caused the cold war?" one can routinely expect a moral evaluation in place of, or at least in addition to, a causal judgment.

Another distinction that must be made by a historian, if she is to avoid ambiguity, is the difference between proximate causes (such as Oswald's shot) and more remote conditions (physical or cultural) that explain the proximate cause. Why did Oswald shoot Kennedy? This question opens up a labyrinth of possible causes of one type or another. If one either asserts generalizations about human behavior or cites various acts by other people stretching far into the past, it may be possible to argue, in a most plausible manner, that Oswald had to shoot Kennedy, that he could not have done other than he did, and hence that the assassination was inevitable. Since Oswald had to do it and since there was no reasonable way for Kennedy to anticipate and avoid the bullet, the event takes on a fatalistic dimension. And indeed, historians often exploit ironic and tragic elements in human affairs, usually by turning away from proximate causes and their immediate context to remote causes that seem so to determine events as to leave no room for individual options and no place for moral judgment.

But such terms as "inevitable" and "could not have done otherwise" are themselves ambiguous and are often interchangeably used in two different ways. For example, to use the familiar old issue, was the American Civil War inevitable? According to the possible meaning of the word, it both was and was not inevitable, as different historians on both sides of the issue have amply demonstrated. As in all human events, retrospective analysis shows ample reasons why varied participants chose as they demonstrably did choose. They would really have had to be different people, with different characters, to have done something other than what they did. In fact, their behavior shows what character they had, and no one can escape this circular, retrospective argument. In this sense, not only the Civil War but all human events are inevitable, and stress on the determinants of human choice invites a commendable sympathy and pity in readers of our stories of the human past. But the word "inevitable" here has a soft or moral meaning, not a strong or mechanistic one. It does not, in fact, lead one to sufficient conditions for human acts, to any past state of affairs that, by the working of uniform laws, of necessity becomes a later state. No mechanical necessity, no determining laws, forced any of the human agents to act as they did in the years before 1865. No physical force compelled Oswald to pull the trigger.

Thus despite remote and even seemingly fully determinate causes for a human act, an individual is still, in one sense of the word, free to do otherwise than he does. No physical impediments block his act; no transformative laws compel what he does (even though the act necessarily exemplifies such laws). For this reason, such an agent, whatever the cultural backdrop, is still rightly held responsible (or else the idea of responsibility has no real meaning at all). A "hard" use of "could" and "could not" applied to the participants in the Civil War shows that they clearly could have done differently. They had options of all sorts, and if they had been better people they would have taken them. If one wants to cast moral stones, then one rightly casts them at their lax character, their manifest incompetence. He blames them for not being better persons, for not being able to make better choices. In this sense of the word, the war was not inevitable. Only physically determined events are inevitable. And in making this judgment, the historian does not, of necessity, assert some standard of conduct of his own invention. He need only emphasize the moral standards affirmed by the participants, the ideals they surely wanted to achieve. One does not have to import value judgments from the present to assert that these people failed. They acknowledged the failure themselves. From this perspective, by this sense of the meaning of such words as "inevitable," the war becomes a case history of human failure—a failure that indeed seems more tragic when we place it against a larger, causal perspective.

By these somewhat subtle distinctions, the Civil War both was inevitable and could have been prevented. The two seemingly contradictory perspectives are not in conflict; they do illustrate the need for greater precision in the causal language used by a historian. And this precision can be found not in the methodological subtleties of the physical sciences, not in textbooks on logic, but in age-old distinctions made in moral philosophy, by far the most relevant discipline for clarifying causal confusion among historians.

Selectivity and Causal Relativity

Despite all these distinctions, a kind of relativity remains. One cannot eliminate all the confusions about causation in history by making a radical distinction between transformative physical relationships and human causes, by asking historians to be aware of two quite different perspectives in the use of causal language, or by an even more treacherous attempt to distinguish and give a preferred place to effect-intentional human acts. All too often the historian must make causal judgments that reveal no clear intent and must, for reasons of economy if no other, isolate one or only a few causes out of many necessary conditions for an event. Assume that the bullet that killed Kennedy had been fired by accident and from some distance away. No intentional act at all appropriate to the end result allows a historian to set up an exclusive and preferred cause. If one wants to explain the event in causal terms, one must turn to quite varied, almost inexhaustible conditions, proximate or remote, for eventually every institution in the society may be implicated. One may, in a given selective context, allege that the failure of Kennedy or of the Secret Service to select a bulletproof automobile caused the accident or, much more remote and embracing, that the gun laws in America caused this and many other useless killings. Obviously, one writing a history of the Secret Service would select the first cause; one writing a history of violence in America would prefer the second. Such causal statements not only are context-determined but also carry with them an unwritten qualification: "This was only one of many necessary conditions for the event."

Causes of this selective type involve no methodological or cognitive issues of great import. Given the above qualifications, they allow no crucial subjective inroads. The historian, by his own intent or interest, chooses the story he will tell and within it selects and emphasizes certain things, including certain causes. As an empirical fact, different historians use varied criteria for selecting causes. One may analyze these criteria, and such an analysis may be of help to historians. In some situations, historians with a certain bent always assume the constant state of affairs and select as causes the unexpected events. Thus "Kennedy really died because a boy accidentally discharged his hunting rifle." But another historian might emphasize a more constant state of affairs, such as gun laws. In an instrumental context, one may stress the curable or eradicable condition over other conditions impervious to our action. Often not only historians but almost everyone gives the unexpected, the extraordinary, the rare condition a preferred place. If they make no special claim, such a selection contributes interest, surprise, and shock to a story. Here, of all places, the historian should not be confused with the scientist, who always has to seek a sufficient condition, or come as close to one as possible. The historian almost always gives a selected cause for a selected event. In a narrative a historian correctly cites a cause if it is one necessary condition and if he neither makes nor implies more sweeping and exclusive claims.

Possibly the distinction, made by Ernest Nagel and by others, between a constant state and unexpected or abnormal events has some relation to two words used (not very clearly, one must admit) by many historians in a seemingly causal way: trends and forces. It is dangerous to try to sum up even what most historians mean by these terms. But they could mean by a trend (or is it a tendency?) a steady increase in choices of a certain type within a group. This would indicate that some unifying

social goal or purpose, some new and significant final cause, was becoming ever more operative in a society and perhaps was already on
the way to becoming a part of some people's working habits. Thus one
might predict an increase in formerly rare or unknown choices or modes
of behavior. In this sense, a historian might say that a society exhibited
a "clear trend toward individualism" (whatever that means).

Likewise, "force" could denote a relatively fixed pattern of choice
and behavior. Then such statements as "Because of economic forces
beyond his control, he did so-and-so" would indicate stable economic
institutions, well-entrenched economic habits, and, perhaps so unconscious as to be beyond criticism, certain internalized goals and purposes.
After this all too neat definitional legislation, one might make almost
meaningful statements of the following form: "Because of economic
forces beyond his control, he had to accept the feudal system before
1688, but by then a clear trend toward individualism enabled him to
launch a new entrepreneurial venture."

Even so brief an analysis has at least demonstrated the complexity of
causal judgment in history and possibly has clarified the following propositions: That any single, exclusive, and fully sufficient condition for
any event, even when cited by a historian, implies some generalizable,
non-time-conditioned order, which, however related by the historian to
cultural events, does not in itself possess any distinctively human traits.
That causal judgments based on agency cannot provide sufficient conditions for an event, and thus can never involve anything more determinate than probabilities and certain necessary conditions. That one
can isolate a primary (and in some cases exclusive) proximate necessary
condition out of numerous necessary conditions only when one can
point to the presence of an agent with intent appropriate to an effect.
That, beyond these distinctions, only the topical context or narrative
demands can guide the selection of certain necessary conditions out of
a vast variety of such conditions. And finally, that there is no conflict
between proximate causes and more remote, more inclusive causes,
although remote causes seem to dissipate options and thus lessen the
sense of responsibility.

CHAPTER 11
OBJECTIVITY

THE so-called problem of objectivity continues to plague historians. Unfortunately, it is not one problem but almost as many problems as there are meanings for the word "objective." Not only do historians use the word "objectivity" in many ways; but also other terms that follow in its wake, such as "relativism" and "presentism." On no other issue have semantic issues been so central and real substantive issues so peripheral.

Can a history really be objective? It can be, but only when the term "objective" has a practical and very restricted meaning. Neither history nor any other cognitive discipline can be objective if "objectivity" entails such impossibilities as certain truths or exact correspondence of concepts to some hidden reality, or such unlikely, undesirable, or absurd requirements as complete neutrality, impersonality, and detachment. If it has any bearing on history at all, "objectivity" means that the clearly cognitive (truth-claiming) parts of a historical narrative must specifically refer to and be inferable from some perceptual evidence of a public sort, and that the cognitive claim must go no further. If it does go further—if one gives evidential weight to nonpublic, personal, intuitive data or to preferences and wishes—then a purported history is not objective, even if it proves later to have been more valid than a more restricted, misleading, but evidentially disciplined account. In this practical sense, objectivity is a criterion for establishing true propositions, but it is not a synonym for truth.

Today even this modest claim is far from fashionable. Never, it seems, have historians faced so many doubts about the cognitive status of their work. The doubts are at two related levels. The first is general and epistemological—the old problem of knowledge itself, of how one can possibly justify any truth claims at all in any empirical discipline. Skepticism on this issue clearly encompasses history as one sort of empirical knowledge. Beyond it is a more restricted issue: Even if one can cite adequate grounds for choosing among contending truth claims in the physical sciences, are these grounds adequate for history? This is another way of asking if historical judgments face more or different hazards than judgments in the generalizing sciences. If so, it is conceivable that well-grounded historical knowledge is impossible. "Knowledge," as the word is ordinarily used, means exclusive, objectively established truth claims. Such claims are either disjunctive—this historical account is true and all differing accounts are false—or weighted—this account is more probable than any alternative. Implicit in the concept of knowledge is the possibility of making and justifying such claims. The word "objective" usually designates the methods or the discipline one has to follow to meet this standard.

This is not the place to investigate forms of skepticism (doubts about the grounds for any knowledge) or solipsism (the idea that all knowledge is inescapably subjective and thus refers only to the person who affirms it). But it is important to note that historians have contributed to one form of skepticism. They have helped to historicize not only the content of knowledge claims but the methods used to verify them. One meaning of the loaded word "historicism" is just this obvious point—all knowledge, in whatever field, and all methods used to procure such knowledge are products of evolving cultures, and thus are time-qualified and always subject to change. By historical inquiry, one can fill in the story of how such methods and such knowledge systems came to exist and how they gained acceptance. This capability would seem to make history the one key to the understanding of all cultural artifacts, of which the sciences are only one. But this special form of reductionism—all knowledge is historical—cannot be exempt from the erosive implications of such an analysis. The historian is also within a historiographical tradition and the product of it, and thus her work is always a subject for what we often call the sociology of knowledge (a focus on how knowledge came to be, not on the criteria of validity internal to it). Such historical reductionism would seem to preclude any universal and enduring foundations for knowledge in any field.

The Subjectivist Challenge

In the twentieth century, at least two updates on this historicist argument have had major impact on historians. Thomas Kuhn, in his work as a historian of science, developed a theory about major scientific revolutions. Each such revolution, he argued, involves a major revision of a complex, interactive body of assumptions, or what he called paradigms. Most inquiry functions within such a body of basic assumptions, which are broad enough to encompass not only concepts and theories but even aspects of method. Kuhn used this theory not to demolish all claims of objective and exclusive knowledge but to identify the major cultural determinants of whatever physical scientists are willing to accept in the way of hypotheses. The time-specific and culturally variable component of any science has to be acknowledged. For Kuhn, this was a needed corrective to the more assertive claims of positivists (those who believed a uniform, shared method, based on formal or logical conventions, would lead to a cumulative, self-correcting, and valid body of knowledge in all empirical disciplines).

In the humanities, it was not formal logic but language theory that, at least for a time, seemed most likely to provide the needed grounding for universal knowledge. For complex reasons, the word "structuralism" came to stand for cultural anthropologists' hope that it would be possible to identify deep structures present in all languages. They then might develop a framework for all cultural studies. But such confidence also spawned skeptical critics, who often used the label "post-structuralism" for their position. Among these critics, the French historian and philosopher Michel Foucault had the greatest impact on historians. Perverse, playful, sometimes obscure, Foucault tried to work out the archaeology of knowledge, which identified major fault lines or discontinuities that appeared through time. He referred to the vast complex of theories, methods, and questions that characterized each cultural period as an episteme. Epistemes are so radically distinct as to preclude meaningful discourse across the fault lines. All knowledge claims, therefore, make sense only within a given episteme. Foucault sensed the waning of one episteme, that which in a sense created "man" and the hopeful human sciences, but of course he could not yet fill in the contours of the coming episteme. All the older knowledge claims, rooted in dead or dying epistemes, were losing both meaning and appeal.

Implicit in such challenges to knowledge is the belief that knowledge ought to be anchored in some justifying ground. Older, simpler, but still beguiling forms of realism rested on the hope that human concepts and propositions could somehow copy a real world, or at least mirror some of its regularities. But such a naive realism has confronted fatal objections. It assumes a "real world," when all that we ever have are the limited, changing conceptual nets that humans devise on the basis of experience, which serves well to guide conceptual invention but does not completely control such invention. Thus conceptual games have a human stamp, reveal creativity if not playfulness. The most developed sciences involve a happy marriage of conceptual inventions and perceptual checks, and neither is in full control. Other attempts to pin knowledge down, to anchor it securely, end up with equal or greater problems. In a purely intellectual sense, skepticism is beyond refutation. None of our knowledge is self-justifying, nor is any of our methods for establishing it. In fact, knowledge might best be defined not as a copy of some prior reality, not as a facet of the cohering mind of a deity, but as active human contrivances that often prove useful in attempts to cope with the opaque world that we keep bumping into. The only controlling justifications for knowledge claims are either esthetic or practical. Some conceptual creations, including some that are deliberately cognitive, are beautiful, and thus good in themselves, and others allow us to solve problems, and as instruments are morally justified. Some are both. This "pragmatic" conception of knowledge is not a solution for all the old epistemological dilemmas, but only a way of avoiding them or of denying that they are meaningful or important.

But even the historian who takes a pragmatic perspective on knowledge has a problem. The instrumentality of most empirical knowledge is clear in a quite technical sense. The generalizing sciences allow prediction, even of impending catastrophes, and at times allow human control over an environment. Knowledge of the human past is not usually so clearly and directly useful. Futility, even death, may follow a lack of scientific knowledge. What is the cost of historical ignorance? From a pragmatic perspective, the ultimate control over our cognitive games is some form of workability—does the theory unify data, allow reliable predictions, give us needed leverage over events? What comparable forms of workability could justify historical knowledge? This is to raise the vital issue of use. What is history for? We defer our complex and extended answer to the next chapter.

But the very need to pose the question suggests, again, the distinction between history and the generalizing sciences, a difference of subject, form, and use, but not clearly one of method. Given these differences, it is not surprising that many arguments for subjectivism peculiarly apply to historical inquiry.

Texts and Narratives

The most sweeping claims about an irreducible and distinctive subjectivity in history involve either the properties of a narrative or the degree of cultural packing in any text. Language and rhetoric relate to both. Historians and philosophers most concerned with narration have not shared the dominating interest of analytical philosophers in problems of causation and explanation. Often they have demoted the importance of truth claims in narratives or argued that truth is not the most important issue for historians. Obviously, a description of events and causal claims about their occurrence are part of almost any history. But they are only parts of a larger whole, and possibly are more determined by the whole than the whole is by them. A historical narrative includes broad themes, patterns, or plots that give it unity. The genius of a historian lies in developing these patterns, not in marshaling analytically separable truth claims. Many aspects of a story may turn out to be false, on certain methological grounds, or at least insufficiently evidenced, and yet the story may be brilliant, innovative, and enduringly influential. To focus on the truth status of individual statements is to misunderstand the inescapable overlap of form and content in a story, and to make the mistake of reducing a history to a series of truth claims.

The emphasis on the distinguishing attributes of a narrative ¬received its most influential support from the historian Hayden White. In *Metahistory: The Historical Imagination in Nineteenth-Century Europe* he argued that the historian, far from copying or literally tracing events in the past (writing a kind of chronicle), rather uses linguistic and dramatic tools to produce a creative and "emplotted" story about the human past. He believed the historian had to choose one of four tropes, or figures of speech drawn from rhetorical analysis, as a perspective on the past, which lead to plots that are variously providential, deterministic, tragic, and ironic. The past is rich enough to allow each type of plotting and never clearly dictates any one, although the tropes match aspects of human experience. The historian's intent, philosophical convictions, and cultural bias determine her plotting strategies, and it is for this reason that historians produce very different histories. Such histories illuminate the past, in some sense continuously enrich it, but do not copy it. What is not so clear in such analysis is to what extent surviving artifacts still constrain this almost rhetorical game, and thus to what extent the component descriptions, however plotted, have to meet a rigorous methodological discipline. If this requirement still holds, then White has cut historical knowledge loose from older copy theories of knowledge, from a naive realism, and has clarified the leeway for creative, imaginative construction or plotting that is part of all storytelling. That is, despite his useful attention to a range of subjective involvements or intrusions, he has not denied the need for objectivity, at least in certifying the bare events that provide much of the content of any story. But such is the complexity and density of the story, of all the interpretive content, that it does not seem meaningful to ask if it is true or false, at least by older conceptions of knowledge.

Another term—"text"—has become omnipresent among historians. Here the fads and the verbal pretension are enough to scare off any beginning graduate student. In some sense, almost all historians read and try to understand texts, by which we mean only written documents of any sort. Their work with such written texts joins that of literary critics, although their purpose varies (rarely is the historian concerned with the literary achievement of the writer). The emphasis on textual interpretation, and on a range of linguistic and rhetorical issues, has led to another loaded term, one now de rigueur among intellectual historians, "hermeneutics." The word comes largely from biblical studies and originally referred to specific canons or rules used to interpret ancient texts. This suggests an obvious point: the rules of interpretation must have something to do with what one finds in such texts. Thus since historians are always interpreting texts, it is as proper to inquire into their "hermeneutics" as it is to analyze their plotting strategies. Of course, historians are rarely self-conscious about such rules. Nor did most past authors fully understand the symbolic rules they followed, and thus what they really said. This realization opens up a complicated game—the game of trying to unearth, or deconstruct, such texts. In literary criticism, this effort has been spearheaded by a somewhat loose body of deconstructionist critics under the influence of the French critic Jacques Derrida.

The faddish popularity of the word "hermeneutics" owes most to a German philosopher, Hans-Georg Gadamer, and beyond him to such seminal philosophers as Friedrich Nietzsche, Charles S. Peirce, and Martin Heidegger. Unfortunately, the verbal fashions have tended to obscure the complex philosophical issues. At times hermeneutics have multiplied faster than flies, and almost no one has bothered with definitions. And "texts" have expanded until they occupy the whole universe of historical inquiry. Some critics have exerted serious efforts to make the whole of the human past a text, and others have wanted to make any human life a text awaiting its interpreter. The game often involves a theory of signs, as well as the latest developments in comparative linguistics. In the 1950s and 1960s, essays about history abounded in the often technical and at times pretentious but usually precise jargon of Anglo-American analytical philosophers, with their generalizations, covering laws, and necessary conditions. Today almost any discussion of history soon degenerates into the less technical, more pretentious, and much less clear language of Continental literary critics, with their texts, hermeneutics, and semiotics.

Most of these seemingly subversive ways of emphasizing the intrusion of a subject into a history are more truistic than profound. Most involve half-truths. After all, the demands of objectivity do not prevent a historian from taking a personal interest in often quite selective historical subjects or from fashioning highly creative and imaginative constructs that are never identical to any past reality, if one can give any meaning to "past reality." Objectivity also is quite consistent with numerous noncognitive, esthetically or morally suggestive, personally or culturally revealing judgments within a narrative. After all, being objective, or even telling the truth, is not the only goal of most historians; it is never the sole aim of any good historian.

Temporal Perspectives and Historical Selectivity

A history is a story about the past; it is not the past itself, although some people use the word "history" for this unrecoverable and possibly undefinable entity. Whether one draws a history with the guidance of memory or of monuments, it cannot exactly mirror the feelings and perceptions of people in the past. We can never, with any adequacy, conceptualize even our own feelings, articulate without ambiguity our beliefs, or recount much more than the outlines of our actions. Existence and concept are never equivalent. This insight has a double import. First, we can never fully conceptualize, or make all possible inferences from, our experience of the symbolically rich human artifacts that seem to represent past human efforts, but at least, in some carefully selected areas, we have to do the best we can if we are historians. Second, inferences from these artifacts to past human feelings are hazardous, so hazardous that historians may avoid inferences about the quality of feeling whenever they can. The experiential past is largely hidden and lost. But one can infer, almost conclusively in some cases, the concepts and acts of people in the past, their articulated beliefs and the ends operative in their behavior. In fact, we can infer ends that they served without knowing they were doing so, or momentous events that they scarcely heeded, for we have the advantage of hindsight. Without it there could be no histories.

Often the most momentous events of our life go unnoticed at the time they happen. In rare cases, we die without having recognized them. The accidental meeting that led to a job, the enjoyable meal that led to illness, the blind date that led to marriage and a family are examples familiar to all. Let a wife and mother tell the story of her life, and these episodes may figure large in it. Every detail of that blind date will become a cherished family heirloom; in nostalgic analysis, every gesture, every word may take on great importance ("Honey, why did I ask you that silly question?"). If she can find language suitable to the task, she can turn such episodes, so full of meaning, into family epics, endlessly recalled and repeated. Unfortunately, a good raconteur may do more than memory allows; she may embellish the epic with dramatic flourishes, with imaginative details that should have been present at such a demonstrably momentous event. Instead of simply claiming significance

("Oh, what a glorious and important evening!"), she adds a moon that never shone, brilliant repartee that never developed, a band that never played. And soon, out of a past that never was, she constructs an illusory self that will never be, one that is pathetic to those who know the truth (historical in this case).

Usually through the revelation of symbolically suggestive artifacts, rather than through memory, historians construct an inferential bridge to events far in the past. And by another class of inferences they calculate the values, purposes, and ends reflected in those events. They cannot rethink or reexperience the past. But they do think it and experience it as a past. Their interest must be selective. The wife who remembers the momentous blind date soon forgets a thousand other events and, in most cases, for good reason. They had no recognizable significance for anyone. The historian finds little of interest to herself or to an audience in most of the past that lies symbolically exposed even to causal inference. Thus she does not think it and construct stories about it. It is not worthy of her art.

But here and there historians do find at least bits and pieces of a seemingly compelling past. Very often this is the past that endures in their beliefs and habits (and who is not interested in oneself?) or that is related to the pressing concerns of themselves, their group, or their country. Here alone are the events that they want to understand and the stories that, given constructive ability and evidential support, they want to tell. These stories have value for them. But to tell such stories or even to hear such stories is not at all like having had the experiences told about. It is not a reliving of the past but a particular way of living in the present (a historically conscious way). In rare cases this historical experience can be more intense than the past experiences thought about (the husband and wife may find more meaning and more exhilaration in the historical experience of their first date than they actually found in the frightening, insecure first meeting). Historical experience is often charged with drama. Very often, even in areas of the past long familiar to almost everyone, a historian sees a new causal relationship (some necessary condition formerly ignored) and thus some new significance in an event. This insight makes possible the telling of an old, old story as it should be told. And in the new perspective, it is really a new story, a history no one has yet created, and often a story never even vaguely understood by any of the actual participants. By such a process, by turning the heretofore forgotten and meaningless into the memorable and significant, historians both rescue and create a past. By so doing, they help in some small way to determine the future. They keep telling children new secrets about their parents and try to convert their sweet innocence into mature wisdom.

Such stories of the past have two closely integrated, mutually conditioning types of cognitive content. The personal (if one wants, the
subjective) intent, the selective aspect in the choice of topic, and the
purposes sought do not play any necessary cognitive role. But any historian asserts something as true about a delimited past: she classifies
subjects and events, locates them in space and time, and serially connects
them by causal relationships or a continuity of identity. Also, if only by
implication in the language used, she also affirms something about how
such events relate to unspecified events in the future (possibly our
present) and to events well outside the temporal span of the story itself.
These not usually explicit truth claims also involve either causes or
continued identity.

When the mother recounts that momentous blind date to her children, she constructs a narrative with a time-limited subject—one evening
in the life of John and Mary Doe. But implicit in practically every word
is the relation that event had to many later events, including the very
existence of Harry and Susan Doe. Such a then-open future has an
indispensable role in establishing a significant past, and thus in guiding
the selection of a story worth telling; it also, as Arthur Danto has so
effectively argued, has a role in the describing and relating of various
episodes in the narrative itself. In the family of our example, the opening
telephone call to set up a date became, correctly in a larger context,
the first act in the John Doe family epic; it became something that it
was not when it actually happened. It is for this reason that even simple
descriptions in a historical narrative may contain some temporal spread
and causal content.

Almost no one denies that historians can reliably infer certain simple
past events from surviving artifacts, or that in many cases they can
reliably date such events according to some conventional calendar. But
simple events, in themselves, are of minor importance in most histories.
One might easily assert that John and Mary Doe dined in a certain
restaurant on that critical evening. But so what? So did a hundred other
couples. We will even assume that John and Mary duly recorded their
visit in a dated guest register. If long afterward a garrulous John Doe
were challenged in his epochal account of that evening, he might even
seek out the old register in order to establish the fact. By this "research,"
he adds public evidence to his account and becomes a more exact and
rigorous historian. But until John Doe consulted the register and used
it, it was scarcely historical evidence, for it as yet evidenced nothing
and supported no history. The surviving effects of past human efforts
are almost infinite; few ever become historical evidence. Only for John
and Mary Doe does the old register (deposited in the local archives)
come to life. Only for them does it have weighty meaning. It bears

witness to the most glorious and momentous episode in their whole life, to the very opening of their history as a united couple.

But one question remains. In referring to a glorious evening, in going beyond the evidenced fact of such an evening together, is John Doe being objective or subjective? By a plausible use of both words, he is both equally and without conflict. What he says is true. It is also charged with intense, personal meaning. Of course, if without qualification, without any clearly implied and limited context, he had claimed that the date was then experienced as the most momentous event in his or in human history, he would be correctly dismissed as a fool.

A historian cannot construct a complete history, either in the sense of including everything or in the sense of completely finishing the story. Not only must we select, but we must face the limitation of being ourselves in process. Even the most ancient history, insofar as it has any continuing relevance, may have a radically different significance for us next week or next year. For example, John and Mary Doe may be divorced next year, perhaps in the aftermath of some serious mental illness and drastic changes in his personality. Then Mary will tell the story of their first date quite differently, but not necessarily less objectively. She may remember it as keenly and even find new corroborating evidence. With the added perspective given by more recent events, she now sees the blind date not only as a glorious beginning to years of happiness (it is still that, although with a tragic tinge) but also as the first episode in what became, finally, a family disaster. In the terms of Hayden White, she may now shift the plot of her story from providential to tragic, and still later in life, with time for reflection, to ironical. Thus her earlier histories were far from being all the truth; now they seem misleading. But they might have been true in all their details, and their truth might have rested on the most careful use of public data. She may indeed have left out what now seems the most crucial knowledge, but she could not have such knowledge until other events took place. And unlike the more abstract and law-determined events treated in the generalizing sciences, she had no possible way of predicting many of these most crucial occurrences.

Mary Doe's plight is typical of the plight of any historian. Judgments in history, even down to descriptive language and class terms, have time qualifications attached to them. The confrontations in the Persian Gulf, a localized conflict as we write, may to the reader already be the opening episode of World War III. But this type of limitation is not relevant to objectivity; it is relevant only to the temporal context and thus to a special type of fallibility or incompleteness ever present in historical knowledge. We may base our present judgments about the Gulf conflict on firm evidence. So did Jane Doe in her earlier judgment that that

first date was the most glorious and momentous thing that ever happened to her. Thus the historian not only must qualify any proposition
with "until new evidence indicates otherwise" but must qualify most
judgments with "until new events reveal new significance and permit
new assessments."

Another issue suggested by Jane Doe's history is a great deal more
subtle. As she told and retold the story of their blind date, she selected
and emphasized some events of the evening over others. In fact, some
remembered details never seemed worth mentioning. They were not
significant to her story. Thus a historian not only tends to tell stories
directly related to her present interests and concerns (surely no less a
motivating factor for her than for generalizing scientists) but will also,
within the broad leeway allowed by the narrative form, select and highlight some events and ignore others. Clearly, in doing so, she may reflect
not only some of her own concerns ("I feel the struggle for female
equality is vital") but also those of her age, her community, and her
culture. Beyond that, as a gifted storyteller, she may shape some of the
details to increase dramatic interest.

Even this interior selectivity does not threaten objectivity, but it does
reveal a critical difference between historical accounts and most scientific hypotheses. In a new context, it simply exhibits the difference
between the generalizable and the human, or often between a search
for sufficient conditions and a search for final causes. Given the values
that often lead to the topic one selects, the generalizing scientist not
only has a methodological discipline that demands verification by public
data (even as the historian) but also has a formal discipline that demands,
within a universe however narrow and arbitrary, a type of completeness
(not certainty). This is simply a feature of all lawlike explanation. Such
completeness, such causal sufficiency, is impossible in disciplines limited
by time and dominated by final causes. The historian can never, however
restricted his topic, compose a complete or fully sufficient account. His
is always, by practical if not by theoretical necessity, a partial story, and
he has no formal reasons to struggle toward a complete story. He looks
for causes but never for all causes. He could never identify all necessary
conditions, and he has no means of recognizing such an achievement
were it possible.

Another way of stating all this, although it may sound sophistic, is to
argue that a historian's selectivity never faces the discipline of some
fixed topic, such as the Civil War. He has no isolable system to explain;
rather, he isolates a system as he explains. Every divergent but equally
objective (a matter of rigor in the making of inferences from artifacts)
account of events in the United States from 1861 to 1865 is a different
history, about some slightly different topic, selected by some different

and in some sense arbitrary criteria. Many of these related but different accounts may carry the label "Civil War." Thus even two historians whose field of inquiry is limited to the Civil War will rarely have a common universe of inquiry; they work in related universes and on various but at points overlapping stories. At places of overlap, one may indeed compare and evaluate divergent accounts by cognitive criteria. On the evidence, which is the true, or truest, account? But it is almost never possible to equate two complete stories, even about purportedly similar subjects, for they are really about slightly different subjects. Thus selection of a topic and selection within a topic are scarcely distinguishable in history. From beginning to end, the historian must select, with no formal demand that at any given point he stop selecting his universe and get on with the story. This is not to deny that, totally apart from formal criteria, historians do face conventionally delimited subjects and professionally favored topics.

This selective freedom requires some necessary caution. Even though no historical subjects await complete description, this must not mean that subjects actually selected by a historian do not have some integrity of their own. Almost any subject will display thematic unity (a continuing personality, characteristic, or flavor), which may well provide the unity of a story. No historian could or would want to write a full biography of John Doe, with a complete description of everything about him (an impossibility) or even a balanced and equal emphasis on all aspects of his career. Only some part of his life may seem important enough to tell. Because of the significance of his beliefs, one may want to do an intellectual biography. John Doe developed a somewhat coherent body of beliefs, some of which very much influenced his society. But it is misleading to abstract these influential beliefs from less influential beliefs and even from nonintellectual aspects of his career. To be at all accurate, the historian must fit the local beliefs into a larger whole, apart from which they could make no sense. Any historian accepts a holistic requirement, an obligation to move at least occasionally from more focal fragments to a cohering whole. Every historian has such an obligation because one wants to understand and not distort the selected few fragments. And their proper relationship is a part of understanding. If one insists on picking and choosing among unrelated fragments, perhaps in behalf of some immediate use in the present, one leaves the field of historical understanding and enters the area of parochial and polemical pleading.

Thus even though a selected subject for historical narration does not carry with it a demand for completeness or set up rigid guides as to what one must tell, it does determine what is integral to it, what one should not fragment and isolate. Even to select out of the unity that is any person or any nation some particular and narrow topic, such as beliefs, demands justification and frequent reference to the nonfocal but always conditioning context. One can justify true (that is, evidenced) but quite narrow histories (the success of John Doe in one endeavor) only by a large body of assumed information already present in an intended audience. Otherwise such histories are unbalanced. They easily mislead by omission, and they distort understanding. However selective a historian is, she faces crucial problems of judgment in determining how much background she must bring into a narrative, how much she can assume her audience to know, and how much, even though relevant and unknown, she must exclude in order to finish her story at all. In this area of judgment, fairness and balance are evidence of a kind of objectivity, but it is clearly an objectivity that has nothing to do with verification by public evidence.

This analysis should help identify a type of historical presentism or relativism, to use two very overused words. Every history has contextual limitations, not the least of which is the ever-unfinished, future-con-ditioned nature of any story. Of course the most pressing contemporary concerns, or at least the areas of present awareness, often correctly govern the selection of a topic and selected emphases within a topic (no one can write a history of some aspect of the past that, because of present cultural blindness, is not even conceivable). But a vicious pre-sentism does not guide selection in history; it precludes history. Instead of making careful inferences from evidence, instead of constructing a true story about some part of the past that now seems significant and worth our reflection, we project our own beliefs and our own standards into some past, and we end up by revealing only ourselves. Such is not history, for the alleged pastness, replete with dates, is a false camouflage; and the alleged evidence, replete with footnotes, is not really historical evidence but undeciphered relics. This type of presentism, perhaps the most tempting pitfall of the historian, always leads to pseudohistories, which protagonists often use to sanction immediate interests or to but-tress naive and oversimplified criticism. Our present interests and our estimate of what is and has been of greatest human significance should direct our backward gaze to those parts of the past worth knowing, and of such vital importance that we must dissipate all illusions by knowing them well. We fail when we let our present concerns blind us to any past that does not mirror our concerns and our prejudices, and thus to almost any past at all.

Because all stories are incomplete and because we lack formal criteria for selection, historians can endlessly compose their stories, even in narrow chronological or topical areas. It is impossible to set a limit to the number of true but somewhat different stories that one can tell about the immense range of phenomena that we loosely group under the label "Civil War." But there are limits to what stories a historian may tell about the war, and these limits are, of course, the evidence that supports all such inferences about the past. But this evidence has no assessable limits, for any number of objects may become appearances for past events. Heretofore speechless and dead objects become evidence in the hands of historians, who search out the mysteries they are ready to tell.

The unending and more or less arbitrary selectivity that enters into every history yields to no cure. In fact, why would one want to cure it or conceal it? Perspective and personality should be clear, not camouflaged or confused. They both add to the appeal of a story. Obviously, there is no general agreement on what is most important, of most value, in our present world. This fact precludes any single, agreed-upon perspective on the past; any perspective may allow a true account. Human tastes vary because of physical differences or, much more often, because of cultural differences. All historians join in finding significance in past events of a cultural sort, or in events infused with value, but this minimal concurrence only testifies to the fact that history is a story of the human past, a past ever replete with meanings and causes.

The only way that one could fully harmonize judgments of historical significance (of greater or lesser significance, of what one should and should not tell) would be for all historians to agree on some object of ultimate value, on some final end. Then, perhaps, all human events would have an assessable significance in reference to this end, and one could then fit limited and parochial judgments to some universal scale. But obviously, because of the very fact of cultural variation, because historians are all conditioned by history, they do not embrace the same ends and never will. Even to accept the objectivity of value (or, more plausibly, an objective method for the determination of goals) does not, with the present diversity of cultures, enable historians to establish any common framework of judgment. Yet, within given ideological, cultural, or national settings, historians do share many common preferences; this means that other historians and lay audiences do have a shared basis for evaluating the selective preferences of historians. They may fault a history not because of cognitive or esthetic issues (Is it true? Is it well written?) but because of the topic selected (Is it really significant? Is it not trivial?). Historians ever face the dismal prospect that in a few decades they will be adjudged foolish in their preferences, shortsighted in their pressing concerns, and be condemned for telling not false stories but the wrong ones.

Value and Historical Language

No methodological horrors lurk in the selective criteria used by a historian. Such selection does not preclude exact description and valid causal judgments. Surely the valuative aspect of selection, even though in history it operates within a topic as well as in the isolation of it, does not force a historian to write fiction or to bend his evidence to support some cause of his own. And although value selectivity determines the story one will tell and what can serve as evidence (only that which relates in a direct way to the story), it does not produce the evidence or provide any magical means of bypassing it.

But the problem of value is not so easily banished. Those who offer the most cogent arguments against historical objectivity may well accept the distinctions heretofore attempted. They may agree that objectivity is in no necessary way threatened by any personal interest that leads to the selection of a historical topic or to the selection of what to highlight within it, by other judgmental criteria located in the present, or by the imaginative and constructive elements of the story that originate in the thinking of a historian and never leap out of any quarry of facts. They will instead insist that value is most compromising not in such selective roles but as integral to almost all the language and to many of the judgments made by historians. It not only focuses interest; it also in part certifies the final product.

To what extent do private or culturally determined valuations affect the language and the judgments of a historian? First, and most obviously, a historian reveals his private preferences in the language that he uses. If he tried to eliminate such self-revealing language, he not only would be doomed to failure but would destroy the literary merit of his story. Since the historian must tell a story in familiar language, he has no recourse to any neutral, unambiguous symbolism. In fact, he often chooses words for expressive rather than cognitive reasons. His very willingness to bare personal taste, to show how he feels about a historical person or event, can add immensely to the dramatic impact of his stories. Few historians would want to dispense with beautiful vistas, compelling speeches, lovely people, or even glorious revolutions.

Such revelations of private taste need not threaten the objectivity of an inquiry in history or in any other discipline. But to advance this argument is to force a distinction between the cognitive, or truth-claiming, language in a completed history and the language that fulfills other purposes, such as esthetic ones. The historian, for example, might assert that monarchical greed was a contributory cause of a glorious revolution which led to national greatness. The causal argument, which asserts an existential relationship, is clearly cognitive. Any historical critic could rightly demand evidence to support it. But the historian would rather think his critic a fool if he demanded: "Prove that it was glorious." Clearly, in this context, the adjective expresses how a particular historian feels about a particular revolution. In the same sense, a biologist, describing a newly discovered butterfly and writing in ordinary language, could or could not give his own personal reaction to its bright colors. He could call it a beautiful butterfly and, in so doing, pose no threat to the accuracy of his description. In fact, his more colorful account would provide an experiential accuracy not usually present in scientific articles (it would reveal how it is for one person to experience such a butterfly). The nature of the historian's storytelling art makes it even more likely that he will frequently exploit such personal and colorful options.

This is not to argue that a critic can always draw a simple distinction between cognitive assertions and self-revealing language. Our language, again, is just not that precise. Expressions of preference are most innocent when they are most obvious, and they are often far from obvious. To say that Lincoln was a great man may mean, in one context, that one admires or likes him; in another, that he made decisions that drastically altered the future of the United States. The first use reveals the historian's taste in people; the second asserts a causal relationship and calls for evidential support. In such ambiguous contexts, the historian has an obligation to make his meaning clear. But there is no good reason for a historian to conceal his own personal reaction to Lincoln any more than there is a good reason for a biologist to conceal his reaction to a butterfly. Surely the obvious warning—that personal reactions must not lead one to ignore or misuse evidence—is almost too gratuitous to mention. What must be emphasized is that the problem of disciplinary integrity is not solved by the deletion of revealing language or by inhuman and impossible efforts at neutrality. Surely no one would suggest to historians the absurd if not impossible assignment of telling stories only about people, or groups of people, that they neither like nor dislike, about which they have no feelings or qualitative reactions whatsoever. This assignment would limit storytelling to blighted and neurotically insensitive people and, if applied to the generalizing sciences, would have the same effect there. The qualitative element is present in any art, including the cognitive ones. To try to suppress it is foolish and inhuman; to conceal it, a mere convention; to express it, a possible adornment; and to misuse it, a crime. In fact, concealment presents the greatest hazards and invites the greatest dishonesty.

The most subtle threat to objectivity—to a history with all its cognitive judgments tied completely to public evidence—is quite another use of valuative language. Even though not compelled by their subject to do so, historians often render verdicts on the acts of individuals and groups. ("His decision was a wise one"; "His solution revealed his brilliance"; "The country reacted rationally to all the threats.") Clearly, such judgments reflect what is often a very private language. Few persons, even in the same society, mean the same thing by such words as "wisdom." But the problem of meaning and thus of effective communication plagues almost all the language of historians. Here the critical issue is not meaning (we will assume that the historian can, if challenged, make perfectly clear what he means) but the type of support he can offer for his judgments. For in each case the historian intends more than a mere revelation of his personal reaction to events, more than "I feel or think so-and-so." Each judgment can be, at least in some sense, cognitive. It may rest on well-established theories and on extensive evidence, which, at least in a judicial sense, fully justifies the verdict rendered. Yet, in other societies, in other ages, the verdict would be different.

Such assessments implicate primarily not private taste but communal standards. On self-conscious reflection, the historian has to admit a valuative content in all such judgments, and he should claim objectivity only for the public, evidential component, which is identical in status to evidence in a court of law. In other words, he could prove that an individual did display the behavior that, in his society and by his own standards, clearly qualified him to be adjudged wise. He cannot prove that such behavior is "really" wise, for he has access to no universal and eternal standard, no infallible lawgiver to whom he can appeal. Just as in a court, in a context of established sanctions, it is meaningful to ask for proof, so a historian can respond to a requirement of proof for his verdicts. Neither in a court nor in a history is it appropriate to expect proof of the legitimacy of the standards assumed. But some understanding of these standards is a prerequisite for understanding the verdict.

The sum of all this is that the word "objectivity," even when restricted to a methodological standard, may still have two slightly different connotations for a historian. In the judicial context, it requires enough public evidence to substantiate a verdict within a set of culturally determined, valuative standards. In a causal context, it requires enough public evidence to substantiate a relationship, and relationships, as such, are not culturally conditioned (the willingness to value such relationships is culturally determined). Objectivity, in the verdict context, functions somewhat differently than objectivity in the generalizing sciences, where such assessments do not occur.

The Properties of Stories

All this chasing after the meaning of an ever more elusive objectivity should not obscure the complexity of a written history. It is a story as well as a purportedly true and objectively based account. One could express much of the purely cognitive content of any history in other ways—as a series of descriptions and as a list of causal hypotheses. But so expressed they do not yet constitute a history any more than a group of isolated melodies constitutes a symphony. A history is not only fact statements but also the complex, time-extended whole that includes them and that, quite often, directed a historian to them. Saying that a history is a story is much like saying that much of modern physics is rational and mathematical. But physics is not all truth; it is only the truth that fits the formal requirements of largely mathematical relationships. And physics is certainly not mathematics; it uses only those selected mathematical constructs that fit some aspects of experience. Likewise, historical truth is a quite limited variety of truth, and true stories about the human past make up only a small portion of all stories. In both cases, form and verity are complementary, and in their interaction they define the discipline. Isolated but true statements about even past human events ("John killed George in 1892") are not historical statements until one fits them into a story, into some history, with a theme and development over a period of time.

One result of all this is clear. A modern physicist must know mathematics. And no matter how many historians work at the bits and pieces of the past, eventually someone must be able to put these pieces together to form the story. Obviously, the form of a discipline does not determine the truth of its propositions, although many a scientist and many a historian, infatuated with the esthetic or moral merit of their latest constructs, have wished that it could. Thus there is no direct relationship between form and objectivity, unless one argues for an ontological rather than some instrumental or esthetic justification for a given form ("Reality really embodies a mathematical order and thus one can describe it only by a mathematical science").

As we emphasized in Chapter 8, it is a serious error, in physics or in history, to attribute a prior reality to the conceptual product of inquiry rather than to the experiential basis for the inquiry. Once invented, of course, the concepts are indeed part of an experienced reality. The mathematical order of the theoretical physicist is a human invention, but it is an order that one can fit to many parts of experience. Once we have fitted it, once the invented order has permitted us to locate uniformities or similarities in our experience, we too easily fall into the trap of seeing what experienced reality allows as what reality requires; we tend to ignore the creative and additive role of our conceptual inventions. They spring from human art, not from physical necessity. Experienced reality probably allows more physical constructs than we could ever imagine. The same is true in history. After finding causes, describing complex wholes, or finally constructing stories and disciplining them to fit evidence, we may come to think of our conceptualized past as a fixed, preexisting structure, awaiting our discovery, rather than seeing it for what it is—an imaginative, time-conditioned, but evidenced human invention. But reality as we experience it severely limits those concepts that we use to understand a part of reality and that we hope brings us into some harmonious, working relationship to that part. And it is in our dutiful respect for those limits that, in any discipline, we are objective.

So long as we do defer to the limits set by experienced reality, or by the aspects of this reality we select for ordering, we must place objectivity and its close relative, truthfulness, above all other goals in our cognitive arts. We often have to sacrifice esthetic and moral goals. A scientist has to dismiss the very hypothesis that, were it only true, would surely win the Nobel Prize and in addition cure all cancers. It may be elegant and beautiful but yet she cannot fit it to reality. The most instructive and entertaining account of the Protestant Reformation may not relate or unify enough of the surviving artifacts to be convincing, even if it does not directly contradict some known evidence. It may make a great novel but one must not advertise it as history. History, more than any other cognitive discipline, allows great scope for formal invention. In it, since no entities require complete explanation, since all causes are partial, since all areas of human experience are potential subject matter, one cannot set limits to the range of possible evidence. Since historians often have no alternative but to build on numerous weak inferences, one correctly judges them as much for the imaginative, intrinsically valuable aspects of their hypotheses and stories as for their truth or significance. One is a great historian not only because he tells the truth, finds the most relevant topic and the richest evidence, or makes the most brilliant inferences from it, but also because he tells a moving and eloquent story.

The narrative form not only is uniquely fitted to the historian's subject matter (they grew together); it also is necessary for what the historian wants to achieve. One tells a story about the past not to get some predictive knowledge, not to gain some direct control over events, but to produce, in the author and in his audience, a certain conceptual experience. A historian tries to get people to experience a particular past in many of its dimensions, often as much in its particularity as in its generality. The story form embraces not only causal relationships but conflict and struggle: dilemmas that await resolution, ironic and tragic situations, paradoxical and surprising events. To bring people to such an experience of a past is not an easy task. It certainly requires gifts of presentation. In many cases, a historian's metaphors are more important and harder to come by than her evidence. Rather than being a handicap, her rich and colorful language is a necessity. If the audience does not become involved in the story—if they do not appreciate it, grasp its significance, and see its relevance—they will lose all that it has for them (no technology flows from the historian's handiwork). In fact, "audience" is a key word for the historian. Unlike many scientists, a historian is not content to record in barely decipherable prose the results of her inquiry so that she will get the credit, so that her work will inform and enrich the ongoing process of inquiry, or so that it will effect some immediate practical return. For the historian, the presentation, in a form for maximum impact on an audience, is all-important, however dependent the finished story is on what she calls research or however many contributory analyses she may have made.

Because a historical narrative is, or purports to be, true (or as true as possible), it does not necessarily lose esthetic value. It can still be a superb work of art, with many features that have everything to do with it as a construct and nothing to do with it as truth. A gifted historian can create a unified whole out of many disparate parts; this is a problem not of inquiry but of organization. Where complexity confounds, she can find the most subtle words; where ambiguity lurks, the most precise; where drama hides, the most colorful. Even the truth she conveys demands such linguistic virtuosity, for she does not ignore but rather emphasizes qualitative aspects of a past (it was really a glorious battle to the victors). But art has to accept its limits and work its way around the immovable and demanding evidence. For gifted storytellers, this may hurt, but not as much as pedestrian historians imagine. Surely a historian must dig and sweat, count and calculate. But unless she is a horrible bore, she will do most of this work offstage. A completed history must not be merely an exhibition of evidence or analysis. Of course, a historian should look well, swim in and through a thousand archives, count carefully, calculate by every strategy of statistical science, let computers grind on for months. But finally she must present her story, now surely as true as refinements of method can make it, surely weighty in significance to justify all the work, and thus in all ways deserving of the respect that only beauty can elicit.

The word "objective" is often associated, misleadingly, with the idea that historians must tell what happened, just as it happened, even if not all that happened, in some human past. If such a statement is qualified in a certain way, it has to be in part true. No one would suggest the opposite—that a historian should tell what did not happen. But "What happened?" is precisely the question. Does it mean all the various experiences involved? If so, we are asking the impossible. Does it mean the past as proximate participants conceptualize and remember it? If so, it might be recoverable but, unless further interpreted in light of more recent events hidden to participants, it would be a past with little meaning to us, a past full of absurd judgments. Does it mean some selected past that lies partially revealed in artifacts, including the recorded words of participants, and a past that endlessly takes on new significance as time passes? If so (and surely it is so), then historians may tell what happened, in a sense, but not just as it happened, and not without many characterizations that reflect present concepts and present understanding.

History as Inquiry

Despite all their distinguishing characteristics, histories result from inquiry. Such inquiry does not reflect any distinctive road to truth (it is rather a road to a distinctive type of truth). To repeat, while history is distinctive in subject, form, and use, it is not distinctive from other cognitive disciplines in method. The historian must conform to the same rules of inference (logic) and to the same canons of inductive verification as any other inquirer. Considered in this narrowed context, history presents, to the logician or to the philosopher of science, the same cognitive demands as physics or biology.

The following somewhat generalized model of inquiry illuminates some substantive methodological issues in history. John Dewey first formulated this model, but Karl Popper and others have subsequently, with slightly altered emphasis, adopted and refined it. When a historian who follows it is confronted with and in some way baffled or disturbed by disparate phenomena that seem to give evidence about some human past, he begins to construct an imaginary account or narrative, one that might include several causal judgments. He uses it to unify and make some sense out of all the confusing phenomena, then checks such an invented story against a residue of acquired knowledge (vicarious verification) as well as against the focal phenomena. He keeps at this game until he is able to construct a story that is consistent with what he already knows and that gives some pattern to the originally disturbing or exciting phenomena (or most of them). Since such a narrative will almost inevitably implicate other, as yet unexperienced phenomena, he must seek them out, either directly or by inferential, deductive chaining (desired phenomenon A necessitates B, and B necessitates C, which if found will have the same evidential significance as A), knowing always that one unpredicted and noncoherent phenomenon will falsify his story. He must keep restructuring his story until, finally, with the most diligent search for all evidence then available, he has so integrated the original phenomena and the induced phenomena as to have a quite unified, plausible, and supported account (as well as, we hope, an eloquent and dramatic story), although he knows that falsifying evidence could turn up at any time and that his story is tentative because of the many probable inferences that had to go into it.

How does this model fit historical practice? Perhaps better than the working historian thinks. The problem-solving aspect, if given quite broad meaning, may be present in any historical inquiry, but of course rarely accounts for the motives of the historian. But since these motives are usually extrinsic to the inquiry (an assigned dissertation, pecuniary goals), they are not directly relevant to the model. The historian, in the often years-long interaction between evidence and imaginative construction, is hardly aware of the complex interplay of invention, deduction, and inductive verification; he may well reject any formal analysis of his procedure. But this also means very little.

The most crucial problem with the model (or is it with historical practice?) is that very often the historian's causal hypotheses and narrative do not (or cannot) attain the precision and coherence needed to permit clear-cut falsification by one or a few exceptional or unanticipated phenomena. Quite simply, he almost always ends up with lower-probability assertions in direct proportion to the scope or importance of his accounts. With near surety, he may say that Oswald killed Kennedy (this assertion, at least, might be refuted by contrary evidence), but, given a series of necessarily weak inferences, what probability and how much precision is there in an allegation that the key remote cause was the violent state of American society? If he could give this causal proposition precise and operational meaning, and if he could find evidence to support it, it is still difficult to argue that, in a sea of necessary conditions, this was in any sense the most determinate cause, and thus to give a quasi-quantitative weight to it. Although supporting evidence might strengthen his argument, it could hardly falsify it. At most, elaborate statistical data might weaken it.

The working historian will almost always respond more avidly to a phenomenological account of inquiry than to a logical account. This tendency is not remarkable; she is the best judge of her own experience and possibly no judge at all in the field of logic. She particularly responds to any account of inquiry that emphasizes creativity and inventiveness. She rarely analyzes the methodological and logical nuances of her art; she is a good historian as a result of good habits rather than of good rules. She is well acquainted with historical inquiry as a type of experience, with all its qualitative blessings and agonies. Perhaps for this reason she can find the language of insight and intuition, of imaginative identification and vicarious re-creation, of reliving and rethinking, quite persuasive. And, insofar as one can conceptualize a creative process, such language may be both ambiguous and yet quite accurate. Only after long contact with a subject area and long intimacy with potential sources, and thus with what seems like the veritable reliving of a past age, can a historian's efforts to construct narratives or to devise causal hypotheses be very fruitful. Thus the intuitionist view of history is most closely related to the formal part of history, to brilliant composition and imaginative leaps, but it is not correctly tied to inferential and evidential issues.

Even the blanket word "research" covers two quite distinctive historical activities, even if historians rarely distinguish them and even though they are rarely widely separated in time. Historians, seeking some correct story about a past that seems somehow important—or, in a more narrow, analytical context, seeking a correct causal explanation for some confusing even if quite narrow problem in well-rehearsed stories of the past—often immerse themselves in the relics of that age or in the possible evidence for solving the problem. They go to the archives; they endlessly read manuscripts; they take notes of material that seems to be relevant. Out of this experiential immersion process comes unifying themes or causal hypotheses. In other words, this type of research contributes directly to fruitful invention, to formal construction, and not to the inductive verification of hypotheses. Even the materials handled are not yet historical evidence or data of any sort. The word "source" perhaps correctly identifies them. Benedetto Croce was most perceptive in characterizing as dead the artifacts that librarians and archivists dutifully, even piously retrieve and store, in the expectation that someone, someday, in conceptualizing a certain relevant past, will convert them into living symbols, finally rich with meaning.

Once the constructive phase of history begins (a schema, a convincing pattern or theme, a crucial causal hypothesis), and it may begin very soon or never, a second type of research becomes possible, and this alone involves true inductive verification. Then and only then do questions need to be answered, problems cry out for solution, and forms demand specific content. Maybe by good guesses or habitual thoroughness, the historian has dutifully viewed all the relevant manuscripts and transferred all relevant data to photographs, recordings, or note cards. Then he can carry out the verification process at his desk. Maybe his memory is acute, and he can make use of what now becomes evidence without any further recourse to archives or notes. In the first phase of research, when the historian familiarizes himself with his material ("familiarization" is a key and precise word in the historian's vocabulary), the process seems to be akin to osmosis, an absorption or intuitive grasp (like getting to know John Smith, a matter of existential encounter and immediate perception, undistorted by concepts). This world of immediate experience is the fount of all conceptual invention. And very often the constructive parts of history—the brilliant narrative patterns or the daring hypotheses—seem to be all-important. They are in the limelight much more than evidential verification, and they usually distinguish the great from the mediocre historian. Here, in constructive invention, is the outlet for historical genius; here the intuitive historian can meet an age in diverse, fragmentary surviving artifacts and see a unifying pattern and likely connections. The verification process may seem as unexciting and as cold as taking John Smith's fingerprints to be sure of his identity, or administering a physical examination to certify the state of his health, or counting his money to attest to his wealth, when one already "knows" that he is John Smith and that he is both healthy and wealthy.

But neither in the present nor even more in constructs about the past can we really know without examining and counting. We only indirectly encounter the subjects of our histories and infer their very existence from deposited and surviving effects. One can preface a characterization of a friend, John Smith, as follows: "If you will go and meet John Smith and carefully observe him, you will find the following. . . ." But for a historical John Smith, the same preface has to read: "If you will go and look in these designated places, you will find the following evidence, which, with the greatest probability, shows John Smith to have been as follows. . . ." In this operational perspective, a historical proposition, even though about something that existed in the past, has the same reference to some future verifying experience as any other existential hypothesis, and it has cognitive meaning only in this reference. However brilliant the hypothesis and however loyal to an existential acquaintanceship with some of the sources, it still prescribes some work to be done. If the work orders are clear, the phenomena of a type in theory perceivable by anyone, then the historical proposition is meaningful, testable, and object-referring. The actual work may be fruitless, the perceptions required unachievable, and the proposition false. But it is of the type that one can objectively test.

Practical Warnings

The sum of all this analysis and qualification is probably the following advice to historians: Unless you are willing to define very carefully, drop all the conventional methodological dualities from your vocabulary. It is usually futile to talk of "objectivity versus subjectivity," of "presentism versus loyalty to a real past," or of "relativism versus positivism." All such dualities rest on arbitrary definitions and thus become snares for the unwary. No one has any compelling reason to doubt that history is a valid cognitive discipline. Propositions about the human past can be meaningful (they clearly indicate the evidence that will vindicate them); one can objectively verify them. One can, with ever higher probabilities, confirm any number of historical judgments by use of evidence. And one can use evidence to falsify claims about clear and precise relationships, or use statistical tools to weaken judgments of probability. Most important, the varied ways in which preferences or values influence historical inquiry (in selection of a topic, in selection within a topic, in expression of self-revealing but noncognitive judgments, in their influence on the choice of perspective or plot, in their revelation of the conventional standards within a society) do not in any way preclude evidenced, objectively justified cognitive judgments. None of the subjective aspects of inquiry make history a form of fiction.

But some final warnings are in order. Objectivity, a matter of methodological rigor, does not guarantee truth. Despite ever-present possibilities of human error or of remote chances for clever forgery or prefabrication of evidence (they are present in any area of inquiry), the historian can conclusively validate the occurrence of simple events, detailed descriptions of events, and even many proximate and simple causal relationships. Here the historian need entertain no more doubts than a physical scientist. But such simple knowledge is rarely a point of controversy among historians; much of it they take for granted. As soon as historians move on to complex patterns and to more sweeping, remote causes, they often move beyond any conclusive evidence. Here their inventive and constructive work is all-important. From long acquaintanceship with the sources, from moving among the scattered artifacts, able historians come to feel confident of at least the suggestively approximate validity of their judgments, even at times when they cannot support them with more than a few fragments of ambiguous evidence.

It is usually easy to demonstrate the tenuousness of the chain of arguments that make up almost any complex historical judgment. In this sense, much of history is a stab into partial darkness, a matter of informed but inconclusive conjecture. The available evidence rarely necessitates our judgments but, if we are responsible, it will at least be consistent with them. Obviously, in such areas of near conjecture, one cannot claim any demonstrably correct "explanations," but only offer, quite tentatively, currently unfalsifiable and possibly correct hypotheses. Here, on issues that endlessly fascinate the historian, the controversies rage, and no one expects, short of the unexpected discovery of a great wealth of new data, to find conclusive answers. An undesired, abstractive precision of the subject might so narrow it as to permit more conclusive evidence. But that would spoil all the fun.

CHAPTER 12
USE

ANY serious consideration of history should end with an answer to the critical question: Of what possible use are true stories about the human past? Definition and delimitation are prerequisites for these answers, but they do not reveal them. If historical knowledge were general, with lawlike regularities and the power of exact prediction, it would provide the same kind of instrumentality as the physical sciences. But it is not and does not. Therefore one must elaborate the quite different uses that a history may serve. Of course, to show its possible uses is not the same thing as to show how people do in fact use it or misuse it.

Intrinsic or Esthetic Values

An obvious, yet in some ways the most complex, use of a history is as a source of various types of satisfaction to those who write it and to those who read it. Some of these satisfactions are intrinsic to the discipline; others are completely or largely extrinsic to it. For the historian, much more than for the consumer of histories, these satisfactions variously relate to motives—to the reasons for her being a historian or for her writing the particular histories that she does write. Such motives or apprehended reasons are of no great methodological import, and they rarely coincide with the extended uses that such a history may have. The private reason that a historian writes a particular book may be far removed from the value that her history, as history, may have even for her, let alone for other people.

People become historians for many reasons. One must emphasize that today the decision to become a historian is generally a decision to become part of a well-defined profession; it is a decision to assume a clear social role; and it is thus a decision that one may make with scarcely any reference to particular histories that one needs to write or to any broad social purpose that such histories might serve. Few students now enter the profession because of any compelling desire to know and reveal a specific part of the human past.

Not too long ago, most historians still believed that the reasons that persons became historians—or, even more, the reasons they selected certain topics—had grave methodological significance. Thus they variously confused psychological and logical issues, as did Charles A. Beard in some of his ill-fated excursions into historiography. Few make such a glaring mistake today. But, at least in the American historical profession, one still senses a rather clear hierarchy of more and less acceptable reasons for being a historian and for writing particular histories. As I use "reasons" here, the word does not mean hidden or compulsive causes; it means the conscious intents of historians, or the ends they seem to serve. For example, historians who write in hopes of bolstering some ideology, of furthering some practical moral or political cause, or of gaining popular esteem or a large income, may risk their professional standing. Their colleagues may suspect them of being nonobjective, if not completely dishonest. But colleagues may honor historians who write because of a quite personal interest in some past (curiosity), to gain self-knowledge, or even for sheer fun. They believe them more likely to be objective and reliable. They reveal this functional hierarchy by such a favored but almost incomprehensible and absurd expression as "history for its own sake" or, to multiply absurdities, "the past for its own sake." Those who use such expressions surely mean something like "history for my sake" or "history for my immediate gratification and enjoyment, without any concern for its further usefulness," or possibly that "historians should vindicate their work by correctly interpreting artifacts drawn from a past, not by any imposition of present valuations." No historian intends what such statements seem to mean: that history or the past has somehow taken on a life of its own or has ends of its own to serve.

It seems that the distinctions between the varied motives of a historian parallel the many distinctions made between pure and practical scientists. At best, all such distinctions embody only half-truths. No inquiry, in any field, is pure in the sense of excluding all extrinsic or instrumental goals. But inquiry, if artfully pursued, is full of immediate value. It is enjoyable; it may be pervaded with an esthetic quality. As people develop skill in any field of inquiry, as they acquire and assume certain personal goals (esteem, salary, professional standing), and as they soothe their conscience by a conventional assurance that the product does serve some moral ends (even though unspecified), then the only focal and conscious ends served by inquiry may be esthetic ones. The vocation becomes a compelling avocation, completely self-justifying. Then scientists or historians might suggest, in all honesty, that they conducted their inquiries out of sheer enjoyment or because of their love of truth (they might even suggest that any other reasons are ulterior and suspect). And, almost always, the best products of inquiry come from persons who are conceptual artists—from those who respond most fully to the demands of their chosen art form. The worst science and the worst history come from nonartists—from people who seek only extrinsic ends, who never love the subject, never see its challenges, and never reap its immediate rewards.

Thus in one sense of the term, historical inquiry is always self-justifying. Intrinsic rewards are always present and may well dominate all others. But such artful and rewarding historical inquiry is not without use, even though the language used to describe it may imply that it is. More important, the returns from doing history are quite different from the uses of the history as product; the prime return from inquiry may be personal and immediate, and the motivation to inquire is often more powerful because of this return. When historians laud truth as the sole object of their inquiry, they really celebrate a form of beauty or something that yields immediate appreciation and value, something that brings joy in itself and not as a result of any of its effects.

Surely, most historians love their work. It is even conceivable (but very unlikely) that somewhere a historical artist seeks fitting topics not because of any expected use, of any moral purposes, or of any professional or pecuniary rewards, but solely because of esthetic and intellectual criteria—the story that will answer the most intriguing questions, unify harmoniously the most evidence, form that most eloquent story, pose the most creative challenges, and permit the most fulfilling resolution. This does not mean that such a person could escape some of the pervasive concerns of time and place, for no one can conceive of topics outside of some spatiotemporal context; nor does it mean that cultural significance does not guide the selection of topic and treatment, for no challenging or broadly unifying topic could fail to reflect this criterion. But one's purpose may not extend beyond the completed history, although one may anticipate some appreciation from other historical artists. Perhaps the historian does not care a whit whether her history has social utility or whether it will win her a promotion. Now, as a matter of fact, such an artful history will inevitably serve other than esthetic ends. If it is a work of genius, it will undoubtedly gain her the promotion and influence thousands of people. It may lead to major changes in a society's goals. But we here assume that our dedicated historian, in her lofty purity, has not been sullied by such gross considerations.

Who has ever known such a pure historian? And if such purity were remotely possible, would it be desirable? A snobbish hypocrisy marks those who, even if they do not attain it, still venerate it. But the partial truth is still there: both the intense interest and the esthetic returns are almost indispensable for any dedicated inquiry. Fortunately, the relationship between esthetic and moral goals is never disjunctive, but often quite complementary. The moral purposes directly intended by a historian (his desire to tell such stories and in such a way as to change and better the goals, tastes, habits, and institutions of a society) are ultimately esthetic goals. But they are much broader ones than those of the pure historical artist. Instead of immediate private value, he seeks a society that is more generous in its bestowal of value on everyone. He seeks a beautiful society as well as a beautiful history. Thus, often, the emphasis on pure history (or pure science) amounts to a form of selfishness, or to some hoarding of intellectual values, or even to a refusal to engage critical but complex moral issues that, whatever the historian's intent, will be somewhat affected by any good history. Conceivably, the pure historian and the morally committed but artful historian might write histories of similar merit, but for different reasons. The morally conscious historian may be the better person, but obviously he is not is not for that reason the better historian. This only indicates what should be obvious: motivation is, in itself, an issue completely distinct from the merit of any historical product. But it is extremely unlikely that either the skill or the effort required by great history will be present when the esthetic goals are missing.

Extrinsic goals of a personal type do not conflict with intrinsic or esthetic goals, but neither do they necessarily complement them. Historians are persons with varied needs. They must earn a living, gain self-respect, find security in some social role. If they cannot find these returns in the historical profession, they may not be able to afford the luxury of composing any history at all. If one's preferred art can secure other than esthetic or even long-range moral returns, then one can give more time to that art and become a better (if not a "purer") artist. And in history, as elsewhere, good art is all too scarce. We need more. But "pure" art is unneeded, even if it were remotely attainable.

Extrinsic goals probably play a larger role in the selection of a career and in the selection and treatment of topics than most historians either imagine or would willingly admit. Of course, everyone remarks the books calculated for a student market or jealously condemns other historians for falling for the bright lures of some publisher. But these focal concerns do not begin to match the extrinsic influences exerted by a self-conscious and organized profession. At least since the late nineteenth century, most historians have functioned as members of a profession, usually in some association with professional organizations and journals, and almost always in an academic intellectual role. Today the product generally labeled history is produced largely in these professional work-shops and according to loose but restrictive professional conventions. Here the historian is at one with other merchants of ideas and knowl-edge. Throughout the modern world, professionalization has standard-ized products in form and content and in many ways has vastly improved the overall product.

The historical profession largely determines the motives that first lead students into areas of historical investigation, even into a lifework. They may write their first book in order to get a Ph.D. and possibly at the behest of a major professor. They may early become involved in in-terpretive one-upmanship and do yeoman work in order to refute great historians and thus gain recognition. They may look for topics that may please convention program chairpersons. Even their courtship of pub-lishers will be motivated less by a zeal for better-informed students or even pecuniary rewards than by a desire for professional status. These professional considerations may push personal interests, esthetic re-wards, and moral purpose ever further into the background. The costs of such concerns include an increase in pedantry, in intramural conflicts of no interest to anyone but the main participants, in the substitution of the form of scholarship for its substance; in an environment that invites selfish career boosting and discourages moral concern and moral perspective among historians. But with professionalization has come an increase in the number of historians, of written histories, and of his-torical publications of all sorts. Above all, at its best, it has encouraged intellectual integrity and rigor in historians, not just as ideals to be sought but as internalized habits.

But even when historians are most influenced by extrinsic goals, they may still respond to intrinsic rewards. Most do. Many people, including some historians, have an antiquarian bent; they enjoy contact with an-cient manuscripts. Perennial detectives may enjoy piecing together evi-dence and finding answers to historical puzzles. Admittedly, neither musty manuscripts nor arts of detection constitute a method, but each may be a part of historical inquiry. Other people, with literary talent, find their reward in composing history, in organizing their insights into eloquent accounts. Masters of inquiry may find their rewards in scholarly exactitude, in the marshaling of conclusive evidence in behalf of sig-nificant causal hypotheses, or in adding their insight to a growing body of historical knowledge. Finally, such inquiry is intellectually fruitful; it bares new and intriguing problems, encourages further thought and analysis, and attracts students with a philosophical turn of mind. When any of these rewarding personal returns are present, historical inquiry has the same justification as a fine art, and it is at least as useful as valued forms of recreation and enjoyable even if pointless intellectual games.

History and Public Policy

Entirely apart from one's personal motives, almost anything one does has some social impact, either in drawing on the resources of society or, through its effect on individuals, in changing their exact role in society. This is as true of recreation as it is of historical inquiry, recognizably so in most societies, which variously support and control both. One may swim simply because swimming is fun. But it also incidentally aids good health. Maybe most individuals compose histories for enjoyment or for completely extrinsic reasons (a career boost). Nonetheless, such historical thinking may change an individual and, if widely indulged in, a whole society. Most historians are a bit skeptical about the uses of their product, for they see how often people outside their profession overlook almost all the individual and social benefits that really derive from histories and how often they offer overt justifications of history which are either mistaken or beside the point. This is sometimes true of justifications offered by historians, usually true of justifications offered by educators, and almost always true of any justifications given by politicians, who after all provide many of the resources necessary for the development and dissemination of historical knowledge. Always applauded for the wrong reasons, called on for the wrong kind of advice, denounced for the wrong deficiencies, historians are indeed tempted to accede to a gigantic fraud not of their own making.

Few historians write or teach for purely personal goals or solely because they both enjoy and get paid for what they do; at least, few think they do so for these reasons alone. They aspire to a more honored social role. Often without rigorous analysis, historians assume that the product of their discipline has some value to other people and even to a whole society. If pressed, they will insist that other people enjoy history and will usually vaguely suggest other uses for it. Consoled by undoubted assumptions of usefulness, they may never bother to identify any specific return from their own inquiry. They are doing history. And history, as everyone knows, is important. In a professional context, only a minority of historians choose their career, select topics for investigation, and emphasize certain aspects of those topics because of some clarified moral goal that they believe their history can or must serve. But there are still exceptions. Some historians want their work, in specified ways, to form better character in individuals or to influence more desirable policies in a society. Yet when historians attain a greater degree of moral self-consciousness and more clearly formulate their goals, they risk censure if their valuations are unconventional (a well-supported story may provoke critical doubt about some revered belief or institution), but they may gain popular praise for more conventional causes (national histories written to induce loyalty and patriotism). Surprisingly, in either case they may provoke professional suspicion, particularly if they seem to be making a special plea, possibly in behalf of some ideology. From this perspective one might conclude, somewhat pessimistically, that historians are most professional when they leave purposes to the professions, to the established order of things, and look to their own immediate tasks and carry out their own assigned role.

Just as a historian may deliberately reveal overt, clearly identified personal valuations, so morally self-conscious historians may become so concerned about how others will use their histories that they try to influence that use by overt sermons, by drawing the moral of the case. Such sermons are not necessary to a history and of course are not cognitive, not subject to proof. Convention, which keeps the scientist from emphasizing desired uses, does allow the historian this option. In any case, such is the transparency of a historian's language that explicit moralizing usually clarifies only what is obviously already present, perhaps in the form of clearly implied policy guidelines. But two qualifications are here in order. The desired moral use must not play any evidential role in inquiry. This is obvious, but the line between correctly permitting moral purpose to guide topic selection and illegitimately permitting it to guide the search for evidence is very narrow. The topic selected and the hypotheses about it do necessarily guide this search. Finally, no historian has very much control over the use of his product. One cannot calculate use by such a simple expedient as pointing out one's preferences. Like scientists, historians must suffer the agony of what they may well conceive to be all manner of immoral and improper uses of their product. Given the diversity of belief and purpose in a society, a true story of the past may convey many divergent lessons and may seem to support many different policies.

History is rarely a magical tool for achieving any of our fondest goals. In fact, quite often historical knowledge seems to impede our efforts to attain our desires. Some of our desires may be of such a nature that no existential truth can justify them. If we want to get rich on quackery, then medical science is a hindrance, although some pseudoscience may be our prime resource. If we wish to exorcise some detested habits or institutions, we may falsely attribute to them an illegitimate or dishonest parentage. Then historical knowledge is an impediment to our purpose; fantasies about the past are excellent armament. And historical quacks are not easy to detect; they too easily camouflage their deceit or blind-ness or too often share it with their audience. The point is clear. Much that purports to be history is indeed fantasy, but it may be valuable propaganda nonetheless. Yet in some cases, history—history as true as evidence permits—may be good propaganda. One cannot establish the integrity of the product by surveying its uses. Clever deceit almost always takes the form of impersonality and detachment instead of fervent com-mitment. And one can at least hope that serious commitment will foster the integrity that eschews illusion and that, whatever the short-run cost, embraces an often hard truth.

History has probably been most misunderstood and most abused as an allegedly simple tool for justifying personal and public decisions. This is the history (or pseudohistory) that is always "proving" something. Indeed, if there were a constant, generalized human nature, then ac-counts of past human effort might be unambiguously instructive. But even in the absence of anything of the sort, there seems to be a certain logic in trying to use history to prove things. Surely, on the basis of past experience rather than of chemical evidence, one can suggest the danger of ingesting arsenic or of trying to do without liquids for thirty days. The example simply illustrates a type of nontheoretical empiricism leading to a loose physical generalization. The examples drawn from the past, although related to human values and policies, only show, by a few examples, the probable relationship between certain chemicals and the human body. Given some policy, such as the preservation of life, such low-level scientific knowledge can indeed justify policy deci-sions, but only in the same way that any scientific knowledge, in clarifying means and consequences, allows informed decision making. In no sense is such a generalization historical; it reveals an invariant relationship of a chemical sort, a relationship not conditioned by time or by meanings, even though data drawn from a past can verify it (one may verify much scientific knowledge by data from the past; the date of the evidence has nothing to do with its verifying role).

It does not make sense to talk about proving a choice true. Choice is not a cognitive issue. But one may justify a choice by a twofold reference—to the end one intends it to serve and to the adequacy of the means one uses to attain it. The end served does implicate history and one can often clarify it only by some historical inquiry—by finding out how it came to be. By clarifying an end, one may be better able to judge critically its relevance to experienced value and thus its desira-bility. Unlike the end served, the means contemplated implicate rela-tionships that hold between events. One can fully justify these rela-tionships only by some type of scientific knowledge, which one can indeed verify. But to validate relationships is not to validate choice, although a choice that does not take into account invariant relationships is blind.

More often, a history supposedly proves something in a quite different sense. Thus many people allege that the aftermath of the Munich conference of 1938 proved the effects that flow from appeasement. This claim involves a minor problem of definition and a major problem of correct analogy. As the word was used after Munich, "appease" soon lost almost all of its generic meaning: to calm, to pacify. It is now dangerous to use it in any context other than that of Munich. "Appeasement" no longer suggests a legitimate aim of diplomatic negotiation but only Neville Chamberlain's sacrifice of Czechoslovakia at Munich. Thus it is a time-conditioned word, a historical label, much like "Renaissance," and we may soon begin referring to the Appeasement with complete accuracy.

The problem of analogy is much more complex and revealing. If Munich teaches us anything, it does so because it shares certain features with other diplomatic conferences. And surely analogies may be drawn. It is a foolish mistake to overemphasize the nonrepeatable or unique aspects of any complex historical event (after all, no event, in its entirety, is repeatable) or to ignore similarities between historical events. But it is the height of wisdom to indicate the complexity of historical events and the minimal chance that many of the features will ever repeat. Any two diplomatic conferences will reveal both similarities and differences; but all too often the similarities have little policy significance, or they reflect common features already assumed by any policy maker (an example might be the well-justified rule that nations usually seek what they perceive to be their self-interest). Almost always, the most important policy guidelines are in the particular and contextual and nonrepeatable features of an event, and these one cannot anticipate by any general knowledge. When politicians use Munich to prove the certain results of appeasement, they almost invariably generalize nonanalogous features and assert them to be true of all diplomatic conferences. They illegitimately transform the actualities of Germany and of Hitler into concealed, lawlike propositions about the behavior of nations, ideologies, dictators, and even all humankind.

We must not then conclude that, in diplomacy or anywhere else, historical knowledge is irrelevant to policy making. But we must acknowledge that its relationship to policy is very subtle. One can often predict both personal and national behavior with high probability. All foreign policy today is based on a detailed knowledge of other nations. Much of this predictable behavior depends on physical determinants, such as geography and climate. But much is tied to cultural influences, and one can account for a developed culture only by reference to a particular history. If one is to predict what John Doe or France will most likely do tomorrow, one has to know quite particular things about the person or the culture; in other words, one has to know about final causes, about purposes and goals, some of which may be quite recent in origin. In a narrow context, such knowledge is descriptive and analytical; in a broader context, it is historical. Historically blind description—however sophisticated one's methods of acquiring and interpreting data, however ingenious one's models or behavioral theories—is much like limited, nonrandom sampling in the physical sciences. Here only a backdrop of theory, of already assumed conditions and possibilities, allows a judgment in one case that fifteen repeated occurrences do not a rule make (or, more likely, that they only a trivial rule make) while in another that only two repeated occurrences exemplify a rule of great scope and highest probability. In the same sense, only a backdrop of historical knowledge can rescue policy studies from a tragically blind empiricism that one can adorn by all manner of formal and statistical aids without relieving it of any of its blindness.

A history in itself, and particularly by analogy, never justifies any policy decision. We have no built-in assurance that any particular aspect of the past will repeat. Not all aspects can repeat. But the past is related to the future, and, at least by setting limits and conditions, does condition it. Without a specific past, some human events are impossible; with a particular past, others are impossible. Before historical knowledge can correctly relate to policy decisions, one must supplement it by the most exact possible knowledge of the decision context. No stories about the past can provide this knowledge; at best, they provide only a framework for making better sense out of such knowledge, for interpreting and applying it. Statesmen should interpret their intelligence in the light of diplomatic history, including Munich. Given the various "lessons" mislearned from Munich, they at least may expect, in carefully defined contexts, certain behavior from a nation such as the United Kingdom. Even though Munich did not prove any rule about diplomatic conferences, it very much changed subsequent conferences.

To relate historical knowledge to policy is a bit confusing. In one sense, now the more typical sense, policy making takes place within an assumed valuative context; it is a matter of proximate goals and correct means. The backdrop for such policy is a vast, slow-changing culture, with habits reflecting goals that few people have thought about for generations; such goals rarely come under review by anyone, much less by policy makers. Nonetheless, any new programs adopted must relate to this backdrop, and in some minor degree each new policy may imperceptibly help to modify it. On occasion, either within a policy-making context or without, we recognize some of the more foundational beliefs and habits and openly affirm or challenge them. At this point policy making becomes much more than a matter of conventional decision making; it is searching and fundamental ethical and philosophical criticism. Such broad criticism encompasses the more restricted policy making and may undercut it at its most vulnerable point—the ends it uncritically serves. At the level of ethics, of moral philosophy, of esthetic appreciation, the specialized policy studies all have to face judgment in a higher court.

Many of the traditional arguments for the social utility of history have stressed its role in abetting rational decision making, at either the individual or the group level. When most history was politically oriented, it was supposed to foster citizenship in an individual, statesmanship in politicians, and wise policies in government. In a context of overarching cultural values, themselves rarely questioned, it surely did play that role. But even here a true story about the past, as well as rigorous general knowledge, can provide only a backdrop for quite detailed, contextually comprehensive descriptions; it can never substitute for them. Both law and history are implicit in any policy decision; each requires its due, whether recognized or not (and nonrecognition may be a prelude to disastrous choice). But lame historical analogies cannot identify the relevant norms or habits; we can determine these only by the most rigorous and thorough analysis of the present context. A political adviser, unaware of the varied effects of the Civil War on voting behavior—on habitual preferences and political goals—might remark a statistical correlation between corn prices and Republican pluralities in an Iowa congressional district. He might then leap to the conclusion that he had located the essential condition for Republican successes and, as a result of this misapprehension, completely mislead a prospective candidate who wished to develop a winning platform. At the very least, only extensive empirical investigation could clarify what a little historical knowledge makes obvious: many voters in the district will vote Republican no matter what the price of corn. But not all will so vote, and possibly not enough to ensure a Republican victory. Without quite an array of supporting empirical data, no historian could cite the effects of the Civil War on voting patterns as the sole or even a major condition for a recent Republican victory. Thus as justifications of policy, historical knowledge and detailed description are always complementary and interactive. Neither can stand alone.

The unraveling of this interaction not only reveals one valid use of history but further clarifies definitional problems in the vague area loosely called the social sciences. All these disciplines have one common point of reference: humanity. Beyond that point the definitions vary. Some political scientists and economists, for example, retain an ancient interest in moral theory; they continue to invent normative models of an ideal political economy in the hope that their essentially philosophical labors will lead to criticism at the most fundamental level of policy, or at the level of ends and purposes. Some social scientists still describe human behavior against a backdrop of historical and cultural understanding. But most reflect not only the analytical sophistication of this century but also some of the disciplinary fads of the moment. Just as social thinkers in the eighteenth century looked to such physical determinants as climate and geography, and in the nineteenth century to culture and history, so they now turn to behavioral theory, which they draw from psychology. They look for the generalizable aspects of human behavior and are often oriented more toward the definition of their fledgling sciences than to immediate policy uses. But many social scientists are incurably addicted to policy goals; they actively advise or serve governments or hope that their research and teaching will directly influence government policies, or that they can develop analytical models (in themselves purely imaginative abstractions) with enough empirical relevance to provide needed policy guidelines.

Abetted by an ever more narrow topical and chronological specialization, many historians work very closely with such policy-oriented social scientists. In fact, their work variously overlaps. For example, a political scientist (the label is here loosely applied) who works in a culturally conditioned area of human behavior (and politics is one such area) needs a historical perspective to clarify many of his problems. When he cannot borrow it from a historian, he may become a historian himself and unravel a particular story about the past. Likewise, a political historian, trying to make sense out of her data, may use statistical techniques developed by political scientists, may see new nuances of meaning in her data by relating them to some borrowed analytical model, and, finally, may want to compare a past context to a present one, only to find no adequate contextual description of the present. In another context she may need a model or an ideal type as a comparative tool for understanding past behavior, only to find that no one has invented such a model. In both cases, she will probably do the work of the political scientist and even use some of his research techniques. The more closely a historical specialty correlates with a social science, the more intimate is the possible interaction. Unfortunately, the interaction can be narrowing as well as broadening. A historian who tells very selective stories and ties them to a cognate social science hardly provides an extensive backdrop for social analysis; she may even unconsciously adopt some of the most myopic perspectives of the social scientist.

With the decline of epochal national histories, and with more specialization and professionalization, academic historians often seem to have a rather narrow policy orientation. But even though historians may deny it, much economic, political, diplomatic, and social history is clearly policy oriented. The changing topical fashions, although variously motivated, reflect this policy orientation. In some histories the policy guidelines are quite explicit. Post–World War II historical monographs in the United States dealt endlessly with such focal policy issues as imperialism, collective security, the welfare state, economic growth, business monopoly, the party system, and constitutional safeguards. In the sixties, varieties of social history bloomed; black history thrived. In the seventies environmental and women's history gained major support. In both decades, more ideologically self-conscious young historians offered a radical critique of American institutions and chose topics congenial to their political goals. But despite these changes, few academic historians make their values explicit, and few American historians have directly challenged their nation's most basic beliefs and values.

The development of a strong nationalism was one of the clear, often overt ends served by many nineteenth-century American historians. Their efforts helped unify the diverse states and regions and surely aided in the transformation of newly arrived immigrants into "good" Americans. But since 1900, a majority of political and economic historians have been concerned largely with the better working of our national institutions, as have many social scientists. Only since the sixties have ideological issues, and with them some searching concerns about ends, moved a few historians to a careful and subtle examination of the final causes that lurk in our institutions, of the beliefs that once were conscious and overtly loved. Actually, few but intellectual historians have been able to operate at this level of conceptual rigor. The average historical monograph of today remains a labyrinth of undefined ideological labels, of liberals and conservatives ad nauseam, but may reflect a careful and thorough search for evidence and a careful statistical weighing of its importance. At least historians are now disseminating, in a more popular guise, some of the latest tools and findings of social scientists. And their technical proficiency in using evidence, their orientation toward issues of proximate policy, when coupled with either ideological naïveté or disinterest, allies them closely with most contemporary American social scientists.

History and Self-Identity

Whereas much contemporary history is policy oriented, most nineteenth-century historians in both Europe and the United States were identity oriented. This observation quite legitimately suggests another use for history, a use that is probably more significant than the guidance of policy. History, as a source of ego identity, has no necessary functional tie to the social sciences or to any other discipline. In a quite personal way, a remembered past becomes a crucial part of our self-image. We may or may not like what we have been and thus what we inescapably are. We can add but never really erase. One may not like being female or white, but these are physical and unchangeable facts. One may not like being a southerner or an American, but, although she can condemn both her region and her country or deny loyalty to them, she can never escape either of them, for they are part of her self-definition and inseparable from her self-image. If concerned, she might learn a good deal from psychology, physiology, or anthropology about being female or white. By descriptive analysis and by history she can learn a great deal about the South and about the United States (and thus about herself), whether this knowledge brings solace or despair. Recent students of American history seem to find about as much despair as solace in their identity as Americans, perhaps in part because of a similar ambivalence among historians. But even a few decades ago, most American historians had few doubts about the United States. They expected to acquaint diverse Americans with an often glorious past and to afford them, at least those who suffered some of the newly discovered dilemmas of being American, both solace and self-confidence.

A confident national history may be dishonest and mythical; it may serve as a deliberate and hypocritical device for stimulating loyalty and sacrifice. At best, even though evidenced, a glorious national past will be narrowly selective and thus unbalanced. Much national history as well as local history is parochial; it affirms basic beliefs and commitments but neither defines nor defends them. Such principles are so confidently held, so secure, as scarcely to need rationalization. The historical parts of the Old Testament—the most influential national history ever written—are a clear example of parochial history combined with sermonic goals. If believable, affirmative national histories flatter those who share them. Such historical knowledge may expand one, give new and affirmative meaning to one's life, inspire one to great efforts, and provoke both self-assurance and community loyalty. Even the most balanced history of a group of people, of a nation or village, or of a church or party, may help create a community, for it broadens the area of common experiences and brings solace even in group penance. Many people need an expanded and clarified past, not to make better choices or as an adjunct of policy, but as an object of their appreciation, as a certification of some meaning in their endeavors, or as evidence of their membership in a community.

As earlier noted, history is a tool for philosophical criticism. In this role it may serve a more fundamental purpose than sheer enjoyment, the limited clarification of policy, or even the buttressing of personal and group identity. This is not to suggest that people often use historical knowledge in a critical way, but rather that when it is so used it has a much greater impact on a society, reaching as it does to the most hidden but most determinative assumptions and goals.

A faint recognition of this critical role is present in the now-popular justification of history as a tool for self-understanding. It is somewhat ironic that as policy-oriented histories have seemed to increase, avowedly and immediately practical uses of history have fallen into bad repute, whereas such humanistic uses as self-knowledge have never received more acclaim. The term "self-knowledge" can be quite misleading, particularly if it suggests some complete and almost impossible isolation of identity issues from policy at any level. But no doubt many people do use it with such an intent and want to repudiate anything broadly practical and moral.

Self-knowledge has at least two aspects, the purely personal and the shared. For the most part, self-knowledge is only an arbitrary designation, since the knowledge one gains necessarily applies to many other selves. Most of what we are is a product of culture. We share it with other people. Only this type of socially pregnant self-knowledge can be gained through the stories of the human past which historians are wont to tell. Of course, in a very private context, each person continuously rehearses his own past, and this private history may indeed illumine aspects of character that are unique to the individual. Unless the person is famous, a hero or a leader, this private history will remain private. Even if it were broadcast, few would be interested in it unless, again, it turned out to be more than private—common to many people, representative, typical, prophetic. Even the uniquely private past, as told on a psychiatrist's couch, can lead to self-knowledge, to more effective functioning in a society, to a clear self-identity, and to strength of character. This type of purely private and particularistic self-knowledge has little to do with written history. But even the most private facets of self-knowledge have social implications. Improved individuals mean an improved social order. It is impossible to draw a sharp line between a private sphere (an often useful abstraction) and a public sphere (another abstraction).

Circumstances and change are unavoidable. For people, so is choice. When people tie choice to knowledge, they may direct changes and take advantage of circumstances. The circumstances that set conditions for human choice are physical, biological, and cultural. The physical and biological circumstances are constant, or nearly so. The cultural circumstances are time-conditioned and historical, although they are often quite stable. At great peril we choose in ignorance of either of these circumstances. Without knowledge of the invariant relationships in matter, of the uniformities of organic behavior, we usually suffer futility. Without an understanding of causes, of cultural determinants, we usually choose rigidified convention; thus we nullify rather than exploit the freedom that is inherent in choice. Accident rather than purpose then determines the ceaseless elaboration and development of culture. Even choices one makes solely in the light of general knowledge, or in the light of well-entrenched causes that are falsely taken to be general and unalterable, are rational with respect only to means, not to final ends; in these circumstances, we do not consciously choose ends but they are still involved in choices.

Thus historical knowledge not only reveals enduring and stable patterns of culturally determined behavior, providing a needed backdrop to many types of social analysis, but, much more important, it clarifies the ends, the causes, that operate in our choices and in our most entrenched habits and institutions. Or it clarifies alternative ends that operate in other cultures. In such a role, history supports reevaluation at the most basic level. Through awareness, it permits a critical judgment on our purposes. In some cases, we see articulated ends as futile and foolish, for they are contrary to scientific knowledge. In other, perhaps more crucial contexts, they are contrary to experienced value, even when value covers the broadest possible context. Then historical awareness is a prelude to moral and esthetic judgment. It aids the development of new tastes and new commitments. And in a sense, what we appreciate, what we love, and what we dedicate ourselves to is who we are. At the level of basic causes or ends, historical awareness is the most potent instrument for the rational development of new cultural forms.

The following example illustrates this use of history. In the United States we live under a distinctive cluster of political institutions, although few of their elements are either uniquely or originally American. These institutions developed over a long time, and at least at one creative point or another they reflected, although never perfectly, certain overt assumptions or beliefs about fact and value. The institutions have changed and are changing, often by force of unrecognized circumstances. Meanwhile, many beliefs and aspirations have changed, in part as a result of cumulative changes in circumstance. But the political habits, reflecting internalized, often long-forgotten ends, remain with us. This complex situation opens two possibilities for criticism based on historical understanding. On the one hand, an appreciative and honest understanding (not easy) of the original ends and purposes that our political forms reflected may give new meaning and validity to those forms. Celebrations of the bicentennial of the Constitution presumably served this purpose. But this understanding may also reveal how often Americans have converted these forms to other, possibly unperceived ends, or in some cases even prostituted them to what present Americans perceive as immoral ends (for example, the sanction of black slavery in the original constitution of 1787). Thus an honest understanding of the original ends reflected in our institutions, ends that surely joined with circumstances in determining their form, may reveal what now seems, in the light of new knowledge or by some significant change in taste, the foolishness or narrowness or blinding self-interest of our progenitors. This knowledge will lead us not to a reinvigoration and repurification of institutions but to a more radical attempt to revise or replace them.

Although history makes a distinctive contribution to criticism, it is not the only discipline that permits and abets such critical evaluations. Anthropology offers other comparative perspectives. Literature and other fine arts offer imaginative alternatives or help shape qualitative aspirations, contributing to the valuative perspectives necessary for criticism. Ideal models developed by philosophers, by social theorists, and even by utopian dreamers often provide the critical perspective. Finally, whereas historical knowledge is necessary for an unobstructed view of the causes that may be operating in our society, only a detailed and rigorous inspection of the present context can determine which causes are actually at work. Even in criticism, one cannot completely separate historical knowledge from contextual analysis.

This critical use of history may seem to place a premium on cultural and intellectual history. It should not. It does place a premium on historical accuracy and on historical breadth, whatever the topical or chronological boundaries of a given story may be. All stories of the human past encompass human values and meanings and reflect some aspects of a cultural environment. All histories implicate final causes of some sort. One must tell the most narrow history against this backdrop; if not, one cannot tell it well. As one must ever emphasize, it is almost impossible to know very well any significant part of the human past. It is comparatively easy to refer our present meanings, goals, and assumptions to a past and thus to conceal the true story (this is the vicious presentism we earlier condemned). By misinterpreting artifacts from the past, we can fashion all sorts of interesting fantasies. Because of an all-too-inviting presentism, many specialized, policy-oriented historical monographs, despite all the forms of scholarship, are scarcely historical at all. One cannot interpret isolated artifacts in a vacuum; too often we misinterpret them by a present, often hazy and ideologically confused conceptual framework that actually distorts the past. Some Ph.D. dissertations are, in this way, unhistorical as well as unphilosophical (the two almost always go together).

To tell a story truly is to penetrate the symbols of a past and to read them correctly. The recorded words and symbolically rich deeds of past actors often meant something quite different from our seemingly identical words and deeds. In order, therefore, to write history at all—to tell true stories rather than superficially persuasive stories—one must have some ability to deal with semantic and conceptual subtleties; to interpret cultural styles; to see the meaning, value, and intent that lurk in institutions and behind human acts. This skill is far more important than any of the tools, statistical or otherwise, that enable historians to draw the most rigorous inferences from certain types of data. It requires conceptual rigor, ideological sophistication, philosophical self-consciousness, and almost always a long and broad acquaintance with a past age, either from reading good histories or from moving, with growing recognition, among diverse artifacts of that age. Any good historian, whatever the topic, must be able and willing to find the thought content, the ever-present even if not articulated meanings, of a past age, even when the focus is on the functioning of institutions or on the consequences of human behavior. But except in quite selective contexts, a historian need not focus on conscious ends or on overt rationalizations. Likewise, the self-conscious and topically selective intellectual historian who abstracts the thought content and focuses on it, and, even more, the historian of ideas, who deals largely with the isolated and usually more artful or rigorous products of human thinking, lose all perspective unless they remark and use as a backdrop the continuum of entrenched habits, the forms of behavior, that are always interactive with and inseparable from deliberate thought.

History and Tragic Experience

At this point the advocate of history may face the charge of naive optimism. Even the effort to relate history to sweeping criticism, to the task of restructuring basic ends, seems to assume the possibility of real progress, of some possible betterment in the human condition. One could show the utility of history for criticism and at the same time suspect an ultimate futility behind the critical games that people play. But this exercise would be pointless. In our day it takes little sophistication to repudiate the very possibility of progress. Ask any sophomore. Even "history," a weapon much used by our children, "proves" the ultimate futility of moral effort. Since history proves nothing legitimately but everything by selective misuse, it now nourishes our despair as faithfully as it used to nourish our most foolish dreams. But one cannot so easily rout the charge of naïveté. For many perceptive people the critical issue today is not finding proper armament for moral criticism; it is finding the courage, the affirmation, that makes possible any moral engagement at all. In a tragic world, nobility is the only worthy human goal, and surely its seekers have never been frightened by futility.

We live in a disillusioned age. We know tragedy; it is a part of our experience. In the very recent past, particularly in the American past, our many illusions and our naïveté successfully camouflaged our dilemmas, our entrapments, our inescapable futility, and thus the only possible ground for tragic experience. We knew failure but not irreducible conflicts of value; sin, but not unmerited and mocking frustrations and horrors. Once free of illusion and from the one overarching illusion (that we are the privileged beneficiaries of some cosmic plan), we cannot, in honesty, ever return to its warm embrace. Thus as an experienced and peculiarly inescapable fact, we will continue to confront tragedy. No strategy save illusion allows us to escape from this hard fact.

We confront two perennial sources of tragic experience: nature and culture. Lightning strikes without a semblance of justice; so does cancer. By what one has to interpret as chance (even though we know that it may not be), misfortune afflicts some and spares others. Our progenitors saw the hidden hand of God, of providential guidance, in acts of nature. This, we assume, was one of their illusions. We find no redemptive purpose, no deserved punishment in our suffering. Of course, we do know more and more about the physical and organic worlds. We have ever more control over them. Even my disease is the physician's challenge. We may find a cure for cancer. But these hopes are small consolation for present victims. They suffer their affliction with little solace; their suffering is rarely the means to such cures. Knowledge and a hope of eventual progress can hardly console them; instead, quite often, it has served to remove the solace of past illusions. Those who suffer have no honest way to dissipate such tragedy, although some philosophical and religious bypasses are still compelling for many people. But saints do not suffer; to them, tragedy is impossible. For the rest of us, such tragic experience is inescapable, but at least it does not preclude progress. It invites it. It does not teach futility; it offers a challenge—that we bring knowledge to bear on these natural afflictions.

Tragedy rooted in culture rather than in physical nature—in causes rather than in laws—is a much greater challenge to any form of moral affirmation. Such tragedy alone implicates history, as Polybius so long ago argued. Again, such tragedy is an inescapable even if rare experience for most people, or perhaps for any intellectually honest person. We cannot exorcise it by any magic. By the interaction of circumstances and human choices, most long forgotten, people have come to serve not only contradictory or futile causes in their own society but causes that conflict directly with those in other societies. Particularly in inter-cultural contacts, but also in the course of internal change, these causes have led to conflict, dilemmas, and often despair. We tend to paint ourselves, or to be painted, into corners. At that point we have no good answers and no way of escape. We are helpless victims of causes un-perceived and beyond our control. However virtuous, we cannot avoid such dilemmas, at either a personal or a communal level. We confront an extraordinary number of them in our Hellenistic age—an age of clashing ideologies and cultures, exposed and naked social systems, and lonely individuals. Neither the isolation of parochial communities nor any creed protects us. From too simple optimism and illusory hope we have often moved to abject pessimism and no hope. Moral achievement seems irrelevant. Where there are no good answers, such achievement is impossible. Where there are no clear values, one cannot measure such achievement.

We can discover causes as well as transformative laws. We can often trace the varied historical developments that clearly account for our present miseries. By this means we at least get rid of all demonic and fatalistic explanations of tragedy, including those explanations that rely on some ambiguous human nature. This maneuver reduces tragedy from a cosmic distortion to a phenomenological affliction. Historical knowl-edge shows us that we suffer not from demonic forces but rather from the mistakes of our parents and grandparents (some contemporary youth invest even those progenitors with demonic attributes). But only we know, or can know, that our parents' choices were grievously mistaken. They often acted in greatest wisdom. They could not have chosen other-wise (here "could not" means not that they encountered physical ob-structions but that, in light of what they knew and valued, they had to choose as they did). Knowledge of this sort cannot dissipate our present suffering (perhaps nothing can) and cannot provide good choices for us (there may be none), but it does place our tragic plight in a causal perspective and lessen its often enervating and cynical import.

When trapped, we suffer. We may avoid other traps, but we cannot escape some of our present ones. Any moral philosophy that affirms a magical solvent for all present dilemmas is based on some illusion. The need of trapped, often futile people is courage, not deliverance. Can they live through (not remove) present tragic dilemmas, and can they possibly escape more tragedy that always lurks in their future? If what grandfather achieved, despite his well-meaning choices, is only this, how can we hope to do better? Look what past generations did to our world. Since better historical understanding will not reveal many devils or conspirators (so simple would it be if it did) but only ignorance and blindness, will not such historical understanding quickly turn youthful commitment into tragic despair (such despair may be wiser than illusioned commitment)? Of course it may, but it need not. And in removing illusions, history invites the maturity that alone can alleviate some future frustrations and dilemmas. Without it we find only the blind, ahistorical naïveté of perennial reformers who see perfection lurking just beyond the final eradication of some favorite clutch of demonic people or forces.

The human past has drama, just as does the human present. It is about people who suffered and knew they suffered, who chose and fully experienced the agony of choice. The human past is haunted by "if"— by a sense that it could have been otherwise. Yet nothing is so set and determinate as the past. We know that, in one sense, it could not have been otherwise. In this case the "ifs" are unreal, except that people intensely experienced them; thus they were phenomenologically real. The past actors, even as we, felt quite confident that they made up their own lines. As historians we agree. They surely did. And they made them up, in part, according to their knowledge of or their illusions about the past. Often they, even as we, tried above all to avoid their parents' mistakes and then learned their history lesson much too well (or rather mislearned it by too little attention to all the subtle meanings), falling into a much more grievous error. And here, in a way easily missed, was how the "ifs" were really efficacious. The choices their parents made became their lesson, and the choices their parents rejected became their choice: without their parents' choice and their historical understanding, they could never have made the choice that they did.

Thus for us in the living present, the drama of the past—of all the contingencies that were present, but really not present—is our drama and our freedom. Every haunting "if" of our parents' world becomes a living option again in ours. But their exact choices are, by our very knowledge, forever beyond our choosing. If we follow them, if we choose the same objects that they chose, it is for us a quite different choice, for we know the past and know that we choose again. The past is indeed finished, but the historical past—the past thought about by us—is ever suggestive and alive. We should not, in honesty and proper piety, be too harsh on our fathers. Their tragedy, when we seek its meaning, is not only very often the perceived source of some of our tragedy but a vital and now recognized circumstance for our choosing. Being what we are, knowing the history we know, we choose as we must. But when knowing is a crucial determinant, when we drive back a bit blind circumstance, we are free and we are responsible in the only meaningful sense of these two words.

We have no assurance that we choose well. We may reap our rewards at our children's expense. We have no complete, objective, hierarchical system of values by which to determine our choices. And we could not have one and be free, for our freedom means continuous redefinition and unending cultural elaboration—it means new ends, new causes, new tastes. People never stay still long enough to be exactly measured by any moral yardstick. But insecurity and a lack of certainty do not mean that we cannot choose by objective criteria, by a science that reveals consequences, by a historical understanding that reveals causes operative in our society. Tragedy, as an existential fact rather than as a cosmic distortion, is ever present; it is a component of our freedom, of our being agents. We cannot escape it or escape being the cause of tragic dilemmas for our as yet innocent children. But we can know tragedy for what it is—a product of as yet unknown or uncontrollable physical circumstances or of accumulations of in part blind even though often generous human choices. Knowing this devil, by far the worst of all, we can at least learn to live with him even though we cannot eliminate him.

This ends a quite lengthy list of appropriate and always in some sense distinctive uses for history. The writing and studying of history have other incidental effects on individuals. For example, historical inquiry has some of the same effects, even social and educational effects, as other types of rigorous inquiry. But the uses of inquiry are quite a different thing from the uses of history, for they constitute a more inclusive class. All intellectual activity, as a class of activity, has its appropriate fruits. But this clearly is well beyond our concern.

No person, no historian even, will gain all the possible benefits either from historical inquiry or from a careful study of completed histories. One who knows no tragedy will not master it by historical understanding. Only one who questions basic goals will find history of use in criticism. One quite secure in his community will hardly need it to buttress his identity. Those who never engage in issues policy, who shrink from politics, will never use it as a backdrop of social analysis. And, alas, those who do not enjoy it, whatever its other benefits, will, most likely, never realize any of its uses.

EPILOGUE

WHATEVER value people find in history, almost everyone in the Western world displays a keen interest in some facet of it. For most of us, to be vitally interested in something is also to be interested in its past. Note the eagerness with which small boys collect incredible amounts of information about the past performances of baseball players or about vintage automobiles, airplanes, coins, and stamps. Note the families that keep heirlooms, the widespread interest in family history (genealogy), the clubs that annually elect historians and cherish records, the towns that zealously treasure every local tradition. As much as physical nature or social relationships, the past endlessly confronts and tantalizes the human mind.

But a rigorous and successful exploration of the human past is not easy. In fact, history can be the most difficult form of inquiry, demanding greater intellectual versatility and more specific skills than any other discipline. Yet one can produce inferior history with little effort and no skill. As in the fine arts, the most critical distinction is not between historians and nonhistorians (if there are any such) but between good historians and bad ones. Good history has to be both supremely literate and rigorously true. Unlike the novelist, the historian cannot make up the story. Only laborious investigation yields an account that other scholars can check.

Even the investigation may demand almost unattainable skills. The historian's potential sources are vast and far-ranging, from a scrap of stone to archives crammed with the miscellanea of modern governments. These materials of history are both complex and unmanageable. Thomas De Quincey once described the two angels that must guide the historian: one, the genius of research; the other, that of meditation. The two qualities seldom combine in the same person. The laborious comber of archives who must "read millions of dusty parchments and pages blotted with lies" is one sort of person; the artist fired with the imagination and literary skill necessary to breathe life into these dry pages is quite another. The good historian must contrive to be both. But one must add the other roles of the historian; that of detective, for one often has to possess the sleuthing abilities of a Sherlock Holmes; of activist, for one should know the world; of adventurer, with the resourcefulness to track down and gain access to elusive sources.

How should historians go about these difficult tasks? Perhaps, to an extent, historians are born and not made ("Some are historians by the grace of God," wrote Albert Schweitzer. "No erudition can supply the place of historical instinct"). But clearly those who have a vocation for it must greatly improve themselves by nurturing the talent. Apprentice historians can best nurture their talents in specialized research seminars, under the guidance of experienced and specialized historians. Such is the diversity of historical subjects that no specific directions can fit all types of historical inquiry. The requirements simply vary too much. The skills required to authenticate an ancient document, or to infer from it great revelations about a civilization, scarcely match the statistical tools needed to extract meaning from census reports or election returns, or the analytical and semantic finesse required to dissect the subtle array of meanings in a single key word or phrase. Some subjects place a particular premium on one skill and not on others; some require a special application of skills. Yet the historian, whatever the field, has to be skillful in three areas: meaning, inference, and verification. For these are the prerequisites of successful inquiry in any discipline.

Perhaps the most neglected and yet the most critical problem in contemporary historical writing is the lack of conceptual rigor, of careful attention to meaning. Historians have, for the best of reasons, rejected a highly technical vocabulary or jargon. Such a vocabulary, even though originally a shortcut to clarity, almost always ossifies and, in vulgar form, becomes the favorite camouflage of mindlessness and mediocrity. But eschewal of jargon makes it even more imperative that historians carefully define their terms, particularly broad categories, periodizations, and labels. Too much contemporary history relies on ambiguous and usually undefined labels, such as rationalism, romanticism, imperialism, naturalism, positivism, industrialism, urbanism, pragmatism, liberalism, conservatism, radicalism, capitalism, socialism, and on ad infinitum. The increasingly heterogeneous audience for most history, resulting from the breakdown of parochial communities with common verbal habits, makes it even more imperative that we subject almost every class term to definitional scrutiny. Even "God save the Queen," a clear enough expression in an insular context, now requires qualification. Which God?

Good inferences make possible valid deductions. Historians, like everyone else, have an obligation to be rigorous in their logic. Logical fallacies haunt almost all our discourse; any text in logic soon frightens us by its endless catalogue of possible pitfalls. Some of these hazards have to do with grammar and meaning, for they involve deceptive sentence structure or ambiguities of language. If we are not careful, we argue in circles, or we unknowingly move from class to subclass and thus attempt to characterize parts by wholes or wholes by parts. By shifts in the meanings of key terms, we even deceive by what appears to be a good syllogism.

But most logical fallacies derive from improper deduction, or the drawing of fallacious conclusions from given premises. If we infer wrongly, then no amount of evidence can rescue us. Any history will contain implicative arguments that have to meet formal criteria. Given a plausible proposition about the past, historians often have to deduce its various implications even before they can begin to seek out evidence to prove it. In concealed language ("therefores" and "thuses"), historians continually draw simple inferences of the form "If a, then necessarily b, c, and d." A typical but fallacious argument of this sort follows: "In 1933, Franklin D. Roosevelt had to devalue the dollar in order to raise prices. He did devalue it in April 1933. Therefore, prices rose." And in fact prices did rise. It may also be true that they could not have risen without devaluation. The premises may be true. Thus as many New Dealers believed, abandonment of the gold standard did, in one sense, *cause* prices to rise (it was a necessary condition). But as stated the argument is still fallacious, for the conclusion does not flow of necessity from the premise (the premise identifies a necessary condition, not a sufficient one). Such examples could be multiplied endlessly. Suffice it to say that all historians, at one time or another, do fall into logical errors and weaken their lines of argument. All the same, their final conclusions may still be true. Then only their statements are wrong. But more often than not, logical fallacies mean wrong conclusions.

Verification, or proof, seems more critical than either meaning or good logic. In one sense it is, for it has a "clinching" quality about it, or a finality not present in semantic and logical achievements. After all, completely untrue propositions may be perfectly clear and allow quite valid inferences. Evidence alone can justify claims to verity. Yet, without clear propositions and valid inferences, no rigorous inquiry is possible and no evidence clearly applies. For sources, artifacts, data, phenomena (use whatever word you want) become evidence only in the context of some question, assertion, or hypothesis that requires them as an answer or as proof. It is nonsense to talk of evidence in general. Meaning and inference not only precede verification but are necessary conditions for it.

A historian may easily confuse sources (as potential evidence for some question historians are wont to ask) with evidence and thus confuse research of an exploratory or topic-seeking and hypothesis-seeking type with the controlled search for verifying evidence indicated by the logical implications of a hypothesis. But despite such definitional confusions, professional historians have rarely minimized the role of evidence and the need for proof. We live in an age of technical expertise, and historians abundantly reflect it. Of course, in history as in most fields we still have our more or less glamorous amateurs, who often rush in where professionals fear to tread. In history they often garner a goodly share of the popular market while perpetuating much ignorance, to the despair of honest yeoman historians. They pay for their popularity by earning historians' scorn. The beginning historian should note the quality of technical criticism in the book reviews of leading historical journals and the devastation that results when a William L. Shirer crosses the path of the professionals and the often savage encounters between authorities, each heavily armed with erudition. Today a historian, in making even a fairly modest contribution to historical knowledge, dealing with a distinctly minor figure or episode, will have pored over scores of collections of unpublished papers in a dozen archives. Large graduate schools, a massive growth of Ph.D. programs, numerous large libraries and manuscript depositories, and even the availability of research and travel grants have encouraged this virtuosity.

But skill in finding one's way to and through archives does not ensure skill in the use of the materials. A naive empiricism always threatens. The would-be historian who is unaware of the need for a unifying theme or hypothesis often accomplishes little more than taking from one pile and adding to another. An ancient scholar, in despair, once said that he had made a heap of all that he found; he is emulated by many Ph.D. candidates. A mere transfer of records hinders the advancement of historical knowledge, for students of history may well take an impressively researched monograph as the "authority" in a given field. An industrious culling of documentary sources does not guarantee perceptiveness; the judgment of a highly skilled researcher can be utterly wrong. The alleged law that decrees an inverse relationship between research energy and philosophical acumen may come into play. Grotesque or inadequate interpretations may accompany impeccable scholarship if scholarship entails only documentation.

Yet the unintelligent drone who has burrowed deep but cannot master his findings is no worse than the clever theorizer who invents striking interpretations (probably revising the received doctrines in order to gain attention) without doing much research. "Without hypothesis, or synthesis, history remains a pastime for antiquarians," wrote the famous

Belgian historian Henri Pierenne, but he added that "without criticism and erudition it loses itself in fantasy." Both are necessary. But professional, academically trained historians are more likely to lack imaginative hypotheses than erudition.

Historians are, by and large, well aware of these problems. They may sigh, with A. C. Bradley, that "research though laborious is easy; imagination though delightful is difficult." They know which libraries to visit in order to find needed primary sources. Indeed, they have probably had their topic determined for them by the existence of the sources. Senator *A* or Foreign Secretary *B* has bequeathed his papers to a library, which has capably organized them. Letters of the same estimable statesman, as can be learned from a national union catalogue of manuscripts, may be found in other collections. (Most published work of a historical nature, examination reveals, is justified because its author has found something new: some interesting person or group, who once perhaps made a splash in the world but has been forgotten, "overlooked.") Before long the fledgling doctor of philosophy is off on an interesting trail that may lead her across continents and oceans. It is laborious but easy to copy the contents of these manuscript collections. But what use to make of all the material? No one really tells her this. She is left to her own instincts and prejudices.

Sooner or later, she will see the need for some hypothesis or organizing principle. It may be quite simple and restricted. She does not have to settle cosmic issues. It does not matter whether historians agree on ontological issues. It does not matter whether they decide that reality is chaotic and must have an order imposed on it by the historian or that there is an inherent structure in events which the historian can discover, or that it is a little of both or (perhaps most sensible) that the issue is meaningless. In any case, we can approach the events of the past only by imagining possible patterns or structures and then checking to see if we can validate them by evidence. It is true that, in most cases, we cannot fruitfully engage in such hypothetical reasoning until we have explored the terrain experientially, but then neither can we do so unless we know a good many things outside the historical theater altogether. At some point we must frame questions or propose some hypothesis; otherwise, we wander aimlessly. Perhaps we should go as far as Ortega y Gasset when he wrote that "facts cover up reality; while we are in the midst of their innumerable swarmings we are in chaos and confusion." We must for the moment turn aside from this chaos and imagine an order; then we must compare it with evidence to see if we can match it to some experience. If we find a match, then we have succeeded; we "have discovered the reality which the facts covered and kept secret." If we find no match, then we have to do some more hard thinking.

Obvious dangers lurk. To love a hypothesis too much may be to ignore contrary evidence or to search only in areas where favorable evidence is likely. All single-minded or monistic interpretations of history, with one primal factor or theme as the key to everything, are subject to this weakness. No one key can unlock all doors, and anyone who thinks it can simply ignores most doors. One must apply hypotheses tentatively and modify them when necessary.

Another danger is our inability to break away from long-accepted and seemingly obvious hypotheses. We freeze our perspectives. Herbert Butterfield, in an essay on the origins of the Seven Years' War, showed that the solution of the problem was delayed for years simply because no one looked in the right direction. Such things often happen. In a richly detailed study of the Dreyfus case, Douglas Johnson showed that the assumption of the complete innocence of Captain Dreyfus as the victim of a nefarious plot—a kind of black-versus-white, good-guys/bad-guys approach—failed to explain all the details of this famous case. Yet such an assumption plagued almost all earlier historians. Of course, we can never divest ourselves of all assumptions. Some of our preconceptions are very dear to us and we can question them only with a great deal of courage. But a flexible and open mind is an asset in any inquiry.

The skills and resources needed by a historian seem frightening in their variety. The historian needs to improve the quality of his mind by wide and intelligent learning in many fields. One confronts no specially "historical" data, which one can master by historical research. The quality of one's mind is involved in every step as one writes history. One may gain valuable knowledge from the social sciences, as many historians now allege. But where can one not seek inspiration and ideas? Poetry and novels deal perceptively with many aspects of a culture and may brilliantly illumine a period, an issue, a human predicament; and so, in principle, historians ought to know all the great literature of the world. Toynbee, who used world literature a great deal, found his leading theme of challenge and response in Robert Browning and built a theory of civilizational decay on some lines from George Meredith. The historian may gain as much insight from a novel as from academic psychology or from the more speculative insights of a Freud. But if literature can be helpful, so also, obviously, can philosophy. One may argue cogently that no competent historian should be without some working knowledge of the methods of the natural sciences. Nor should she be without wide travel and acquaintance with the practical affairs of the world.

In brief, historians ought to know as much as they can of everything, so that they can bring to bear the greatest possible amount of wisdom on the materials they handle, in order to shape them into the most illuminating account possible. In principle this fertilization of mind has almost no limits. It might be thought that a diplomatic historian could profit only from studies in political science, but there seems to be no reason why she could not derive benefit from a novel dealing with situations of rivalry comparable to those that arise between states, from a sociological analysis of game theory or of the contours of popular belief, or even from an awareness of the precepts of Confucian ethics in regard to statecraft. Many other forms of knowledge might be applicable to the historical episode or process that concerns her. Almost any knowledge in her tool kit may be useful at some unexpected moment. She must not be a slave to any of her tools or try to force one to do everything. Wisdom consists in knowing when to apply a tool.

But this observation suggests a final irony: even versatility and brilliance have pitfalls. History is such a fluid subject, with so many possibilities, that even a small subject offers almost unlimited possibilities in both conception and research. One can see heaven in a grain of sand. And one is never done. The case of what Philip D. Jordan called "the palsied hand" reveals one peril. Able scholars familiar to all of us for some reason never finish a work. Lord Acton was a celebrated example; though in fact this great man wrote much of high quality, he never published a major book-length study. His "History of Liberty," for which he long collected materials, remained unfinished at his death, thus becoming, as one wit remarked, the greatest book never written. In Acton's case the trouble lay in his very genius; he not only was an able researcher, keenly aware of the value of original materials, but also had a subtle and searching intellect. How could such a mind ever finish such an ambitious project?

Other historians, without his brilliance, enjoy research but lack the analytical or imaginative skill to turn their findings into a synthetic whole. Others so value perfection that they cannot publish so long as relevant sources remain unexamined, as some always do, since one can never exhaust any topic of importance, at least not in one normal lifetime. Finally, one often meets richly imaginative persons who see innumerable interesting subjects and develop a fresh enthusiasm each week, flitting from one to another excitedly but never able to fix their attention for long on one. They have to learn to curb their imagination and enthusiasms. Boundaries, limits, rules, and discipline are necessary to all great art. Historians must strike a balance somewhere between an unseemly haste to finish and an obsessive drive for perfection. The palsied hand is as useless to society as a compulsion to publish everything. In all these issues, balance and moderation are the rule, along with candid self-analysis.

SELECTED BIBLIOGRAPHY

General

The Classic European Historians series, general editors Gordon Wright and Leonard Krieger, and Classics of British Historical Literature, edited by John Clive, are both published by the University of Chicago Press and include editions of such famous historians as Hume, Herder, Macaulay, Michelet, Mommsen, Treitschke, and Acton. There are of course many other editions of the classic historians, from Herodotus, Thucydides, Polybius, Tacitus, and Livy to Bacon, Machiavelli, Gibbon, Ranke, Burckhardt, Parkman, Prescott, and Adams.

General histories of historical thought and writing: R. G. Collingwood, *The Idea of History* (New York and London: Oxford University Press, 1946); Ernst Breisach, *Historiography: Ancient, Medieval, and Modern* (Chicago: University of Chicago Press, 1983); John Barker, *The Super-Historians* (New York: Scribner's, 1982); Frank Manuel, *Shapes of Philosophical History* (Stanford: Stanford University Press, 1965); Arnaldo Momigliano, *Studies in Historiography* (New York: Harper & Row, 1966); Peter Gay, Gerald Cavanaugh, et al., eds., *Historians at Work,* 4 vols. (New York: Harper & Row, 1972–1975); Herbert Butterfield, *Man on His Past* (Cambridge: Cambridge University Press, 1955); J. H. Hexter, *On Historians: Reappraisals of the Makers of Modern History* (Cambridge: Harvard University Press, 1979).

Ancient World

Herbert Butterfield, *The Origins of History* (London: Methuen, 1981); John Van Seters, *In Search of History: Historiography in the Ancient World and the Origins of Biblical History* (New Haven: Yale University Press, 1985); Michael Grant, *The Ancient Historians* (New York: Scribner's, 1970); Charles William Fornara, *The Nature of History in Ancient Greece and Rome* (Berkeley: University of California Press, 1984); Truesdell Brown, *The Greek Historians* (Lexington, Mass.: D. C.

Heath, 1973); Chester Starr, *The Awakening of the Greek Historical Spirit* (New York: Knopf, 1968); M. I. Finley, ed., *The Portable Greek Historians* (New York: Viking); J. H. Finley, *Three Essays on Thucydides* (Cambridge: Harvard University Press, 1967); Virginia J. Hunter, *Past and Process in Herodotus and Thucydides* (Princeton: Princeton University Press, 1982); M. L. W. Laistner, *The Greater Roman Historians* (Berkeley: University of California Press, 1947); F. W. Walbank, *Historical Commentary on Polybius* (Oxford: Clarendon, 1957); P. G. Walsh, *Livy: His Historical Aims and Methods* (Oxford: Clarendon, 1974); T. J. Luce, *Livy: The Composition of His History* (Princeton: Princeton University Press, 1977) Ronald Syme, *Tacitus*, 2 vols. (Oxford: Clarendon, 1958); Ronald Martin, *Tacitus* (Berkeley: University of California Press, 1981); Donald R. Dudley, *The World of Tacitus* (Boston: Little, Brown, 1968); G. A. Williamson, *The World of Josephus* (Boston: Little, Brown, 1965); Andrew Wallace-Hadrill, *Suetonius: The Scholar and His Career* (London: Duckworth, 1984).

Medieval

R. L. P. Milburn, *Early Christian Interpretations of History* (London: Adam & Charles Black, 1954); Herbert Butterfield, *Christianity and History* (London: G. Bell, 1950); C. A. Patrides, *The Grand Design of God: The Literary Form of the Christian View of History* (London: Routledge & Kegan Paul, 1972); R. H. Markus, *Saeculum: History and Society in the Theology of St. Augustine* (Cambridge: Cambridge University Press, 1970); A. H. Thompson, ed., *Bede: His Life, Times, and Writings* (New York: Russell & Russell, 1966); Joseph Dahmus, *Seven Medieval Historians* (Chicago: Nelson-Hall, 1982); R. H. C. Davis and J. M. Wallace-Hadrill, eds., *The Writing of History in the Middle Ages* (Oxford: Oxford University Press, 1981); Denys Hay, *Annalists and Historians: Western Historiography from the Eighth to the Seventeenth Century* (London: Methuen, 1977); Antonia Gransden, *Historical Writing in England, 550–1307* (Ithaca: Cornell University Press, 1974); and *Historical Writing in England II: c. 1307 to the Early 16th Century* (1983); Indrikis Stern, ed., *The Greater Medieval Historians: A Reader* (Lanham, Md.: University Press of America, Inc., 1983); Beryl Smalley, *Historians in the Middle Ages* (London: Thames & Hudson, 1974); Nancy Partner, *Serious Entertainment: The Writing of History in Twelfth-Century England* (Chicago: University of Chicago Press, 1977); Paul Archambault, *Seven French Chroniclers: Witnesses to History* (Syracuse: Syracuse University Press, 1974); J. J. N. Palmer, ed., *Froissart, Historian* (Totowa, N.J.: Rowman & Littlefield, 1981).

Renaissance and Reformation

Peter Burke, *The Renaissance Sense of the Past* (New York: St. Martin's Press, 1969); Eric Cochrane, *Historians and Historiography of the Italian Renaissance* (Chicago: University of Chicago Press, 1981); Mark Phillips, *Francesca Guicciardini: The Historian's Craft* (Toronto: University of Toronto Press, 1977); Felix

Gilbert, *Machiavelli and Guicciardini: Politics and History in the Sixteenth Century* (Princeton: Princeton University Press, 1965); Peter Bondanella, *Machiavelli and the Art of Renaissance History* (Detroit: Wayne State University Press, 1974); Harry Levin, *The Myth of the Golden Age in the Renaissance* (Bloomington: Indiana University Press, 1969); Nancy S. Struever, *Language and History in the Renaissance* (Princeton: Princeton University Press, 1970); Donald R. Kelley, *Foundations of Modern Historical Scholarship: Language, Law, and History in the French Renaissance* (New York: Columbia University Press, 1970); Arthur B. Ferguson, *Clio Unbound: Perception of the Social and Cultural Past in Renaissance England* (Durham, N.C.: Duke University Press, 1979); E. H. Harbison, *The Christian Scholar in the Age of the Reformation* (New York: Scribner's, 1956); C. K. Pullapilly, *Caesar Baronius: Counter-Reformation Historian* (Notre Dame: Notre Dame University Press, 1975); John L. Lievsay, *Venetian Phoenix: Paolo Sarpi and Some of His English Friends* (Lawrence: University Press of Kansas, 1973); Julian Franklin, *Jean Bodin and the Sixteenth Century Revolution in the Methodology of Law and History* (Cambridge: Cambridge University Press, 1973); George Huppert, *The Idea of Perfect History* (Urbana: University of Illinois Press, 1970); Fred J. Levy, *Tudor Historical Thought* (San Marino, Calif: Huntington Library, 1967); F. Smith Fussner, *The Historical Revolution* (London: Routledge & Kegan Paul, 1962); Joseph M. Levine, *Humanism and History: Origins of Modern English Historiography* (Ithaca: Cornell University Press, 1988).

Seventeenth and Eighteenth Centuries

Orest Ranum, *Artisans of Glory: Writers and Historical Thought in Seventeenth-Century France* (Chapel Hill: University of North Carolina Press, 1980); J. G. A. Pocock, *The Ancient Constitution and the Feudal Law: English Historical Thought in the Seventeenth Century* (New York: Norton, 1967); Martine Watson Brownley, *Clarendon and the Rhetoric of Historical Form* (Philadelphia: University of Pennsylvania Press, 1985); J. H. Brumfitt, *Voltaire, Historian* (Oxford: Oxford University Press, 1958); Leon Pompa, *Vico: A Study of the New Science* (Cambridge: Cambridge University Press, 1975) and (ed.) *Vico: Selected Writings* (Cambridge: Cambridge University Press, 1982); A. P. Caponigri, *Time and Idea: Theory of History in Vico* (Chicago: Regnery, 1953); J. B. Black, *The Art of History: Four Eighteenth Century Historians* (New York: Russell & Russell, 1966); David P. Jordan, *Gibbon and His Roman Empire* (Urbana: University of Illinois Press, 1971); Victor G. Wexler, *David Hume and the History of England* (Philadelphia: American Philosophical Society, 1979).

Nineteenth Century

John D. Rosenberg, *Carlyle and the Burden of History* (Oxford: Oxford University Press, 1985); John W. Burrow, *A Liberal Descent: Victorian Historians and the English Past* (Cambridge: Cambridge University Press, 1983); H. A. L. Fisher, *The Whig Historians* (Oxford: H. Milford, 1928); Jerome Buckley, *The Triumph of Time* (Cambridge: Harvard University Press, 1966); John Clive, *Macaulay: The Making of a Historian* (New York: Knopf, 1973); A. Dwight Culler, *The Victorian Mirror of History* (New Haven: Yale University Press, 1985); Rosemary Jann, *The Art and Science of Victorian History* (Columbus: Ohio State University Press, 1985); Friedrich Meinecke, *Historism: The Rise of a New Historical Outlook* (New York: Herder & Herder, 1972); Roger Wines, ed., *Leopold von Ranke* (New York: Fordham University Press, 1981); Leonard Krieger, *Ranke: The Making of History* (Chicago: Chicago University Press, 1977); Georg Iggers, *The German School of History* (Middletown, Conn.: Wesleyan University Press, 1983); Theodore Von Laue, *Ranke: The Formative Years* (Princeton: Princeton University Press, 1950); Hayden White, *Metahistory: The Historical Imagination in the Nineteenth Century* (Baltimore: Johns Hopkins University Press, 1973); Melvin Rader, *Marx's Interpretation of History* (New York and London: Oxford University Press, 1979); Michael Ermath, *Wilhelm Dilthey: The Critique of Historical Reason* (Chicago: Chicago University Press, 1978); Andreas Dorpalen, *Heinrich von Treitschke* (New Haven: Yale University Press, 1957); F. Engel-Janosi, *Four Studies in Nineteenth Century French Historical Writing* (Baltimore: Johns Hopkins University Press, 1955); William R. Keylor, *Academy and Community: The Foundation of the French Historical Profession* (Cambridge: Harvard University Press, 1975). S. W. Halperin, ed., *Some Historians of Modern Europe* (Chicago: Chicago University Press, 1961); Roland N. Stromberg, *Arnold J. Toynbee* (Carbondale: Southern Illinois University Press, 1972); Hans A. Schmitt, ed., *Historians of Modern Europe* (Baton Rouge: Louisiana State University Press, 1971).

Recent, General and European

Georg Iggers, *New Directions in European Historiography* (Middletown, Conn.: Wesleyan University Press, 1984); Felix Gilbert and Stephen Graubard, eds., *Historical Studies Today* (New York: Norton, 1972); Donald C. Watt, ed., *Contemporary History in Europe* (New York: Praeger, 1967); Robert W. Fogel and G. R. Elton, *Which Road to the Past? Two Views of History* (New Haven: Yale University Press, 1983); Theodore K. Rabb and Robert I. Rotberg, eds., *The New History* (Princeton: Princeton University Press, 1982); Lawrence Stone, *The Past and the Present* (London: Routledge & Kegan Paul, 1981); T. Stoianovich, *French Historical Methods: The Annales School* (Ithaca: Cornell University Press, 1976); Jacques Barzun, *Clio and the Doctors* (Chicago: Chicago University Press, 1974). Olivier Zunz, ed., *Reliving the Past: The Worlds of Social History* (Chapel Hill: University of North Carolina Press, 1985); James B. Gardner and George R. Adams, eds., *Ordinary People and Ordinary Life: Perspectives on the New Social History* (Nashville: American Association for State and Local History, 1985); Robert Forster and Orest Ranum, eds., *Selections from the Annales,* 7 vols. (Baltimore: Johns Hopkins University Press, 1975–1982); Gerda Lerner, *The Majority Finds Its Past: Placing Women in History* (Oxford: Oxford University Press, 1979); Berenice Carroll, ed., *Liberating Women's History* (Urbana: University of Illinois Press, 1976); Joan Kelly, *Women, History, and Theory* (Chicago: University of Chicago Press, 1984). Peter Loewenberg, *Decoding the Past: The Psychohistor-*

ical Approach (New York: Knopf, 1983); Philip Pomper, *The Structure of Mind in History: Five Major Figures in Psychohistory* (New York: Columbia University Press, 1985); David Stannard, *Shrinking History* (Oxford: Oxford University Press, 1980); George M. Kren and Leon H. Rappoport, *Varieties of Psychohistory* (New York: Knopf, 1983); Geoffrey Cocks and Travis Crosby, eds., *Psycho/History: Readings in the Methods of Psychology, Psychoanalysis, and History* (New Haven: Yale University Press, 1987); R. J. Brugger, ed., *Our Selves/Our Past: Psychological Approaches to American History* (Baltimore: Johns Hopkins University Press, 1981). Peter Temin, ed., *The New Economic History: Selected Readings* (Harmondsworth: Penguin, 1973); Leo F. Schnore, ed., *The New Urban History: Quantitative Explanations by American Historians* (Princeton: Princeton University Press, 1975); A. Dorpalen, *German History in Marxist Perspective: The East German Approach* (Detroit: Wayne State University Press, 1985); Georg Iggers, *The Social History of Politics: Critical Perspectives in Western Historical Writing since 1945* (Warwickshire: Berg, 1985); Harvey J. Kaye, *The British Marxist Historians* (London: Basil Blackwell, 1985); Mark Poster, *Foucault, Marxism and History: Mode of Production versus Mode of Information* (Cambridge: Blackwell, 1985); Charles Delzell, ed., *The Future of History* (Nashville: Vanderbilt University Press, 1977).

American

John Higham, with Leonard Krieger and Felix Gilbert, *History: The Development of Historical Studies in the United States* (Englewood Cliffs, N.J.: Prentice-Hall, 1965); Robin Winks, ed., *Pastmasters: Essays on American Historians* (New York: Harper & Row, 1969); Peter Gay, *A Loss of Mastery: Puritan Historians in Colonial America* (Berkeley: University of California Press, 1966); David Levin, *History as Romantic Art: Bancroft, Prescott, Motley and Parkman* (Stanford: Stanford University Press, 1959); George Callcott, *History in the United States, 1800–1860* (Baltimore: Johns Hopkins University Press, 1970); Richard C. Vitzthum, *The American Compromise: Themes and Methods in the Histories of Bancroft, Parkman and Adams* (Norman: University of Oklahoma Press, 1974); Jurgen Herbst, *The German Historical School in American Scholarship* (Ithaca: Cornell University Press, 1965); Richard Hofstadter, *The Progressive Historians: Turner, Beard, and Parrington* (New York: Knopf, 1968); Cushing Strout, *The Pragmatic Revolt in American History: Carl Becker and Charles Beard* (New Haven: Yale University Press, 1958); Burleigh T. Wilkins, *Carl Becker* (Cambridge: M.I.T./Harvard University Press, 1981); Wilbur Jacobs, *The Historical World of Frederick Jackson Turner* (New Haven: Yale University Press, 1968); Ray Billington, *The Genesis of the Frontier Thesis* (San Marino, Calif: Huntington Library, 1971) and *Frederick Jackson Turner* (Oxford: Oxford University Press, 1973); W. H. Jordy, *Henry Adams: Scientific Historian* (New Haven: Yale University Press, 1952); Paul Conkin and John Higham, eds., *New Directions in American Intellectual History* (Baltimore: Johns Hopkins University Press, 1979); Michael Kammen, *The Past before Us: Contemporary Historical Writing in the United States* (Ithaca: Cornell University Press, 1980); Peter Novick, *That Noble Dream: The "Objectivity Question" and the American Historical Profession* (Cambridge: Cambridge University Press, 1988).

Non-European

A. A. Duri, *The Rise of Historical Writing among the Arabs* (Princeton: Princeton University Press, 1983); Franceso Gabrieli, ed. & trans., *Arab Historians of the Crusades* (Berkeley: University of California Press, 1969); Daniel F. McCall, *Africa in Time Perspective* (Boston: Boston University Press, 1964); David P. Henige, *Oral Historiography* (New York and London: Longman, 1982); Jan Vansina, *Oral Tradition as History* (Madison: University of Wisconsin Press, 1985); W. G. Beasley and E. G. Pulleyblank, *Historians of China and Japan* (Oxford: Oxford University Press, 1962); Charles S. Gardner, *Chinese Traditional Historiography* (Cambridge: Harvard University Press, 1961); Arif Dirlik, *Revolution and History: The Origins of Marxist Historiography in China, 1919–37* (Berkeley: University of California Press, 1978); Albert Feuerwerker, ed., *History in Communist China* (Cambridge: M.I.T. Press, 1968); Peter Hardy, *Historians of Medieval India* (London: Luzac, 1966); R. C. Majumdar, *Historiography in Modern India* (Bombay and New York: Asian Publishing House, 1970); Sida Pada Sen, *Historians and Historiography in Modern India* (Calcutta: Institute of Historical Studies, 1973); John Barber, *Soviet Historians in Crisis, 1928–1932* (New York: Holmes & Meier, 1981); Cyril E. Black, *Re-Writing Russian History: Soviet Interpretations of Russia's Past* (New York: Vintage, 1962); Nancy Whittier Heer, *Politics and History in the Soviet Union* (Cambridge: M.I.T. Press, 1971); George M. Enteen, *The Soviet Scholar-Bureaucrat: M. Pokrovskii* (University Park: Pennsylvania State University Press, 1978).

Theory and Philosophy of History

Much of the bibliography on the history of history relates to philosophic issues. Among the most relevant earlier citations are those on the German idealists, particularly Dilthey, Burkhardt, Hegel, and Ranke; on Marx; on the work of such Americans as Beard, Turner, and Becker; on Collingwood and Croce; and most citations on contemporary history.

Some Continental philosophers not included in the preceding bibliography deserve special mention: Heinrich Rickert, whose turn-of-the-century *Science and History: A Critique of Positivist Epistemology* (New York: Harper & Row, 1967) was in the Kantian tradition: Ernst Cassirer, whose *The Logic of the Humanities* (New Haven: Yale University Press, 1960) has had wide influence; and the Spanish philosopher, José Ortega y Gasset, who takes an even more humanistic approach in *History as a System* (New York: Norton, 1941).

The extended debate over covering laws in history began with an article by Carl G. Hempel, "The Function of General Laws in History," in the *Journal of Philosophy* in 1942, but now most easily available in Patrick Gardiner, ed., *Theories of History* (Glencoe, Ill: Free Press, 1959). He broadened his argument in "Explanation in Science and History," reprinted in William H. Dray, ed., *Philosophical Analysis and History* (New York: Harper & Row, 1966). The largely epistemological issues raised by Hempel dominated the field until the 1970s, and together constitute the most prominent subject of debate in a number of now classic but outdated anthologies, including the above ones edited by Gardiner and Dray, plus Ronald H. Nash, ed., *Ideas of History*, 2 vols. (New York: Dutton, 1969); Sidney Hook, ed., *Philosophy and History* (New York: New York University Press, 1963); and George C. Nagel, ed., *Studies in the Philosophy of History* (New York: Harper & Row, 1969). Two excellent recent anthologies are Richard Rorty, J. B. Schneewind, and Quentin Skinner, *Philosophy in History: Essays in the Historiography of Philosophy* (New York: Cambridge University Press, 1984); and Bernard P. Dauenhauer, ed., *At the Nexus of Philosophy and History* (Athens: University of Georgia Press, 1987).

Most of the better essays in the philosophy of history appear in journals. They are most concentrated in the one major journal devoted exclusively to the subject, *History and Theory*, vols. 1–26 (1961–1987). Other articles appear frequently in *Clio*, in the *Journal of the History of Ideas*, and occasionally in all major philosophical and historical journals. Unfortunately, space does not permit a listing of even the most significant articles in these journals.

In retrospect, a number of books, most dating from the covering-law debates of the fifties and sixties, have become recognized classics in the field. Textbooks are few: they include W. H. Walsh, *An Introduction to Philosophy of History* (London: Hutchinson University Library, 1951), and William Dray, *Philosophy of History* (Englewood Cliffs, N.J.: Prentice-Hall, 1964). Dray also launched a major attack on Hempel's covering-law arguments in *Laws and Explanation in History* (New York: Oxford University Press, 1957). The idealistic tradition of Collingwood has been updated by Allan Donagan in, *The Later Philosophy of R. G. Collingwood* (New York: Oxford University Press, 1962), and by Louis O. Mink in *Mind, History, and Dialectic: The Philosophy of R. G. Collingwood* (Bloomington: Indiana University Press, 1969). Other standard works include Patrick Gardiner, *The Nature of Historical Explanation* (New York: Oxford University Press, 1961); W. B. Gallie, *Philosophy and the Historical Understanding* (New York: Schucker, 1964); Arthur Danto, *Analytical Philosophy of History* (New York: Cambridge University Press, 1965); Morton G. White, *Foundations of Historical Knowledge* (New York: Harper & Row, 1965); R. C. Stover, *The Nature of Historical Thinking* (Chapel Hill: University of North Carolina Press, 1967); and Murray Murphey, *Our Knowledge of the Historical Past* (Indianapolis: Bobbs-Merrill, 1973). In a sense the grandparent of such analytical philosophy of history was Maurice Mandelbaum, who wrote stimulating essays and even a book before World War II. His final, climactic work is *The Anatomy of Historical Knowledge* (Baltimore: Johns Hopkins University Press, 1977).

The analytical tradition lives on. But by the 1970s, concerns over the language of historians and the properties of narratives began to complicate the ongoing debates about history as a form of knowledge. The following books reflect some of the most sophisticated thinking of the past two decades, but few fit easily into any one philosophical mold: Haskel Fain, *Between Philosophy and History* (Princeton: Princeton University Press, 1970); G. H. von Wright, *Explanation and Understanding* (Ithaca: Cornell University Press, 1971); Leon J. Goldstein, *Historical Knowing* (Austin: University of Texas Press, 1976); Rex Martin, *Historical Explanation: Re-enactment and Practical Inference* (Ithaca: Cornell University

Press, 1977); Burleigh T. Wilkins, *Has History any Meaning? A Critique of Popper's Philosophy of History* (Ithaca: Cornell University Press, 1978); Frederick A. Olafson, *The Dialectic of Action: A Philosophical Interpretation of History and the Humanities* (Chicago: University of Chicago Press, 1979); J. L. Gorman, *The Expression of Historical Knowledge* (Edinburgh: University of Edinburgh Press, 1982); F. R. Ankersmit, *Narrative Logic: A Semantic Analysis of the Historian's Language* (The Hague and Boston: Martinus Nijhoff, 1983); Arthur Danto, *The Transformation of the Commonplace* (Cambridge: Harvard University Press, 1983); Paul Ricoeur, *Time and Narrative*, 2 vols. (Chicago: University of Chicago Press, 1984); C. Behan McCullagh, *Justifying Historical Descriptions* (New York: Cambridge University Press, 1984); and Michael Stanford, *The Nature of Historical Knowledge* (London: Basil Blackwell, 1987). On the venerable subject of history's practical value, an interesting contribution, associated with the recent growth of interest in 'public history,' is Ernest R. May and Richard E. Neustadt, *Thinking in Time: The Uses of History for Decision Makers* (New York: Free Press, 1986).

To understand the most extreme subjectivist views, one must start with Thomas Kuhn, *The Structure of Scientific Revolutions* (Chicago: University of Chicago Press, 1970), although Kuhn never applied his theory about paradigms to history or supported any extreme skepticism about the sciences. Related, but more far-reaching in implications, was Michel Foucault's conception of epistemes, best argued in *The Order of Things: An Archaeology of the Human Sciences* (New York: Vintage, 1973). But, at least in the United States, the most influential thesis of all appeared in Hayden White's *Metahistory: The Historical Imagination in the Nineteenth Century* (Baltimore: Johns Hopkins University Press, 1973), which should be supplemented by his *Tropics of Discourse: Essays in Cultural Criticism* (Baltimore: Johns Hopkins University Press, 1978), and by Peter Munz, *The Shapes of Time: A New Look at the Philosophy of History* (Middletown, Conn.: Wesleyan University Press, 1977). The now fashionable discussions of various hermeneutics date from a study by Hans-Georg Gadamer, *Wahrheit und Methode* (Tübingen, 1960); in English, see Gadamer's *Philosophical Hermeneutics*, translated and edited by David E. Linge (Berkeley: University of California Press, 1976). The most determined critic of such subjective perspectives has been Adrian Kuzminski, who adheres to a realist position, as in "Defending Historical Realism," *History and Theory*, 18, no. 3 (1979), 316–349.

Methods

Jacques Barzun & Henry F. Graff, *The Modern Researcher*, 4th ed. (New York: Harcourt Brace Jovanovich, 1985); Allen Johnson, *The Historian and Historical Evidence* (New York: Scribner's, 1926); J. H. Hexter, *Doing History* (Bloomington: Indiana University Press, 1971); Marc Bloch, *The Historian's Craft* (New York: Vintage, 1953); Allan Nevins, *The Gateway to History*, ed. Robin Winks (New York: Garland, 1985); David H. Fischer, *Historian's Fallacies* (New York: Harper & Row, 1970); Emmanuel Le Roy Ladurie, *The Territory of the Historian* (Chicago: University of Chicago Press, 1979), and *The Mind and Faith of the Historian* (Chicago: University of Chicago Press, 1981); François Furet, *In the*

Workshop of History (Chicago: University of Chicago Press, 1984); Oscar Handlin, *Truth in History* (Cambridge: Harvard University Press, 1979); Jacques Le Goff and Pierre Nora, eds., *Constructing the Past: Essays in Historical Methodology* (Cambridge: Cambridge University Press, 1985); Robin Winks, ed., *The Historian as Detective* (New York: Harper & Row, 1969); Philip C. Brooks, *Research Archives: The Use of Unpublished Primary Sources* (Chicago: University of Chicago Press, 1969); Roderick Floud, *An Introduction to Quantitative Methods for Historians* (London: Methuen, 1979); Edward Shorter, *The Historian and the Computer* (Englewood Cliffs, N.J.: Prentice-Hall, 1971); G. R. Hawke, *Economics for Historians* (Cambridge: Cambridge University Press, 1980); J. Dennis Willigan and Katherine A. Lynch, *Sources and Methods of Historical Demography* (New York: Academic Press, 1982); Anne Chapman, ed., *Approaches to Women's History: A Resource Book and Teaching Guide* (Washington, D.C.: American Historical Association, 1979); Arthur L. Stinchcombe, *Theoretical Methods in Social History* (New York: Academic Press, 1978); Philip Abrams, *Historical Sociology* (Ithaca: Cornell University Press, 1982); Peter Burke, *Sociology and History* (London: Geoge Allen & Unwin, 1980); Quentin Skinner, ed., *The Return of Grand Theory in the Human Sciences* (Cambridge: Cambridge University Press, 1985).

Reference

Susan K. Kinnell, ed., *Historiography: An Annotated Bibliography of Journal Articles, Books, and Dissertations* (Santa Barbara: ABC-CLIO, 1987), 2 vols.; John Cannon, R. H. C. Davis, William Doyle, and Jack P. Greene, eds., *The Blackwell Dictionary of Historians* (Oxford: Basil Blackwell, 1987).

INDEX

Acton, John E.E.D., 77, 81, 245
Adams, Henry, 71, 87, 111
Adams, John, 18
Aeschylus, 9, 10
Alcuin, 22
Alexander the Great, 13
Alison, Archibald, 81
Ambrose, St., 21
analogy and history, 225–26
Althusser, Louis, 108
Apollinaire, Guillaume, 99
Aquinas, Thomas, 24, 33
archaeology, 67–68
Aretino, Bruno, 36
Aristophanes, 11
Aristotle, 12, 16, 17, 33, 177
Arnold, Matthew, 76, 84
Aron, Robert, 37
Asellio, Sempronius, 18
Augustine, St., 21, 23, 25, 26

Bacon, Francis, 57
Balzac, Honoré de, 76, 77, 111
Bancroft, George, 42, 69, 76, 78, 111
Barnes, Harry Elmer, 5
Baronio, Cesare, Cardinal (Baronius), 38, 40
Barraclough, Geoffrey, 106
Barthes, Roland, 108
Barzun, Jacques, 109
Baudouin, François, 38
Bayle, Pierre, 37, 47, 59
Beard, Charles A., 86, 89, 90, 218
Beard, Mary, 114
Beauvoir, Simone de, 114
Becker, Carl, 89, 90
Bede, the Venerable, 21–22, 27, 70
behavioral theories, 180–81
Bentham, Jeremy, 56, 79
Bentley, Richard, 41

Berdyaev, Nicolai, 98
Bergson, Henri, 87, 88
black history, 42
Blanc, Louis, 61, 80
Bloch, Marc, 87, 94, 95, 111
Bodin, Jean, 38, 40
Bolingbroke, Henry St. John, 22, 48
Boniface, St., 22, 23
Booth, Charles, 81
Bradley, A. C., 243
Bright, John, 81
Browning, Robert, 76, 244
Bruni, Leonardo, 34
Brunner, Emil, 98
Buckle, Thomas, 70, 71
Bultmann, Rudolf, 98
Burckhardt, Jacob, 80, 83, 92
Burke, Edmund, 43, 53, 61, 76
Bury, J. B., 12
Butterfield, Herbert, 16, 65, 81, 102
Byzantine historiography, 27–28

Calvin, John, 36
Camden, William, 41
Cannadine, David, 124
Carlyle, Thomas, 67, 69, 74, 76, 78, 79
Carr, Edward H., 37
Casaubon, Isaac, 38–39
Cassiodorus, 21
Cassirer, Ernst, 155
causation in history, 170–91
Chadwick, Owen, 34
Chamberlain, H. S., 102, 120
Charlemagne, 22, 23, 42
Cheyney, Edward P., 94
Christian approaches to history, 3, 4, 5, 6–8, 20, 21, 22, 23–28
Churchill, Winston, 125
Cicero, Marcus Tullius, 16, 17, 18, 32
Clarendon, Edward Hyde, Earl of, 44, 53

Cohen, Morris R., 73
Cohn, Norman, 25
Colet, John, 33
Colie, Rosemary, 35
Collingwood, R. G., 8, 15–16, 47, 55, 92, 93, 94, 103
Comnena, Anna, 28–29
Comte, August, 25, 55–56, 61, 69, 70, 71, 86
conceptualization and history, 137–43, 151, 240
Condorcet, Marquis de, 25, 51, 58, 61
Copernicus, Nicolaus, 40, 55
covering-law model of explanation, 163– 65, 174–75
Coulanges, Fustel de, 82
Crane, Stephen, 77
Croce, Benedetto, 55, 88, 92, 93–94, 214
culture, concepts of, 154–56, 157, 158, 159, 160, 161, 162, 164, 165, 166, 169,178– 79

Danto, Arthur, 200
Darwin, Charles, 68, 72, 73
Darwinism, 71–73, 82, 90
De Quincey, Thomas, 245
Derrida, Jacques, 197
Descartes, René (Cartesianism), 40, 55, 149–50
determinism in history, 159
Dewey, John, 56, 90, 212
Dickens, Charles, 76, 77, 111
Diderot, Denis, 49, 50
Dilthey, Wilhelm, 88, 92
Diodorus, Siculus, 12
Dionysus of Halicarnassus, 13
Disraeli, Benjamin, 76, 81
Döllinger, Johann I. von, 81
Dostoevsky, F., 123
Dreiser, Theodore, 77, 98
Dreyfus Case, 244
Dryden, John, 16
Duchesne, André, 52
Dumas, Alexander, 77
Durkheim, Emil, 86

Edwards, Philip, 69
Einhard, 23, 27
Einstein, Albert, 97, 125
Eliade, Mircea, 3, 4
Eliot, George, 67, 77
Eliot, T. S., 111
Elizabeth I (Elizabethan age), 41, 42, 78
Elton, Geoffrey R., 107
Emerson, Ralph Waldo, 76
Engerman, Stanley L., 105
Engels, Friedrich, 72, 75

epistemes (Foucault), 194
Erasmus, Desiderius, 33, 83
Eratosthenes, 41
Erikson, Erik, 120, 122
Euripides, 10
Eusebius of Caeserea, 7–8, 21
evolution, 71–73
explanation in history, 130, 151–69, 172– 76

Fairbairn, Ronald, 123
Febvre, Lucien, 87, 111
Ferguson, Adam, 53
Fichte, Johann, 62, 65
final causes, 159–60, 177–83
Fischer, Fritz, 105
Fisher, H. A. L., 98
Fiske, John, 76, 81
Fogel, Robert W., 105
Fontenelle, Bernard, 54
Foucault, Michel, 194
Frankl, Victor E., 121
Freeman, E. A., 77, 78, 89, 111
free will, 159–60
Freud, Sigmund, 86, 119, 120, 121, 122, 123, 244
frontier hypothesis (Turner), 89, 103
Froissart, Jean, 25, 26–27
Froude, J. A., 69, 77, 78
Fussner, F. S., 69, 77, 78
Fustel de Coulanges, N. D., 82

Galileo, 40, 149
Gardiner, Patrick, 55
Gardiner, Samuel R., 77
generalizations and history, 149–69, 170, 178, 180, 181
Geoffrey of Monmouth, 22
Geyl, Pieter, 78, 101
Gibbon, Edward, 47, 51, 52, 54–55, 100
Gilbert, Felix, 33, 35
Gilby, Thomas, 24
Gladstone, William E., 77–78, 82
Gobineau, Comte de, 69, 102
Goethe, Johann W. von, 65, 123
Gransden, Antonia, 23
Grant, Michael, 80
Greek historiography, 3, 4, 8–13, 15, 16– 17
Green, J. R., 89
Gregory of Tours, 21, 22, 27
Grote, George, 78
Guicciardini, Francesco, 18, 35–36
Guizot, François, 42, 62, 63, 64, 66, 76, 78

Hammond, Mr. and Mrs. J. L., 90
Handlin, Oscar, 105, 107

Harbison, E. H., 22, 24, 33
Hardy, Thomas, 77, 98, 111
Harrison, Frederic, 78
Hebrews (Jews), 3, 4, 5, 11, 17
Hecataeus, 9
Hegel, G. W. F., 26, 39, 55, 57, 58, 61, 62, 63, 65, 66, 67, 71, 73, 74, 94, 98, 147
Heidegger, Martin, 197
Hempel, Carl G., 163–65, 174
Herder, Johann G. von, 11, 55, 58, 59, 66
hermeneutics, 197–98
Herodotus, 8, 9, 10, 11, 13
Hexter, J. H., 75, 103
Hippocrates, 10
historicism, 61–69, 93, 193
history
    in ancient times, 3–18
    causation in, 170–91
    critical philosophy of, 129–30
    definition of, 130–48
    during the Enlightenment, 47–59
    generalizations in, 149–69
    in the Middle Ages, 20–30
    in the nineteenth century, 61–84
    objectivity in, 192–216
    professionalism in, 218, 220–21
    in the Renaissance and Reformation, 32–39
    research methods in, 88–92, 211–15, 239–44
    role in public policy making, 222–29
    scientific approaches to, 69–75, 111–19
    speculative philosophy of, 47–48, 100–103
    in the twentieth century, 86–109
    uses of, 217–38
Hitler, Adolf, 87, 92, 120
Hobbes, Thomas, 18, 41
Holmes, Oliver W., Jr., 18, 41
Homer, 8, 9
Horace, 15
Houghton, W. E., 76
Hugo, Victor, 76
Huizinga, Johan, 83
humanism in the Renaissance, 32–35
humans, attributes of, 133–37, 153, 154–55, 156
human nature, concepts of, 146, 156, 168, 224, 236
Hume, David, 47, 49, 50, 53, 54, 61, 75, 150
Hus, John (Hussites), 39
Huxley, Thomas H., 72
Huxley, Julian, 95

idealism, philosophical, 61–68, 135
identity and history, 229–34

imagination in history, 140–42
India, history in, 5
inference and history, 212–14
inquiry, model of, 212–15
intellectual history, 118–19, 229, 233–34
intuitive method in history, 213–14
Isaiah, 147
Isidore of Seville, 21
Islam, 4, 5, 22
Islamic historiography, 29–30

James, William, 87, 90
Jaspers, Karl, 88
Jaurès, Jean, 80
Jedin, Herbert, 39
Jerome, St., 21
Joachim of Flora (Fiore), 25, 27, 75
John of Salisbury, 22
Johnson, Douglas, 64, 244
Johnson, Samuel, 38
Joinville, Jean, Sire de, 25
Jordan, Philip D., 245
Josephus, 11, 21
Joyce, James, 102, 125
Judaism, 3, 4, 5, 11, 17
Julius Caesar, 18, 34, 80
Jung, Carl G., 86, 119, 121, 123
Justinian, 28
Juvenal, 14

Kant, Immanuel, 55, 58–59, 62, 65, 66, 150, 155
Karamzin, Nikolai, 63
Kautsky, Karl, 80
Kennedy, John F., 184–86, 187, 188, 189, 190, 213
Kepler, Johannes, 40, 70, 71, 149
Keylor, William, 96
Khaldun, Ibn, 29–30, 33, 57
Kingsley, Charles, 76
knowledge, definition of, 193–94
Kuhn, Thomas, 193–94

Lafayette, Marquis de, 48
Lamartine, Alphonse de, 76
Lamprecht, Karl, 83
language and culture, 135–43
La Popelinière, Henri de, 38
law-like explanation. See explanation.
learning theory, 158–59
Lecky, W. E. H., 72
Lefebvre, George, 103
Leibniz, Gottfried W., 38, 40
Lenin, V. I., 87, 97
Lessing, Gotthold E., 58
Levi-Strauss, Claude, 155
life, concept of, 153–54

literature and history, 197, 208–10
Livy, Titus, 10, 11, 14, 15, 18, 32, 33, 35
Locke, John, 41, 44–45, 47, 48, 50
Loewenberg, Peter, 121
logical analysis, 150, 172–74, 241
Loria, Achille, 87
Lovejoy, Arthur O., 49, 51
Lucian, 17
Luther, Martin, 32, 40, 120, 122

Mabillon, Jean, 52
Macaulay, Thomas B., 38, 42, 43, 63, 68, 69, 76, 79, 81, 88
Machiavelli, Niccolò, 18, 32, 33, 36, 48, 70
McMaster, John B., 89
McNeill, William, 106
Maitland, F. W., 43
Marcellinus, Ammianus, 21
Marcus, John T., 98
Maritain, Jacques, 6, 8
Marrou, H. I., 90–91
Marx, Karl (Marxism), 18, 25, 26, 39, 55, 56, 57, 58, 61, 67, 68, 69, 70, 71, 72, 73–75, 80, 82, 86, 87, 90, 96, 97, 102, 103, 106, 108, 120
mathematics, 141–42, 209
matter, conceptions of. See sciences, physical
Medieval historiography, 20–30
Meinecke, Friedrich, 64
Mercier de la Rivière, 53
Meredith, George, 123, 244
Michelet, Jules, 67, 68, 69, 76, 88
Michels, Robert, 86
Milton, John, 38, 123
mind-body problem, 159–60
mind, concepts of, 153, 154–59, 160–63, 178
Momigliano, Arnaldo, 9
Mommsen, Theodor, 67–68, 79, 80, 82, 125
Montesquieu, Charles Louis, 30, 38, 47, 48, 49, 51, 57, 72
moral judgments in history, 176, 186–87, 223, 227
moralism and history, 187, 223
Morley, John, 76
Motley, John L., 76, 78
Mueller, Adam, 62

Nagel, Ernest, 190
Napoleon I, 54, 65, 68, 81
narration and history, 117, 130–35, 195–98, 208–12
natural history, 133–34, 146
Nebuchadnezzar, 4
new history, the, 89–90, 111

Newton, Isaac, 40, 41, 47, 48, 50, 70, 71, 75, 150
Niebuhr, Barthold, 67
Niebuhr, Reinhold, 98
Nietzsche, Friedrich, 57, 72, 79–80, 82, 84, 87, 102, 197
Norris, Frank, 77

objectivity and history, 192–216
operationalism, 215
Ortega y Gasset, José, 47, 106, 243
Orwell, George, 98
Ostrogorski, M. I., 86
Oswald, Lee Harvey, 184–87, 188, 213
Otto of Freising, Bishop, 25–26
Owen, Robert, 70

paradigms, 193–94
Pareto, Vilfredo, 86
Paris, Matthew, 24
Parkman, Francis, 68, 76
Pater, Walter, 183
Paul, St., 33
Peirce, Charles S., 197
phenomenology, 213–14, 237
Pirenne, Henri, 103
Plato, 4, 10, 12, 16, 24, 40
Plumb, J. H., 107
Plutarch, 18
Pocock, J. G. A., 38, 48
Polybius, 10, 13–14, 18, 32, 33, 99, 235
Popper, Karl, 61, 102, 212
positivism, 69–71, 92, 94, 101–02
Powell, York, 78
pragmatism, 88–90, 195
Praxiteles, 10
Prescott, William H., 76
presentism, historical, 204, 233–34
Procopius, 11, 28
professionalism in history, 218–21
Psellus, Michael, 28
psychohistory, 119–23
psychology, 119, 160–63
Puritan revolution, 42–44

quantitative history, 117–18
quantum theory, 160

Racine, Jean, 49
radical history, 113
Ralegh, Walter, 42, 69
Ramses II, 4–5
Ranke, Leopold von, 17, 63, 65, 66–67, 80, 92
reductionism, 164–65
Reformation historiography, 33, 35, 36–39
relativism, historical, 189, 204

Renaissance historiography, 32–36
Renan, Ernest, 42, 84
research methods, 88–92, 212–15, 239–44
Rhodes, James Ford, 78
Ricardo, David, 80
Richelieu, Cardinal and Duke de, 52
Robertson, William, 53
Robinson, James Harvey, 89, 90, 111
Rogers, Carl G., 121
Roman historiography, 10, 11, 13–15, 17
romanticism and history, 63–65
Roosevelt, Franklin D., 181, 241
Rostovtzeff, Michael, 100
Rousseau, Jean-Jacques, 50, 51, 54–55
Rowse, A. L., 42
Ruskin, John, 77
Russell, Bertrand, 95

Saint-Simon, Henri, 56, 61
Sallust, 11
Santayana, George, 140
Sarpi, Paoli, 38–39, 70
Sartre, Jean-Paul, 121
Savigny, Friedrich, 64
Scalinger, J.-J., 41
Schevill, Ferdinand, 91
Schliemann, Heinrich, 68
Schmoller, Gustav, 81
Schweitzer, Albert, 240
sciences, physical, 130, 131, 145–46, 149–53, 155, 159, 160, 166, 167, 171–72, 173, 192–93, 209
sciences, social, 115–17, 149, 161, 162, 227–28
Scott, Walter, 76, 77
Selden, John, 43
Shakespeare, William, 41, 42, 123
Shirer, William, 242
Sidgwick, Henry, 125
Smiles, Samuel, 77
Smith, Adam, 53, 54
social history, 111–19
social sciences. See sciences, social.
Socrates, 10, 33
Sophocles, 9, 10, 123
speculative philosophy of history, 100–103, 147–48
Spencer, Herbert, 69, 70, 71–72, 86
Spengler, Oswald, 99–100, 101
Spinoza, Benedict, 40, 41
Stampp, Kenneth, 104
Stannard, David, 120–21
Stark, Johannes, 97
Steward, Dugald, 58
Stone, Lawrence, 103
Stubbs, William, 77
subjectivist views of history, 193–98

Suetonius, 11, 23
Syme, Ronald, 15
Symonds, John A., 73

Tacitus, 10, 14–15, 17, 18, 70
Taine, Hippolyte, 71
Tawney, R. H., 86, 90, 103
Tennyson, Alfred, 63, 76
Thiers, Adolphe, 77
Thompson, James W., 15
Thucydides, 8, 9, 10, 11–12, 13, 15, 16, 18, 28, 33, 54, 70
Tillich, Paul, 98
Tocqueville, Alexis de, 68, 78
Tolstoy, Leo, 111
Toynbee, Arnold J., 29, 30, 57, 73, 78–79, 80, 94, 95, 96, 98, 100–102, 103, 123, 147
tragedy and history, 234–38
Treitschke, Heinrich von, 42, 63
Trevelyan, Charles, 81
Trevelyan, George M., 79, 81
Trevor-Roper, Hugh R., 103
Trollope, Anthony, 111
Trotsky, Leon, 97
Turgenev, Ivan, 111
Turgot, A. R. J., 51, 58, 59
Turner, Frederick Jackson, 89, 90, 103

universal history, 100–103, 167
USSR (Soviet Union), history in, 97–98

Valéry, Paul, 102
Valla, Lorenzo, 34, 35
value and history, 206–08, 226–27
Vasari, Giorgio, 35
Veblen, Thorstein, 86
verification in history, 212, 214, 241–42
Vico, Giambattista, 30, 38, 47, 55–58, 92, 102
Victorian historians, 75–79
Villehardouin, Geoffroi de, 25
Vincent, John, 81
Virgil, 14
Viollet-le-duc, Eugène, 77
vitalism, 159
Voltaire (François-Marie Arouet), 47, 48, 49, 50, 51, 52, 53, 54, 57, 59, 65, 69, 70, 98
Vryonis, Speros, 28

Wallace, Henry A., 181
Wallas, Graham, 86
Watson, E. W., 21
Waugh, Evelyn, 100
Webb, Sidney and Beatrice, 80–81, 90

Weber, Max, 86, 87, 88, 103
Wells, H. G., 94–95, 100, 101, 102
Westermarck, E. A., 72
Whalley, Peter, 50
White, Hayden, 196, 201
William of Malmesbury, 24
Wilson, C. T. R., 125
Winsor, Justin, 78
Wittgenstein, Ludwig, 103
Wollstonecraft, Mary, 114
women's history, 113–14

Woodward, E. L., 102
Woolf, Virginia, 114
World War I, 96–97

Xenophanes, 9
Xenophon, 11, 12

Yeats, W. B., 100

Zola, Émile, 77, 98, 111

Heritage and Challenge: The History and Theory of History was copyedited by Barbara Salazar. Computer and proofreading assistance from Michael Kendrick and Andrew Davidson. Production manager was Judith Almendáriz. Sponsorship and editorial management by Maureen Hewitt. The book was typeset by Impressions, Inc., and the first run was printed and bound by Capital City Press, Inc.

Cover design by Roger Eggers.